On Foot
Grand Canyon Backpacking Stories

On Foot
Grand Canyon Backpacking Stories

edited by
Rick Kempa

Vishnu Temple Press
Flagstaff Arizona

Cover design by Sandra Kim Muleady
Cover photographs by Larry Allison

Vishnu Temple Press
P. O. Box 30821
Flagstaff, Arizona 86003
(928) 556 0742
www.vishnutemplepress.com

Contents

V Encounters

Introduction

A wealth of adventures and discoveries await the readers of this, the first-ever anthology focusing on the Grand Canyon backpacking experience. In it, twenty seven writers offer authentic, close-up views of what it is like to be afoot on particular days in particular places within the vast canyon wilderness. Many of their stories illustrate as well a truth that veteran canyon hikers come to know: time spent beneath the rim, out of the press of human time, can change who you are and re-direct how you live your life. The canyon does not just invite transfor-mation; it all but guarantees it, the way a full moon guarantees a high tide—provided you can shut down the brain factory or stay beneath the rim long enough for it to wind down on its own.

There's plenty of high drama to be found in these pages. Dillon Metcalfe, caught up on the flank of Isis Temple one blazing day, comes too close to dying of thirst. Not far away (as the raven flies) in a dif-ferent season, David Zucconi nearly drowns in a plunge pool. Bob Bordasch gives a matter-of-fact account of a group hike gone terribly wrong. Nic Korte tells a harrowing tale that will sober anyone who, flushed with good fortune at being in the canyon, might mistakenly feel immune out there. Indeed, part of the allure of these stories is the knowledge that what happened to these hikers could happen to any of us. Even the worst could happen, as Nathaniel Brodie comes to know in the course of a grim recovery mission.

In a wilderness as vast and as intricate as Grand Canyon, the pros-pect of discovery will never fade. Arnie Richard's vivid tale of how a trio of teenagers, decades ago, found a way through the cliffs above Deer Creek Valley in what became known as the Cranberry Canyon route, will charge the engine of any youthful spirit for whom even the wisp of a trail is unwelcome. So will Scott Thybony's crisp story of a rugged expedition in Marble Canyon, in search of the fossilized tracks of ancient animals. But one need not range so far afield to break new ground, as Kate Watters shows in her account of botanists scouring upper Phantom Creek for *Agave phillipsiana*, a cultivar whose presence suggests prehistoric trade routes with peoples in Mexico.

The trials may not always shrivel one's tongue or break one's bones, but they can be every bit as acute. With Rick Jurgen we suffer first the agony and then the woodenness of coming face to face, alone in the canyon, with a loved one's loss. Nor will all of the triumphs be as striking as Mark Jenkins' account of attaining the summit of Zoroaster Temple; the canyon novices who, under the guidance of Wayne Ranney, are led one "bite-sized" switchback at a time back up the Bright Angel Trail experience an euphoria every bit as genuine.

Speaking of the corridor trails, NPS employees Matt Berman, Marjorie "Slim" Woodruff, and Kristi Rugg offer uncommon perspectives on that most-trammeled section of the canyon. Berman's account of a surreal season on a trail crew is a cross-section of exertion, suffering, and death. We simmer with Slim as she stoops for the thousandth time to pluck micro-garbage from the trail. And thanks to Ranger Rugg's "Night Hike, South Kaibab," we are reminded that, no matter how many millions of hooves and boots may pound the trail dirt, the canyon's greatest treasure—solitude—can be readily found if you know when to claim it.

Threaded throughout the book are essays grounded in the quiet rhythms of days, weeks, lifetimes of putting one dusty boot in front of the other, on trancelike journeys where nothing in particular happens, except that you are being transformed, slowly, just as a lump of limestone under certain conditions grows into a crystal. Your eyes uncloud. Insights arrive on all levels–personal, interpersonal, cosmic. Thus, Sara Whitestone finds in the canyon's topography a perfect metaphor for the layers and the overlays of her own life. In D.J. Lee's "The Edge Is What We Have," a daughter and father see each other most clearly in a pivotal moment of shared danger. And Molly Hollenbach, in her visionary essay "Rock Bhakti: Dreaming the Vishnu Schist," sees in that most ancient of canyon rock the many faces of the Hindu god for which it was named: at one moment, "beautiful and soft," like blue-bodied Krishna; in another, "something greater and more fearsome, more like the thousand glittering eyes, mouths, and limbs of the god."

Truths such as these shimmer in every corner of this collection, like shards of precious stones at the edge of the trail.

The main virtue these essays share is clarity of vision, trained outward. Whatever happens to these hikers, be it a head trip or a body trip, happens in place. Any essay could serve as example. Jurgen's grief is witnessed by a tribe of bighorn sheep ("The Girls") and underpinned by the thunder of Boucher Rapids. Any of us who have failed—as all must—to capture a Grand Canyon sunrise in words will appreciate Ranger Molly McCormick's go at it: "Light cascaded outwards, caressing and dancing along the sheer cliffs, expansive flats, dramatic highs and lows of the canyon layers." John Yohe's celebration of "Holy Water" on the North Bass Trail is guaranteed to provoke flashbacks to some of our most cherished moments alongside dripping springs or gurgling creeks or bellowing rapids. And Thea Gavin, looking back on her barefoot rim-to-rim adventure, focuses neither on the plentiful pain nor the thrill of finishing, but on a rare moment by the waterside, when, with her "feet feeling the pull of the Colorado River," she "watched raindrops evaporate before they could become part of the current. How they caught the light, if only for a few seconds; how they made a high sparkle against the dark eroding shoulders of the old cliffs."

Veteran canyoneers will nod their heads in recognition of many of the precise places conjured in these pages: the cleft of solid shade at the foot of the Tanner Trail where Rick Dean leans back to watch the eddying river; the one and only monolithic sandstone block on the traverse of the "nameless side canyon" on the Escalante route, where Chris Propst finds temporary relief from his fear of falling. And if you ever find yourself wandering the Tonto Platform south of Holy Grail Temple, you will surely know on sight the chunk of Redwall big as "a cathedral-ceiling living room," within whose cracks Eb Eberlein and his companion wedge themselves to escape the inferno. It's not going anywhere soon!

Equally authentic are the emotional truths that arise in the course of a canyon hike. With Laurie McClellan, we will descend to the bottom on our first canyon hike wrapped in a trance of beauty. We will feel Clint King's pain as he plunges broken-hearted, malnourished, and bloody-footed toward his redemption. My own small essay, on backpackers' encounters with river runners, may provoke a twinge of gastric memory. With Sara Whitestone, we may find "discouragement in switchbacks." And we will all recognize the note of reluctance in Seth Muller's voice as he turns his back on his beloved canyon on the climb out.

It is my hope that these stories may serve as companion for many a new canyon excursion, to be enjoyed in the shade of a boulder on a beach or by headlamp in a tent; or that they will provoke memories of days well-spent beneath the rim and anticipations of journeys yet to come.

My thanks go out to each and every writer who sent me his or her canyon-centered words. What a pleasure and a privilege it was to read them—despite the inevitable pain of having to say no to so many. A special thanks to the writers whose essays appear in this book, for their hard work and good will as I invited them to revise and re-revise their work. Gratitude goes as well to Tom Martin and Hazel Clark, publishers of Vishnu Temple Press, for their enthusiasm and input all along the way; to John N. Gibbs, the project's first editor, who found several of these essays; to Betty Upchurch, past curator of Grand Canyon Research Library, for her help in locating sources; to Tay Audevart of Rock Springs and Hannah Winward of Farson, Wyoming, my brilliant student interns; and to my partner Fern, who smooths the way. Thanks, finally, to the North Rim Artist-in-Residence Program selection committee and to the friendly tribe of NPS employees up in that blessed forest. Time, as we all know, is our most precious commodity, and the opportunity to spend several weeks in solitude at the canyon's edge infused this project with energy and momentum.

Rick Kempa

I
Passages

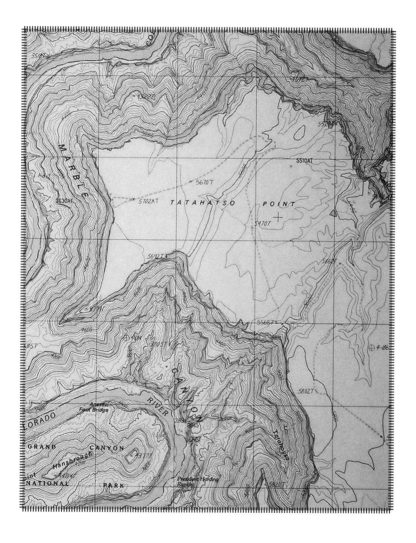

Fifty Mile: A Search for Ancient Tracks
by
Scott Thybony

Winds kick up and cirrus clouds sweep high overhead as we make final adjustments to our packs before descending. When all is ready the four of us stand on the brink of Marble Canyon, joking about the impossibly steep route we are about to tackle. It's a moment of pure anticipation when anything from wild euphoria to abject terror is still possible. I'm counting on it landing somewhere in between, but you never know.

"This is great!" says Barry Albright, looking nearly straight down at the Colorado River thousands of feet below. "This is so unreal!" The curator of paleontology and geology at the Museum of Northern Arizona is about to make his first backpacking trip into Grand Canyon. And I'm not sure if he knows what he's getting himself into.

Time to get moving. The sun already hangs high overhead, and we need a couple of hours to hunt for the tracks of animals millions of years older than dinosaurs. The year before, I came upon a major fossil tracksite in a branch of Marble Canyon, and now the National Geographic Society has decided to support our efforts to locate new sites.

Years ago I asked Harvey Butchart, the authority on the backcountry of Grand Canyon, what he thought was the shortest rim-to-rim route. The question interested him, and he considered various possibilities before settling on a traverse from Eminence Break on the eastern side to Boundary Ridge on the west. As I watched, he slowly traced the route on a map with his finger, letting the motion unlock his memory of the terrain. This route, I decided, would make an ideal transect to link track-bearing formations on opposite sides of the Colorado River. A crossing of Marble Canyon would give us an idea of the frequency of trace fossils and any key differences between locales. It would also require negotiating thousands of feet of talus, balanced at the angle of repose, while carrying all the normal backpacking gear plus rafts for a river crossing. Following no trails, we would finish with a 3,200-foot ascent out of the gorge.

Friends, who were veteran trekkers, were surprised to hear I was taking a novice canyon hiker on such a demanding trip. But Barry has scrambled over lots of rough terrain in search of fossils, and more importantly he has the right attitude, an eagerness to face whatever comes along. I have no concerns about our other geologist, Christa Sadler, a top canyon guide who wrote her master's thesis on fossil tracks. On an earlier trip I came to appreciate her unshakable good nature even in difficult circumstances. And besides, she carries a heavier pack than I do. Having worked with Bill Hatcher on other assignments, I have full confidence in his abilities. He's more at home in the vertical world of cliffs than any photographer I know. As we begin the descent a white-throated swift zips past Bill's head and disappears into the void. "It sounds like rockfall on a cliff face, zinging past a climber," he says.

We head down Eminence Break, a major fault breaching the rim cliffs. The route takes us through a steep notch, past veins of calcite crystals to a massive block of limestone wedged between cliff walls. Shattered rockfall piles up below like drifts of shore ice. Under heavy packs, the four of us continue down a cone of loose talus and soon reach the Coconino Sandstone. It formed when ancient climates shifted, causing a low-lying desert to grow hyperarid. As winds increased in velocity the dunes thickened and spread across 32,000 square miles of near-coastal lowlands. Then seas flowed in to cover the dunes, turning grains of sand to stone and adding another layer to the geological record.

Below the Coconino we drop our packs and hunt for a track-covered slab as large as a billboard that tumbled from above and landed edgewise. I've seen it before, and the excitement hasn't diminished when we relocate it. Several long trackways cross the vertical face in double lines of footprints, along with dozens of smaller, clawed tracks. Inspecting the most prominent trackway, I notice something odd. The claws on one foot curve radically back. The animal must have been lame, struggling up the loose sands with one foot turned inward.

"Sitting here," Christa says, "you can really get a sense of how these animals moved. You can really see them plodding up the dunes." Barry walks over and adds, "What we are seeing are vertebrate tracks on the down-wind slope of a sand dune in a near-coastal environment. There's a great, vast sea to the south of us and we're now near the equator, too. We're talking about 265-million years ago."

Ichnologists, the scientists who study trace fossils, classify these Permian tracks as species of *Chilichnus*. No bones of the creatures have been recovered from the sandstone formation, only tracks. "They're totally alien to anything we know," Barry says. "In a general sense these animals are called mammal-like reptiles." And Christa offers a comparison closer to home. "It had a long body and short legs," she says, "like a rez dog. You know the type, a dog with the body of a German Shepherd and the legs of a terrier."

We now concentrate our efforts on the bedrock exposures nearby, scrambling up shelving ledges, zigzagging across the cliff as the bedding planes change direction. On one slab we find a set of small tracks where a reptile was side-stepping across what was then a dune face, struggling to find enough purchase to continue upward. And a wider search turns up dozens of other track-bearing slabs.

Needing to reach the river before dark, we resume our descent through a vertical maze of boulders and weathered cliffs. And suddenly, while down-climbing, Barry loses his footing and takes a head-over-heels tumble. Luckily, he's back on his feet as quickly as he left them with only a few scrapes. We continue descending, and I notice far below an oasis of color where a patch of flowering cactus has burst open in florescent pink. Reaching it we take a water break, and Barry starts picking out the cactus needles stuck in his knee like a pin cushion. "This is amazingly beautiful," he says, gazing at the canyon setting and ignoring the pain. Our route threads through a break in the Redwall Limestone, taking us to the river near President Harding Rapid. "President Harding isn't much of a rapid," says Christa, "but hey, he wasn't much of a president."

Sheltered from the wind by a massive boulder split in two, we make camp and watch the clouds stream across the gap of sky between the rims. I stretch out, thinking about deep time, not such an unusual thought at the bottom of Grand Canyon. Passing the ancient footprints on the way to the river has drawn us into a lost world, not only unimaginably distant in time but one shifting in space. These deposits formed near the equator and now lie far to the north. Over time the earth's surface changed as tectonic plates collided and continents drifted apart like sea ice during breakup.

Dawn light strikes the highest band of rock as we get an early start, moving downstream at a good pace. Cliffs on both sides of the river soon close in, forcing our hand. I planned on crossing farther down canyon, but this will have to do. The four of us bushwhack through a tamarisk thicket to reach a small beach. "Dr. Livingston, I presume?" says Christa to no one in particular as she thrashes through the riparian jungle. We stand at the river's edge a moment, watching the big water flow cold and clear, and then each of us begins rigging a pack raft. Weighing five pounds and about the size of a watering trough, they have just enough room for one person and a pack. Pushing into the current we let the river carry us away. Our intention is to float only beyond the sheer cliffs, but finding strong eddies and boulder-choked banks we stay on the water until Saddle Canyon several miles downstream. Barry has never seen the beautiful Redwall narrows here, so we secure the boats and hike up the side canyon.

"This is unreal!" he says, looking back at the river from a high point. "No," Christa reminds him, "this is real. This is truth."

Our inflatables have proven to be stable enough for us to continue floating down to camp. We encounter a stretch of whitewater, and the last riffle above 50 Mile Canyon proves to be the most exciting. I ship a few splashes from the biggest waves before landing at the upper beach, five miles from the start. We set the boats out to dry, only to find ourselves rushing to stow them away when a rainstorm hits. Showers continue through late afternoon and turn heavy that night. During a lull in the storm, I ask Christa about her first time down the Colorado. She tells us about falling in love with the place on a commercial river trip. "I cried all the way back on the flight to California," she recalls, and before reaching home she decided to become a river guide.

We get an early start the next morning and pick our way up 50 Mile Canyon through a choke of boulders. To find a way out, we will need to piece together just the right combination of talus slogs and rock scrambles. When the four of us reach the base of an unscalable cliff in the Redwall, Bill goes to investigate a bighorn trail disappearing around the corner.

"It probably goes," he shouts back a few minutes later.

"Probably goes?" Christa asks with a laugh, knowing his skill as a climber. Probably for him could easily mean probably not for us.

Rejoining us, Bill describes "a devious little route" hugging a narrow ledge and running above a sheer drop with uncertain handholds. This being our only option we decide to give it a shot, but first Bill instructs Barry on the proper technique. "Make sure you stand straight up," he says. "Weight your feet and watch where you place them. Only use your hands for balance. If a handhold pulls out, even an experienced mountain climber will be thrown off balance with this kind of weight on his back."

Bill leads, climbing with one hand on the rock and working his camera with the other. The narrow ledge curves above a crumbling chute and then twists up an exposed point to reach more solid footing. A rock rolling over the edge will fall 50 feet before taking the first bounce. How many bounces it will need to reach the bottom I don't lean out far enough to see. One by one we cross and scramble to the top of the cliff, relieved to be past the crux.

Pushing on, we locate the water cache Bill and I placed two weeks before on a trip down from the rim. The four of us dump our packs and spread out to check the blocks of fallen sandstone. An hour's search turns up very little. We still face a hard climb to reach the rim by dark, but don't want to leave this side of the canyon without locating a track or two. So we move higher, traversing slopes of red Hermit Shale where the footing becomes tricky. On a narrow ridge mantled with rockfall, we immediately begin finding a variety of fossil imprints in the fractured sandstone. Most have weathered into faint depressions, vague blobs with only the stride pattern making them recognizable. Ghost tracks. Others appear so fresh I expect to turn a corner and see some reptilian creature scrabbling up a dune.

"There's something so charming about these tracks," Christa says, after crawling under a boulder to view the protected underside. She studies several sets of reptile prints and something more unusual. A small trackway, exquisitely preserved, matches the tracks of a scorpion. In experiments with a living scorpion, Christa was able to duplicate tracks nearly identical to those made millions of years before. "That's a beauty," Barry says. "Very nice, very nice. Look at the detail." Christa points out a line as thin as a pencil lead where the tail dragged through dust many centuries before.

Nearby she finds a set of spider tracks similar to those made by Rose, the pet tarantula she used in her studies. "One, two, three," she says, counting the line of prints, "and one in." The next set follows the same pattern, and the next. Spider tracks are a small detail in the fossil record, but one that bridges an immense span of time. We usually focus on the strangeness of the past, on the monstrous creatures so different from those now living. But here, recorded in the rock, are tracks of a spider climbing a dune, and millions of years later the pattern holds.

"I like tracks better than bone," Christa tells me, "because they're the remnants of an action. Bones are so difficult to get a sense of something living, but these traces show motion and let you imagine the actual animal. You can imagine it walking, and feeding, and breeding."

Considering the slim chances of a track surviving intact for so many millions of years, I'm amazed we found any. First they were left in dunes constantly reworked by the wind with only those on the sheltered, leeward sides lasting. Fine layers of sand sealed the prints before more dunes buried them and encroaching seas submerged the site. Carried north from the equator with the drift of continents, they were uplifted a mile high and finally brought to light when the covering rock eroded away. Scientists talk about the accident of preservation, but with such a long chain of improbables, it comes closer to being a miracle of preservation.

As we pass one of the rare bivouac sites along the route I'm surprised to find a Boy Scout insignia. Then I remember an incident from 1996 when a group of scouts ran into trouble on this route. At the hottest time of year they attempted a three-day descent from Saddle Mountain to the river. They carried heavy packs, lost the route, and finally ran out of water. Desperation set in. When the leaders were unable to continue, one of the scouts went ahead to find water. Becoming delirious, he collapsed of heat stroke within sight of the river and died a few hours later.

For us, the last leg of the canyon traverse means a long, uphill slog through a stack of rock formations. We don't pass a level spot for another 1,300 vertical feet. The four of us find ourselves kick-stepping up talus, climbing cliff faces, and hauling up packs with rope. At one point we use a stone step left by prehistoric Indians whose potsherds are scattered on the rim above.

Reaching the top, we set up camp on the extreme end of Boundary Ridge. The river makes a wide curve directly below us, and the low roar of Nankoweap Rapid rises on the still air. Spur ridges stand outlined, one behind the other, and snow still hangs on the highest slopes and ledges. To the south a chain of temples and buttes break the horizon in a dramatic skyline, punctuated by the lone pinnacle of Mount Hayden set off from the North Rim. The canyon grows deeper, older in the fading light. And as night comes, the color lifts from the bottom of the gorge, leaving darkness in its wake. Moving upward it abandons the river first, and then the cliffs, before brushing the undersides of the clouds for a long, final moment.

"This is so glorious!" Christa says.

"Unbelievable," Barry adds. "This is one of the best trips I've ever done. And now that I've made it across on my first rim-to-rim, you guys have to teach me the secret handshake." He pauses, noticing our blank stares. "Isn't there a secret handshake?"

At dawn the cry of a peregrine brings me awake, and the dark clouds ignite overhead with the same flaring pink we saw in cactus blossoms along the way. The four of us pack up and leave, walking through the blackened landscape of a recent wildfire, past the ruins of prehistoric pueblos and scatters of broken pottery now twice fired. Taking the Saddle Mountain pack trail we traverse a slope thick with Indian paintbrush, leaving our own tracks in the dust behind us.

Time's Factory
by
Laurie McClellan

My husband has some friends who live in Arizona, about two hours from the Grand Canyon. One year a friend of theirs, a geologist named Dave, came to visit, and they proudly drove him to see the national park. Many people feel overwhelmed the first time they glimpse the Grand Canyon, but for geologists, visiting it is like finally beholding the Holy Grail. Earth hides most of her history, burying it underneath mountains or sinking it below oceans. The Grand Canyon is one of the few spots where the planet's past is laid bare for anyone to see.

Dave needed to leave in an hour, so he couldn't hike the eight-mile Bright Angel Trail that winds down to the canyon floor—but he wanted to walk the first quarter-mile, just to get a taste. His friends sat down on a park bench, and Dave trotted off in his sneakers, carrying a small water bottle. An hour later, they were worried. Two hours later, they started down after him. It was 95 degrees that day, and a hiker needs a gallon of water just to make it to the bottom. In an average year, two or three hikers die from dehydration, sunstroke, falls off sheer cliffs, or heart attacks brought on by attempting to walk to the bottom and back in one day, a 16-mile journey that drops more than 4,000 feet—about four-fifths of a vertical mile—from the rim to the Colorado River, then gains it back on the way up.

It was after dark when they finally spotted Dave, heading back up to the canyon rim, walking by moonlight under a starry sky. They were furious to see him smiling. When they asked what had happened, he shrugged. "You know, I kept meaning to turn around. Then I would see something ahead I wanted to look at, something I'd never seen before, and I'd say to myself, OK, I'll turn around in five minutes. I kept doing that, and before I realized it, I was at the bottom." Other hikers had taken pity on Dave all day long, doling out sips from their water bottles to the jubilant, dusty man who had never seen the Grand Canyon before.

In a way, it's not surprising that the Grand Canyon can make you forget time, because time is what the canyon is all about. Not seconds and minutes and hours, the stuff that human time is made of. The Grand Canyon is a factory of time, manufacturing oceans of the stuff, time stretching forward and backward, limitless. To the canyon, a human being is pretty much the same thing as a mayfly, an insect that can mate, reproduce and die, all between one sunrise and the next.

Time isn't some abstract concept in the canyon, but a story that you walk through. You take your first steps over the Kaibab Formation, a creamy stone speckled with fossil worms and fish teeth. These are the youngest rocks in the canyon, but they pre-date dinosaurs by 25 million years. Go another mile, and you're walking on rust-colored Hermit Shale, imprinted with fossils from the planet's first ferns.

Down you go, descending into a well of time. Each formation striping the canyon walls is a different color. Every time you walk into a new shade of tan or ocher or burnt sienna, you've moved deeper into the past. The names of the rocks sound like a mantra that takes you back to the beginnings of the planet—Toroweap, Coconino, Supai, Vishnu.

I hiked to the bottom of the Grand Canyon once myself. It was the first vacation I ever took as an adult, with my own money. When my boyfriend proposed this plan—we would fly to Phoenix, drive to the canyon, hike to the bottom and camp out there—it held the allure and bravado of a jail break. We arrived at the park just as the sun was setting, and Patrick made me close my eyes as he parked our car at the rim. He led me, blind, all the way to the overlook. He wanted my first sight of the Grand Canyon to be the whole thing. That night, we went to sleep with snowflakes pinging off our tent. The next day, the temperature at the bottom hit 85 degrees.

Our hike didn't start well. Packing up took longer than expected, and we had to run with fully loaded backpacks to catch the last hikers' shuttle bus to the South Kaibab trailhead. After an hour of walking, I realized I'd forgotten to bring any tissues. I took off my boot, rolled off one dusty sock, blew my nose on the clean bit at the top, and put it back on. When you're walking through deep history, little things don't seem to matter as much. It was mid-May, and the desert was blooming. I had expected the canyon to be something magnificent, but desolate.

Instead, its slopes were washed with magenta and orange flowers, humming with bees, hung with miniature waterfalls leaping from the cliffs.

Like Dave, I discovered the unexpected. The view changed constantly, beckoning me deeper inside the canyon. With each step, the walls soared higher overhead, a cathedral of red and orange rock. The trail wound around twisted spires of rock that hid the canyon from view, then suddenly emerged onto cliff edges that looked out over vast stretches of space. Collared lizards skittered across the path, leaving behind the tiniest footprints imaginable. When we finally crossed the Colorado River on a suspension bridge, the sight of the churning green water under our feet was shocking after a day spent gazing at the desert. But even after hiking for eight hours, knees protesting every step, the sight of shade in the side canyon that was our destination made me speed up. We went to sleep under a moon that was bright enough to read by, the Colorado River chuckling softly as we drifted off.

The hike out the next day was another story. The trail climbed relentlessly skyward, like hundreds of flights of stairs strung together. I wasn't used to the heat, the elevation, or the desert air. My knees were throbbing, the sun was blinding me, and there was no shade. Three miles from the top, I sat down on a rock to cry, convinced that I couldn't make it. Patrick took my backpack, strapped it on top of his, and carried it up. To this day, I consider this the nicest thing that anyone has ever done for me. We went into a snack bar, and I drank a root beer. I was so tired, I sat without speaking for an hour, chewing on the crushed ice in an ecstasy of contentment.

Of all the places I've ever traveled, the Grand Canyon is somehow the hardest to pin down. Although it's pictured on millions of refrigerator magnets, postcards, and coffee mugs, the canyon is impossible to truly capture in snapshots. As a place, it's more like a movie than a photograph. Sunbeams break against the walls, clouds cast down shadows, and the colors ripple and shift like an ocean of light. The sheer vastness of the space never comes across in pictures. Once you've been there, looking at a photo is like looking at a disappointing picture of a friend, the kind where you shake your head and say, "No, this one doesn't really look like you at all."

Perhaps Einstein was right, and time spirals in on itself. That would explain why one summer in your childhood can last forever—and how a man can accidentally hike clear to the bottom of the Grand Canyon, five minutes at a time.

Rock Bhakti: Dreaming the Vishnu Schist
by
Margaret Hollenbach

Day dawns, and all those lives that lay hidden asleep
Come forth and show themselves, mortally manifest:
Night falls, and all are dissolved
Into the sleeping germ of life.
—the god Vishnu, in the *Bhagavad Gita*

A light wind carries scents of pine duff and beer from the saloon in the breezeway. Voices drift up from the trail below. Here on the patio of the North Rim Lodge, the Grand Canyon opens out before us to the east and south in all its colorful complexity. The earthquake fault that splits it north to south lies deep in shadow, and above it three buttes—Deva Temple, Brahma Temple, and Zoroaster Temple—blur into beige and pink tapestries. As somewhere in the west, behind us, the sun sinks an inch closer to the horizon, a green and gold canyon snuffs out and a high rocky butte leaps into foreground, flooded in salmon-colored light. The man sitting next to me gasps at the same moment I do. The earth moved. We saw it.

He takes a swig of his beer and I lean over the wall, staring down past the layers of white Kaibab Limestone jutting out below us, searching for the thin line of the trail, remembering the feel of it under my boots, its dust on my skin. Darkness obscures that line soon, as shadows creep up over the Tonto Plateau.

I had no idea that rocks go through their own cycles of birth, death, and rebirth until I opened a book on the geology of Arizona at the North Rim bookstore. Lava, pushed up from the molten core, cools and hardens, but that's not the end; it will be pressed down under later flows, broken by wind and water, forced under the weight of mountains or oceans back into the core, to transform and break free again. The three types of rock—igneous, sedimentary, metamorphic—which sound so perfectly distinct, are all in the process of becoming each other, in a gargantuan time frame.

Here I can see the earth's transformation happening all around me, in dust blown around by the wind, pebbles rolling against the creek bed, an insect that will die soon and become part of the record of dust; I see movement in this curving, contrasting, layered rock; I see my own bones falling away, littering the path, becoming moments, no matter how enduring they seem in their present state. It is Thanatos and Eros, death and life, visible, present, all at once. In the Grand Canyon, geology is the ecstatic science.

In the middle part of my life, roughly my forties, I hiked rim-to-rim several times, mostly alone; it was a pilgrimage, and I didn't know anyone with the same religion. My parents were vaguely Protestant, my friends and I were vaguely nothing. My study of anthropology had given me a certain distance from all belief systems. Hiking in the Grand Canyon, I simply felt the most at home of anywhere I had ever been, the most connected, the most alive.

One October I decided to hike from the North Rim to the South Rim, and then, instead of taking the shuttle around to my car, to hike back again, staying as long as possible in the canyon. It is usually necessary to apply months in advance for a backcountry permit, but a certain percentage is reserved for walk-ins. I counted on that process to get me in. I arrived and set up camp at night and was in line at the Backcountry Office when it opened at 7:30 AM. There were already ten people ahead of me. Once my name and request was on the list, my day was free. I would return the next day and the next, until I reached the top of the list.

The nearly level, paved trail to Bright Angel Point starts just below the lodge and follows along the top of a narrow, rocky promontory that extends a quarter mile out to the southeast, offering spectacular views of the canyon on either side. I love to go there to look and listen, get used to the feel of the place, and contemplate the days of hiking ahead. For most of the way there is no guardrail. I walk on a white dust ledge hanging over infinity and realize I could easily step off to become bits of flesh and cloth. This trail, like many in the canyon, makes it clear that life is a choice.

People do sometimes fall or jump from the rim. I can understand that. Falling is one of the risks of the place. But jumping is different: it has a certain attraction that can't be explained entirely as a desire for death. Jumping off a 1,500-foot cliff would be an amazing experience. That's the twist: the jump would be an *experience*; the word implies that there is someone still there, a consciousness, going on before, during and after. Part of me believes that. The other part clings to the wall or makes me steer to the middle of the path—as far away from the edge as I can get.

At the lone guardrail at the tip of Bright Angel Point, I stand among other tourists scrutinizing the light-and-shadow mysteries before us. Our feet are on Kaibab Limestone, the top layer at both the north and south rims. Beneath the Kaibab Limestone, a succession of nearly vertical, fossil-rich layers of sandstone, limestone, and shale culminate in the sheer Redwall cliffs. These cliffs are accessible only on the few trails carved through them by the Ancestral Puebloan people, shored up by the miners, and maintained by the Park Service; but beneath the Redwall cliffs is a wide, green plateau, horizontal enough to support a hiking trail for some ninety miles. The Tonto Plateau pushes out beneath the Redwall cliffs like a great, heaving bosom, then slopes down to rest on top of horizontal blocks of Tapeats Sandstone. Bright Angel Shale, a greenish layer of mud from shallow seas, erodes from above to paint the Tonto green. Desert plants—sagebrush, burro bush, Mormon tea—also color it green, not a kelly green but an ancient, hardened green thinking about becoming black.

Beneath the Tapeats Sandstone crouches the Vishnu Schist, the two-billion-year-old metamorphic rock that forms the Inner Gorge, the bottom of the canyon. Its thousand-foot walls frame the Colorado River for forty miles. Its colors change as the sun crosses the sky. It is jagged black in the morning, and then, paradoxically, the harsh noon light softens it to brown and salmon, with highlights of pink from vertical streaks of Zoroaster Granite, a younger rock "interbedded" in the schist. At sunset the gorge returns to eggplant-purple-black.

Returning from Bright Angel Point, I'm walking slowly, looking west into Transept Canyon, a narrow crenellation that can only be reached from the mouth of the creek that carved it, four thousand feet below. A raven calls out, floating along the far wall.

Rounding a corner formed by a large boulder, I meet a thin, grey-haired woman who stands quietly against the rock, holding a cigarette to her lips, the other hand in her pocket. She says hello. Then she says, "I've been thinking of jumping."

I stop beside her, my smile fading. Only a few feet separate us from the edge.

"My life hasn't really amounted to much," she says, as if speaking of her bowling score. Her face shows the patternless weathering produced by years of sun, wind, and smoking. She wears a checkered wool jacket of beige and brown, sensible walking shoes—all compact and orderly. She looks like someone who usually does what she says: not at all the person I imagined attracted to the brink, her calm accounting not the way I thought it would be.

"But all this," I say, taking in with a gesture the canyon walls, the raven, the golden light. "It's worth something, isn't it? Just to be here?"

She gazes out into the vast air before us, past boulders and bushes that cling to the cliff below the trail.

"Yeah, but we're messing it up." She drags on her cigarette and exhales a thin wisp of smoke. "They're going to build a huge hotel complex at the North Rim."

"I can't believe that would happen. People would stop it."

"No, they wouldn't. I live in Santa Fe," she says, glancing over as if I should know what that means. I don't have an answer to that. Perhaps my dismay shows on my face.

"I admit it's not so bad for me," she says, allowing herself, or me, one crumb of consolation. "I live in the junipers outside of town."

"Well, that must be comforting. It's so beautiful there."

She smiles thinly. "My son was killed in a climbing accident when he was twenty-four. In his short life he did a lot more than I ever have."

"I'm sorry," I say, not sure whether I mean sorry for her son's death or sorry for her.

She dismisses me with a twitch of her hand. "I'm fine."

I stand there, uncertain.

"I'm fine," she says again. I move on. Later, at the lodge, I see her buying postcards in the bookstore.

On the third morning I get my permit to hike from the North Rim down to the Colorado River and up the Bright Angel Trail to the South Rim—three days and two nights in the canyon. I will then have to sleep one night at the South Rim and stand in line there for a permit to stay two more nights on the way back. I set off down the North Kaibab Trail: four thousand feet down in seven miles to Cottonwood Campground.

The descent focuses my attention on the downhill muscles of thigh and calf, hot feet in wicking socks, brown boots scuffing at white Kaibab rubble, beige Coconino pebble, red Supai Group dust. The gentle sloshing of the four heavy water bottles in my pack is the only sound other than my footsteps, until I hear the clopping of a line of mules behind me, taking tourists on what they hope is the easy way to explore the canyon. Mules going up the trail, mules coming down. The dense smell of mule poop and urine drying in the sun.

In the second and third miles, the trail drops steeply through layers of limestone and sandstone, across dry watercourses, past bouquets of cerulean flowers set in round green clumps. I catch the scent of lemon, search for it and find it in clusters of pale starflowers growing up out of crevices in the rocks.

Descending through the Redwall Limestone, the trail is little more than a ledge hacked across the face of a cliff. My old-fashioned backpack hangs the load rather high on my shoulders, so that I feel topheavy, born to teeter. I survive by not looking down to the outside, instead admiring the rock wall close to my shoulder and the trail ahead of my feet. Below the Redwall, the way becomes gentler, switchbacking down through sloping layers with few openings into wider views. I will not see the Inner Gorge again until tomorrow.

All the layers I'm passing through now—in fact, all the layers of the Grand Canyon except those of the Inner Gorge—are sedimentary, laid down over many millions of years of wind, erosion, and the lapping waters of inland seas. In contrast, the Inner Gorge schist and granite are metamorphic, transformed by heat and weight as mountain ranges are thrust up, subside, and thrust up again. The Vishnu Schist began as sand, silt, and clay in a two-billion-year-old sea, while the Zoroaster Granite started as lava shot up from the earth's core into the already ancient schist. The 5,000 to 7,000 feet of sediments we see above the schist today, its staggering burden of shale and limestone and dolomite, chert and sandstone, siltstone and gypsum, were laid down in the last, brief interval of the schist's existence. At its birth, the only witnesses were bacteria and algae. Everything else was wind and water, fire and rock.

The Grand Canyon place names borrowed from Asian religions pique my curiosity: Why, I wonder, do we have the Deva, Brahma, and Zoroaster temples, but no Jesus, Mary and Joseph buttes? Why would a geologist name the ancient metamorphic rock at the bottom of the canyon the Vishnu Schist? Could these names suggest experiences, spiritual, religious, or other, that don't have words in our vaguely Christian culture, our vocabulary that separates spirit from matter?

More than one traveler has written of the Vishnu Schist as if it were alive: as if it not merely *gave* feelings but *had* feelings. "Down in these grand, gloomy depths we glide," wrote John Wesley Powell of his passage through the Inner Gorge. "One cannot imagine anything more uncanny than these inner Canyon walls," wrote John Van Dyke, a canyon traveler in the 1920s. "They are grim and unearthly . . . almost too creepy for enjoyment."

I don't find the Vishnu Schist creepy, but I do feel a presence in it.

Traditionally, in both scientific and Christian thought, projecting human emotions onto the landscape has been considered anthropomorphism or the "pathetic fallacy," based on the belief that in reality we are alone in the world, the only beings who combine spirit and matter. But is it projection or perception? What if it's both? And what do we project—life, death, or one after the other, as Helios drives his chariot across the sky and the light moves over the earth, illuminating now one and now another face of the rock, the earth, ourselves?

In the late nineteenth century Clarence Dutton, who wrote the first geological treatise on the Grand Canyon, gave many of the canyon features their Hindu names. Dutton found a 5,000-foot butte in the inner canyon "so admirably designed and so exquisitely decorated that the sight of it must call forth an expression of wonder and delight from the most apathetic beholder." He named it Vishnu Temple. Following his lead, Charles Walcott, a paleontologist, applied the same name to the oldest layer at the temple's feet. Apparently it was Walcott who named the Vishnu Schist.

According to historian Stephen Pyne, Dutton thought that although he himself appreciated the canyon's beauty, other visitors might need help interpreting this landscape; like the early Spanish explorers, Americans might find it an ugly wasteland. Educated at Yale, Dutton was likely familiar with the writings of Emerson and Thoreau on Hindu and Buddhist philosophies. He probably knew of the European fad for art and religion of the "Orient," as Asia was then called in the ethnocentric west. In short, he drew upon Asian religions for exotic names to match exotic land forms.

There is no evidence that either Dutton or Walcott was motivated by religious feelings in naming this rock; the name, however, has deeper resonance for me because of my early experience as a student in India, in the ancient, holy city of Varanasi. There I saw the followers of Vishnu practicing their religion of renunciation and devotion as wanderers on the streets or bathing in the waters of the Ganges: clean, shaven-headed Brahmins in saffron-colored robes or wild-looking, skinny men with ragged, filthy coils of hair. In Hinduism there are many gods and many different paths to salvation.

Vishnu, called the Preserver, is one of the three primary Hindu gods (with Brahma the Creator and Shiva the Destroyer). All three have multiple aspects, some compassionate, some vengeful and destructive, expressed as different personas or avatars. Vishnu's most prominent avatar is Krishna, a beautiful, blue-skinned young man playing a flute. In popular culture in India, a deep-blue Krishna is depicted in colorful posters, disporting with a group of maidens, cowherds whom he seduced with his beauty and the music he played on his flute. The passion these maidens feel is *bhakti*—the passion for God. It is both sexual passion and pure, egoless, limitless devotion. *Bhakti* is one of the three main paths to salvation and by far the most popular.

But to see the face of Vishnu is terrifying. Krishna is only one of Vishnu's faces. Vishnu is the whole universe, the "unmanifest," all being, all nonbeing, all creation, all destruction, all that is wonderful and all that is horrible, too. "I am come as time, the waster of the peoples/ ready for that hour that ripens to their ruin," Vishnu warns his frightened devotee, Arjuna, in the *Bhagavad Gita*.

Like its namesake, the Vishnu Schist can appear as Krishna in one moment, beautiful and soft; but with a shift in the light or a turn of the river, it becomes something greater and more fearsome, more like the thousand glittering eyes, mouths, and limbs of the god.

Five miles down from the North Rim, I stop to admire Roaring Springs, the water source for all the developments at both rims. A few paces down the trail is a large thermos set out on a rock with a note written in a child's hand: Free Lemonade! It's not there every day, so I feel particularly blessed. Artist Bruce Aiken and his family live here to tend the pump house, and the lemonade is his children's gift to thirsty hikers.[1]

As the sunlight is leaving the lower canyon walls, I arrive at Cottonwood Campground, a scattering of tent sites nestled in cottonwoods and scrub oak along Bright Angel Creek. I take the last campsite, a flat place with a wooden picnic table, encircled by prickly scrub.

The white noise of the creek makes the campground silent. I see a bent head at the next campsite, moving hands—no soundtrack. Down by the water tap, three hikers chat companionably as if at a village well, standing close together to be heard over the creek. A tanned man in a dust-streaked T-shirt and khaki shorts straightens up and caps his canteen. I see it is Pete, who stood behind me in line during our final wait for permits at the Backcountry Office. Pete is an Englishman in his mid-thirties who lived in the Bay Area for a couple of years and is now on a car-camping vacation with his girlfriend. In line he told me he hadn't planned on hiking in, but once he got to the North Rim and saw the trail he couldn't resist. He would carry only a blanket, a water bottle, and a small bag of food.

1. Aiken lived at Roaring Springs for more than 30 years, oversaw the production of the park's water supply, and made the Grand Canyon the subject of his life's work. The Aiken family has since moved on, and, alas, there is no more lemonade.

Pete flashes me a smile. He's a slender, wiry man. The red bandana around his neck is stiff with sweat and dust. Dried red dust has plastered a few strands of fine brown hair across his forehead.

"I camped here last night and hiked to the river and back today," he says.

"Fifteen miles? Wow."

"Worth it, though." As if suddenly remembering a secret, he takes a step closer and locks his eyes on mine. His nostrils flare, his lips part. I smell his sweat, sharp and clean.

"Have you been there?" he asks in a husky voice. "Have you seen the Vishnu Schist?" His hands mime an awestruck exploration of the wall.

"Oh, yes," I say, my voice matching his, almost a whisper. Meeting his eyes, brown like my own, I feel lit up inside, my self expanded into a larger, more open space. This man feels the way I do about the rock. We hang motionless, facing each other, until someone comes up to the pump with an open canteen and Pete and I move aside. I ask if he'd like to come by the campsite later.

Around dusk, Pete emerges through the prickly branches that rim my camp. I cut up some smoked salmon and he sets down some crackers.

"I wish my girlfriend could see this," he says, "but she's really not a hiker, and I don't have a tent." I ask about his vacation and his job. He asks about mine. When it's truly dark, I set my combination flashlight/lantern on the table, throwing our faces into weird light and shadow. We trade notes on the geology of the Grand Canyon, the age of the Vishnu Schist.

"Well, I'll be off," he says. I imagine him curling up in a blanket under the scrub oaks, whose leaves pierce like thorns, rolling on the hard, dry earth at eye level with the scorpions.

I boil up my freeze-dried dinner, then tie my backpack high on a metal pole to keep it away from critters. To make sure I don't meet any scorpions, I spread out my ground cloth and sleeping bag on the picnic table, rustle down into my bag and lie flat, looking up at the near wall and beyond it the high cliffs, now brilliant in moonlight. I think again of Pete in his blanket. The wind fingers my hair.

After some time I edge out of my sleeping bag, slip on my sandals, and walk back along the trail, which is limned in moonlight down to each speck and pebble. Although I, too, am no more than a speck in the gaze of the cliffs that rise in thousand-foot terraces on either side, I feel large, exposed in this ruthless light, connected with the silent life around me, desert plants doing their night work, breathing in, breathing out. I search for anything of human scale. A mesquite tree spreads its sketchy shadow ahead. In the chiaroscuro near its trunk I slip off my shirt and shorts and offer myself to the cool bright wind.

In the morning at the water tap, Pete, blanket wrapped around his shoulders, says he had a good night. Shortly after that he heads back up the trail to the North Rim. I pack up and set off in the opposite direction, following along Bright Angel Creek about seven miles to the Colorado River and then up five miles to my next campsite at Indian Garden.

Indian Garden is a green oasis tucked into a fold of the Tonto Plateau, partway up toward the South Rim. After making camp and eating dinner, I walk out to Plateau Point, a mile and a half across the Tonto desert from the campground, to watch the sunset.

Plateau Point is a pile of broken-up chunks of Tapeats Sandstone perched at the edge of the Inner Gorge. I join a handful of hikers pressed against the guardrail and look down past thirteen hundred feet of Vishnu Schist to the Colorado River. Imagine jumping from here…. I wobble back and sit down on a flat block of sandstone. The upper canyon walls across from us and in all directions out over the river blaze under a crimson and purple sky. Behind us, the long green arms of the Tonto Plateau lie as if underwater in a calm and eerie light. A person silhouetted on a rock to my right looks so concentrated, so stilled in meditation that I stare for a moment and realize I know him; it's Damon the Desert Rat.

"Well hullo sweetheart," he rasps, and folds me up in a hug.

It's so natural to see him here, I can't stay surprised. Since he lives in Phoenix, it's easy for him to make a short trip down for the sunset and a night in camp. He has hiked every major trail in the canyon, but now, he says, his overused ankles and hips are giving him trouble.

When we first met, I was on a rim-to-rim trip with my friend Carol, a psychologist from New Jersey, and Damon was hiking with his buddy Al, both of them retired meat cutters from the Phoenix Safeway. We found ourselves at adjacent campsites. Carol and I were not eager to meet the Good Ol' Boys next door, but they won us over with their jolly, silly talk. We gave in to the second invitation to come over for a chat. It quickly became clear that Damon had a genius for the landscape. He knew more about the Grand Canyon, from his boots to his sharp blue eyes, than I would ever know. Damon loved the canyon so much that he was carrying the additional weight of a video camera on his shoulder (long before they became light enough to hold in one hand) to record his trip. The next morning these experienced hikers left before Carol and I had our coffee, but we caught up with them again at Bright Angel Campground and again at Ribbon Falls.

As we sat companionably in the cool shade of the overhang next to the falls, Damon reminisced about hiking the Boucher Trail, which he said was by far the hardest but also the most beautiful, even more beautiful than my favorite, the South Kaibab.

"That's one place I'll never go," I said. "I've heard so much about the exposure on the Boucher—sending your backpack down on a rope—I would never do that. I'm too afraid of heights."

"So am I," said Damon. "I've got acrophobia. I get dizzy if I'm not careful."

"You? After all the hiking you've done?"

"Yep, I'm afraid of heights, always was."

By the time Damon asked for our addresses so he could send us a copy of his tape when he got home, we were lifelong friends.

And here he is again at Plateau Point. Age has limited his hiking but never his love for this place. We sit side by side among the rocks until the buttes and temples swell up with darkness, then walk the mile and a half back to camp.

Damon, as usual, leaves before I do, even though I pack up and set out in the dark for the steep, five-mile climb to the South Rim. Dawn pulls sunlight down the Redwall cliffs. Mules carry anxious-looking tourists around blind corners, forcing hikers to the wall. Cigarette butts, bits of trash, and salty-smelling mule shit litter the trail. At last I emerge, sweaty and triumphant, to walk through a crowded Disneyland of tourist lodges to the South Rim campground.

Back from the hotels and parking lots, in the quiet forest at the rim, light filters down through juniper and pine; birds gather around the water taps to drink. To them, this human construction means water in the desert—a sacred business.

I use the nearest tap to wash my socks and shirt in a plastic wash basin. As I walk away, a raven coasts in and dabbles at the water running down the wooden post. Another waits nearby. Then a pygmy nuthatch, a tiny, blue-grey bird with a stubby tail and a sharp beak, takes its turn.

Three pygmy nuthatches flutter in the slender trees where I'm hanging my short clothesline. As I pin up a shirt, the little birds harass me, twittering, flying a few feet away then coming back to nearly land on my shoulder. Maybe they're trying to tell me I'm too close to a nest, but I can't see anything in the sparsely needled branches. They aren't treating me like a human, though—more like a big, stupid nuthatch. That evening in the cafeteria I find dried bird droppings on my sleeve. I decide they are a compliment, or maybe an initiation.

The next morning, instead of returning down the Bright Angel Trail through Indian Garden, I descend by the South Kaibab Trail, a shorter and steeper route to the Colorado River. It is the only trail on the main corridor that sticks to the ridges instead of following sheltered watercourses and the fault that crosses the canyon from north to south. The South Kaibab is a waterless trail that offers unobstructed views up and down the canyon and into the Inner Gorge.

Down zigzag switchbacks through red earth, my boots pull me along pell-mell toward the cleft of the canyon, the Colorado River, the bottom of the world. I stop for a long look where the trail tumbles off the gentle slope of the Tonto shelf and threads down between blocks of sandstone to the first sharp points of Vishnu Schist.

But below me, in the midday light, the Inner Gorge is not black. After the fall rains, young plants have sprouted on the pinkish-brown Zoroaster Granite, in tiny pockets of soil; pale green, arrow-shaped leaves lay their tracery across it, giving the cliffs the texture of soft corduroy. What before seemed jagged, menacing, phallic, today could be the labia of the goddess. The birthplace of life could be here, as the Hopi believe; the first humans could emerge in a season like this, the first ravens could fly out from somewhere below these paradoxical cliffs.

The river, too, is green today, a bright emerald slash from above and a roaring, swirling, juggernaut as I emerge from the tunnel at the base of the trail and cross the metal grates of the footbridge. It is a short walk to Bright Angel Campground, and from there another five minutes to the cluster of stone cottages and the canteen-dining room of Phantom Ranch. Vishnu Schist rises some 1,500 feet on both sides of this narrow oasis.

At Bright Angel Campground I find a site tucked in against the dark rock, shaded by young cottonwood trees and willows. I heave off the Kelty onto the picnic bench and sit down beside it, just taking in the warm, still air, the talk of the creek, which flows rapidly here along cobbles, and, in the background, the deeper voice of the Colorado.

Here beside me, the Vishnu is not so much jagged as made up of an interplay of rough surfaces and obsidian-like, smooth, linear pitches. Taken together, the effect is like a great compound eye. As I fix my freeze-dried dinner, wash up, arrange my usual bed, I feel that I am in the presence of an indifferent but noticing being. It is a kinesthetic sense, a sentience. It doesn't feel weird or ominous or sinister or threatening: it feels present, in the same way that I am present.

That night I fall asleep quickly. Sometime before dawn I awake, hearing the sound of my own slow breathing and sensing the comfort of other humans asleep somewhere nearby. Beside me the long, parallel planes of Vishnu's face glitter in moonlight.

After a slow, easy day with a side trip to Ribbon Falls, I once again arrive at Cottonwood in late afternoon. The sun has withdrawn to the top of the rim by the time I drop my pack on a picnic table under a low scrub oak.

At a group campsite near the water tap, eight or nine men gather around a flat rock to look at geological maps of the canyon. Their leader, a husky man in khaki shorts, is explaining competing theories of the canyon's origin. I hover on the edge, listening, then fade away to boil water for my dinner.

Later, at the water tap, I recognize Mark, the geologist, and ask him some questions about the surrounding strata. It is almost dark; the stars are out but the full moon hasn't yet appeared above the canyon wall. It's too dark to make out the details of the upper tiers of cliffs, and I can barely see his face. Not tired of explaining basic geology, Mark doesn't mind telling me that at Cottonwood we have ascended some 1,500 feet from the river and are now standing in the Grand Canyon Supergroup, brightly colored sediments ranging from 740 million to 1.2 billion years old that were laid down between the Tapeats Sandstone and the Vishnu Schist. I am astonished to hear this; throughout most of the Grand Canyon, the Supergroup layers are missing and the sandstone rests directly on the schist.

John Wesley Powell, who first explored the canyon by boat, called this contact between layers of radically different age the Great Unconformity. "Unconformity" is a geological term meaning that some layers are missing because of a long period of erosion. But who can imagine seven hundred million or a billion years simply disappearing—perhaps literally gone with the wind? I had seen the Great Unconformity pointed out with excitement on a trail or in a streambed where one could stand right next to the horizontal line of sandstone lying across the vertical schist. But I had never before realized that Cottonwood Campground is located in one of the few places where those layers still exist. Here we are, in the dark: tiny living creatures standing among the missing hundreds of millions of years.

A sudden cracking and rumbling jerks our heads up. *Thunder*, I think, but the sky is clear. Voices on the far side of the campground call back and forth indistinctly. Then Mark shouts: "Rockfall!"

We turn and see sparks somewhere up in the dark, and somehow perceptible, the falling shadow of locomotive-sized blocks—liberated, collapsing vertically like a building imploding.

Mark shouts again to his students camped under the trees. The rumbling stops. We stand side by side staring against the blackness, as a white triangle expands in slow motion against the cliff face. Like a silk parachute billowing in the wind, a dust cloud floats silently upward across the invisible walls.

Finally Mark murmurs, "I've never been present at a rockfall. It's a geologist's dream. You know they're happening constantly somewhere in the canyon, and you see the fresh scars, but I've never seen one happen. Other geologists I know have."

I'm bemused to think that he has yearned to see what the yellow highway signs have warned me against all my life: *Danger! Rocks!* Here, the natural movements of the earth go unremarked and unsigned unless a geologist is lucky enough to see them.

His voice grows more urgent. "Geology isn't just something I do for a living, you know. This is my connection to the earth." His skin seems to glow Krishna-blue in the starlight. "Biologists talk about the living green planet, and yes, there's a lot of wonderful life on the surface, but to me the whole planet is alive. It's the moon that's dead. We're lucky to be here on a planet with a living, molten core."

We stand a while longer in silence. As I move away I stumble; he catches my arm and we give each other a commemorative hug.

The next day, I stop to sit on a rock about a mile up the trail toward the North Rim. The high canyon walls blaze gold and red in the morning sun. Near the creek is a soft green landscape of feathery vegetation and above it increasingly drier and steeper talus slopes in the rainbow colors of the Supergroup. On the far side the talus crumbles out from a stratum of chunky red sedimentary rock. On the near side, a deep purple and lavender shale has formed boulders next to the trail.

Soon Mark appears, hiking along effortlessly under a large backpack. He identifies the lavender rocks beside me as Hakatai Shale, then lengthens his strides and passes out of sight. Miles later, on the long, red switchbacks above the Redwall Cliffs, he slows down, and, side by side, we drift into conversation. We talk about our work and the work not getting done: his two or three papers waiting to get written, my book.

We trudge, trudge, breathe, up the trail, which seems to steepen in the hot, still air. A raven far above us near the North Rim blows out bubbly calls like smoke rings. At the two-mile water tap Mark stops again to wait for his students. He roots around in his backpack and finds a small, wrinkled notepad and a pen.

"Here's how you can find me," he says. "Call me and I'll send you my paper on the Great Unconformity." Not a pickup line, exactly, but certainly an opening—a small, human-scale opening. I laugh and put the note in my pack, shoulder it and move on.

That evening, clean and free of the backpack, I walk again down the pavement from the North Rim Lodge to Bright Angel Point to watch the sunset. It is again a pleasure to look down from the rim after hiking in the canyon, to possess the distant thread of trail. If the woman who thought of jumping had hiked into the abyss instead, would she see a different canyon now?

In the cold early morning, I pack the car and drive slowly out of the park, not quite ready to let go. I turn onto a Forest Service road to a campground on the edge of the east rim. There, bundled up in a camp chair with my feet on a fire grate, I wait for a sign to release me or keep me here forever.

From where I sit, a forested valley in brilliant fall colors plunges down, perhaps two thousand feet, and gradually gives way to a wide flat plain stretching out some fifty miles, beige and golden in the morning light. The black, jagged line of Marble Canyon tears it in two. Beyond the plain, the Vermillion Cliffs rise up, and beyond them, the mesas and mountains of southern Utah.

A grasshopper flashes yellow wings, clicking as it flies, lands, and flies again. A raven cuts somersaults overhead. A wind stirs the ashes beneath the grate, and the air gradually warms.

Nothing is happening. And in that nothing is the fullness of life.

Stephen J. Pyne's cultural/intellectual history, *How the Canyon Became Grand*, inspired and informed parts of my essay, as did Clarence Dutton's *A Tertiary History of the Grand Cañon District*. Late in my process, I stumbled on a scholarly paper by Vinay Lal, a professor of history at UCLA: "Ambiences of Hinduism in the Wild West of America: Perspectives from Two Citadels, the Grand Canyon and Las Vegas." Lal examines in greater detail Dutton's thinking in choosing Hindu names for canyon landforms, and ponders a surprising resonance between the built excesses of Las Vegas, the natural excess of the Grand Canyon, and the grand spiritual excesses of folk and scriptural Hinduism. There's so much more to be said!

Falling Down First
by
Clint King

I always think of the Grand Canyon, and the Grand Canyon never thinks of me. I want to thank the Grand Canyon for not caring about me. For not caring where and why I have lived. What woman I deeply love. Why she broke my heart the way she did. What stuff fills my apartment. What job pays my bills. What technology I pretend to be hip with. What music inspires me. What friends I have neglected. What money I have utterly wasted. People I have helped. What liability I have created. What car I drive and repair. Why I am so optimistic. What memories I wonder will last beyond the grave.

It is nice, every once in a great while, to live and to not be cared for. The grip of caring replaced by the harsh reality: what is ultimately and irreplaceably beautiful is not necessarily yours. It is not something you possess. It is not on a talk show filled with nonsense temporarily labeled as "expert" or "truth." It is not in a book club or a motivational speaker or a new home.

The Grand Canyon will not remember you, but you will remember the Grand Canyon—and to paraphrase poet Robert Frost, *that makes all the difference.*

I had not eaten a full meal in well over a month prior to stumbling down the North Rim. A meal-less state is not the kind of pre-trip training recommended by your hiking professionals, and especially not for a lanky kid. Humbly speaking, though, what I lost in weight I made up for in heart. Problem there, too: there wasn't much left of my heart. So, I guess without calories and without heart, one is forced to rely pretty much on will.

Three of us went to the Grand Canyon, but in the end we all hiked alone. The drive past Vegas was a rowdy one. Talks of geography. And the geography of women. Discussions about the existence of God. Debates if God sculpted the Grand Canyon. I stood alone in belief with heavenly optimism. Time spent staring out windows, looking at the American West, the ugly interstates and the glorious state roads. Led Zeppelin played loudly, mainly "Immigrant Song" on repeat. Pearl Jam blasted, followed by some acoustic blues and soulful harmonicas as the sun began to sink. It's funny how the clichés can be so true—some of the best thinking gets done on the American road.

Egomaniacs, crybabies, investors, folks temporarily on top of the world, folks heartbroken, cell-phone-talkers, day-planners, immortal-feeling, 401K-responsible, debt-ridden, stuck or thriving, and undernourished . . . the Grand Canyon does not care. The beauty of the Grand Canyon begins with a simple premise: it owes you nothing. Nothing. It does not owe you a sunset. A place to dispose of your blood-drenched socks. A filter for its ancient water. Duct tape for your blisters. A full course dinner of fresh fish and organic vegetables grown near the river. It does not owe you the lover you've always dreamed of waiting for you at the end of the journey. It does not stop your sleeping bag from falling into the river and ripping. It does not supply direct deposit. Even with a map, the Grand Canyon visually defies your plans. You may desire to get to the river by sundown, but like life itself, you are not owed your timely destination.

The Grand Canyon is beautiful for this and a million other reasons. But if you are careless, you wind up with a bunch of pictures, bragging about the miles you conquered, boasting credit for that which is not yours, and in the end take nothing with you. The Grand Canyon gives you everything.

When you stand at the edge of the North Rim on a cold, sunny October day at the beginning of a trip, you feel invincible. You feel like you are standing on the edge of challenge. You check your eyes to make sure you haven't left earth and arrived on some other breathtaking planet. You don't even think, "Can I do this?" You know you can. The backpack is fresh, the bottles are full, the knife clean. Your muscles are stiff from the car ride; otherwise, you are a force to reckon with. And you know you are in the presence of good friends when you don't have to say much. You know the trip itself will be a brush with eternity. In the end, a mortal scrape with the natural elements is lonelier and deeper than any fist fight, any revenge, and certainly better for the human spirit than dwelling on the ways we are betrayed in this lifetime.

I purchased the usual trip food, nothing noteworthy, except for a couple items. First, I bought more Cliff Bars than I'd ever hope to consume on the trip—little did I know I would eat them until the very second the journey ended.

Secondly, I bought a bottle of Bushmills Irish whiskey. Each of us brought a hard alcohol of choice. John and Matt each brought vodka, while I poured a rationed amount of Irish whiskey into a Nalgene plastic bottle for the celebratory moment of reaching the Colorado River. The glass Bushmills bottle stayed at the trailhead, a trophy set aside before the adventure even started. Perhaps I imagined what I would *deserve* when I finally reached the car and the trip was over. Perhaps I would grab the Bushmills, swig it, and say, "Take that, Grand Canyon!"

Turns out I would barely have one sip of this expensive whiskey.

So we took the trail. First, John, an old friend who is now officially addicted to knowing every corner of the Grand Canyon. John will someday bring his bride to the Colorado. There, eventually, he'll summon a well-traveled midwife, and all his children will be born and baptized in the waters of the Colorado. Maybe he'll even teach them to crawl out of the Grand Canyon like I did. Second on the trail was Matt (a friend brave enough to step into the canyon with two people he barely knew; in the end, he probably would have had a better trip if John or I had fallen into the Colorado and drowned). Finally, I took the path, ate a Cliff Bar, and tightened my backpack, already halfway through my first bottle of water.

As I mentioned, no matter how many hikers go with you, you spend most of the time by yourself. Staring at the pebbles kicked by your boots. Watching the heat change color in the sky. Thinking of the next time you'll kiss her. Thinking of the last words you said before goodbye. But it's good to know you're in good company. It's good to know, even when the horizon in front of you is empty for long stretches of time, good friends are waiting for you by the river.

The first couple of the miles down from the North Rim, we hiked in close proximity. Conversation flowed. Confidence poured.

"Do you think we can drink right from Thunder River?"

"It will taste good. Shouldn't need a filter, kid."

"Let me go in front."

From this conversation you can tell a lot from our perspectives. From the start, I was already thinking about ice-cold water. John was upbeat about the trip, feeling good about drinking unfiltered water straight from Thunder River. But he wanted to earn the water. Matt was understandably a bit impatient with my pace. Heck, I was impatient with my pace. Usually I am a good lead hiker. Grew up an athlete. Long strides. Not today, though. Strides of an infant or an old man moved the arches in my feet.

After dropping down some two thousand feet of vertical scorched earth, my left hip was raw with pain. I figured I was most likely doing permanent damage at this point. Would I always walk with a limp from now on? Make no mistake, heartbreak is physical. Heartbreak is an honest rip of tendon in your hip. A clenched fist. A broken rib. A ruined liver. You can't smooth it over with self-help tips from people who know nothing about your heart in the first place. Heartbreak is not emotional. Not philosophical. Heartbreak is as raw as shadeless Arizona. And the only relief is helping your self find the river again.

I climbed down through a hot planet, where Nature looked fierce and unforgiving and raw. By Surprise Valley the heat was biblical. When you think about it, you either survive the desert or you don't. You either put a foot in front of the other or you don't. I'm not being poetic. In a place where you must drink water like air, you suddenly realize what's important.

A couple months of not eating, not exercising, listening to miserable love songs, and constantly shifting between 1st and 2nd gear in gridlock L.A. traffic made for legs strong as a neglected bird. That's being generous. I'm no doctor, but it felt like no muscle, cartilage, or tendon existed between my hipbone and my upper thigh. To have this feeling only a few miles into our hike was not encouraging. I complained. I thought about turning back. Then, democracy decided a course of action. Matt and John would venture on ahead. I would go slowly, find my own two feet.

John found a good stick for me. Looked like one Moses would use. Honestly, I never got the hang of the stick. But it stuck with me and made the miles seem measurable.

The only sound I gave a damn about was my breath pushing against the unforgiving trail. My memory cleared itself with each step. My heart re-set like an ancient internal clock.

John and Matt moved on. Even allies need to make room. What is it about a horizon that is so damn humbling? It stretches out before you, looks you in the eye. You move toward it, it moves away. You see its face. Just then, a cloud overtakes the sun and, in the time it takes you to move your stick from one spot to another, you get a hint of what real darkness looks like, how shadows blur an entire landscape and erase your footprints. The Grand Canyon, in particular, has this ability to fake you in to believing you are making progress. *Hah! Think again*, the canyon roars.

John once told me how he hiked alone a couple times into remote parts of the canyon. Spent two nights surviving at the bottom and almost needed a helicopter rescue. He'd run low on supplies and had to make do with the grace his gear provided. I respected John's ability to face the proportion of this place on his own.

The Grand Canyon is no stroll in the woods. No trot around the golf course in fresh white tennis shoes, with a plastic water bottle crinkled in your hand. The hours spent alone hiking the Grand Canyon feel eternal. Stretches of the canyon are epic. Endless. Depending on the time of year you go and the path you choose, you can go hours without seeing another face. Moreover, it is a challenge—psychologically and metaphysically—to know you are essentially climbing down into a hole. You are not achieving summit. You are not moving toward a vista, but away from one. You are falling down *first*. Down the most beautiful staircase you've ever known.

John and Matt had already sipped Thunder River by the time I arrived. Good to see other countries, the sound of friends, after you've spent time in the nation of your own skin. Their packs rested on the edge of a steep drop, away from the heat of Surprise Valley. From the looks of it, they had eaten lunch, packed, and were ready to head down toward the Colorado and set up camp. Thunder River was music to my hip. I sat down in the middle of the trail to hear the water. I pulled the bloodless knife from my pack and cut a slice of meat and put it on a piece of smashed, fingerprinted wheat bread.

Thunder River comes from nowhere and rushes cold. It makes you remember how water is *everything*. How water shaped this whole place. Whereas other hikers tentatively sipped drops of the unfiltered river, I gulped. I drank the Thunder without filter or fear. It is a primal moment, an ancient act, devouring water in an hour of need.

Hiking the Grand Canyon is a return to profound simplicity. The feeling of sitting in the dirt and letting your sweat dry. The feeling of your skin worn and well-earned on your frame. The feeling of blisters on your feet. Like roots ripping through concrete, the terrain finds a way under your skin. Even with thick hiking socks and duct tape on pivotal rubbing spots, all shields prove useless to wear. Skin toughens, without permission.

On our way to find a campsite, with canyon walls broad in all directions, my sleeping bag left my backpack. I was on a lip of trail slightly above John and Matt. Rolled tightly, the bag slipped from the straps and bounced off flat red rock. Like a dead body. *Thump*. Even with good reaction time, there was nothing I could do but watch it fall into the swift Deer Creek below. The Colorado just waited somewhere downstream to take away whatever remained.

Matt dropped his pack and ran down the water's edge. John crossed the creek with swift feet. I, meanwhile, stood stupidly frozen, finding a way to be still that would best soothe my raging hip. Watching my friends switch into search-and-rescue mode filled me with gratitude. Maybe I was wrong. You aren't totally on your own in the realm of Nature. Those Jack London stories weren't right after all. Nature doesn't always have the final say, does it?

The sleeping bag, now soaked and heavy, hit a large branch in the water, came to an abrupt stop, and ripped. The white down interior, like scrambled egg whites, splattered in bright sunshine. Matt fished the sad pathetic mess out of the water. I knew it would be my job, though, to squeeze out the water, re-roll the bag, and fasten it back on my forty-pound pack. It was the least I could do. Grand Canyon scores, takes the lead again. Only in the wilderness do people make an effort to chase after the things that slip away from us. Effort may be all that Nature allows.

After a day of red dirt, alien plant life, silly lizards, and unwavering sunlight, nightfall is a gift. By the early light of stars, you lean against cold walls so steep you could swear there was no way to hike up the way you came down. John fired up his stove, mixed together some tuna and rice, and filled my aluminum bowl before his own. Humanity scores. After all, Nature does not have propane stoves and a good friend willing to cook for you. The best tasting tuna and rice I've had in my entire life. My stomach was bottomless.

The next morning, we angled down to the river's edge, and then the three of us split up again, found our own corners in which to sit and refuel, our own piece of infinite red wall to stare down. The banks of the Colorado River are a welcome home, a return to green leaves and filtered sunlight. You can finally put your cursed sunhat away. I found a place near a wide-open stretch of the river. Took off my bloody socks. Crawled into the arm of a short tree. I opened the knife, unclean from my last snack, and cut slices of peppered salami for another dented piece of bread. Wished a rattlesnake or scorpion would have showed up near my bare feet. Maybe smelled my blood on the river breeze. I would have waved my knife and barked, "Hey, I'm finally eating here!"

The Grand Canyon collects light and decides what to do with it. In the evening, the Colorado looked prehistoric. Depending on your perspective, it is the force that holds the canyon up, the force that carves, and the force that destroys. It weaves forcefully and flattens rock. It cares not for centuries or for dams. Other riverbeds dry up. This river does not give up. This river finds a way.

The last evening, just before sundown, John caught a small fish. He placed it in a small pan of water and prepared a tidy area to filet the catch. Rafters downstream were cooking pork chops and icing down beer. Their anonymous laughter was pleasant, caught on a small river wind, along with the smoky smell of the chops. What else could we do but laugh too? We made it—somehow—down to this Eden by the river; we were lucky enough to be eating within this cathedral. We didn't camp in clusters and crowd up the river, but rather spread out along it. Humanity scores.

John and Matt went upstream to check on the pork chops and grab some cans of beer. I wandered away from the campsite. Barefoot, I glided along the edges of the river. Felt the cuts on toes and heels sting with relief. Right above the campsite, a small rock cliff looked like the perfect spot to just sit and breathe. A blue-green photogenic light hovered in all directions. I returned to camp, put on my boots without socks, and for the first time, opened the cheap disposable camera I purchased a few days ago. When they returned, I handed John the plastic camera and asked if he'd snap a picture of me up on the small cliff above the Colorado.

Looking at the picture now, it appears like a wind could blow through me. My ribs are pressed against the fabric of the shirt. My eyes are shut and there is a breeze against me, the same one helping to push the river along. At first I wondered if the trip could have been better documented. Now, I'm glad there are few photos from this solitary trip. It means *more* to have clawed, crawled, spat and sweat, cursed, almost given up, cursed giving up, marveled, and jabbed that Moses stick in the throat of the Earth over and over again. If anything, the one photo is a reminder that living is never really recorded, only lived.

I returned to camp, where the blue light from gas stoves and the aroma of boiling curry seemed a comfort and luxury. I took a small sip of whiskey. Finally, I was able to rest. Only a day and a half had passed since we left the car. For me it had been weeks, months, and years. One sip of whiskey—only one—because I was hiking out alone before sunrise. I was the slowest, so I would have to take the pre-dawn lead. I tightened the cap on the whiskey.

Even if my boots left marks in the dirt on the way down, even if a trace of my blood or sweat was stained somewhere on these canyon walls, fusty pain would not be something I could use to find my way back. The journey up would be map-free. All the old steps unreliable. Let all fools know—every step in the natural world is a new one.

I shut off my head lamp just to see how dark it really was. It was *dark*. The sun had not merely set, just an hour ago, it was *gone*. The Grand Canyon extinguishes light and gives the stars a reason to exist. I took a deep breath. Whatever hurt and joy remained, exploded and scattered in all glorious directions. I heard the river murmuring as my eyes closed.

September was a month without sleep. A month of understanding why Blues music was written. But in two days in October, the Grand Canyon took me and shook the soot from me. Wore me down and fried me in the sun. Blistered me, even as it blessed me.

Grand Connection
by
Molly McCormick

Each day on the trail in the Grand Canyon is a multi-faceted sensory carnival. This ride of adventure is the root of my love affair with the Grand Canyon. But there is more to the story than just adventure. Having recently turned 30, I have been reflecting on the decade of my life just past. The immensity of my time spent at the canyon has filled up the better part of that reflection. Through my experiences in one of the largest holes on earth, I have come to understand and gain confidence in myself. With each step of the thousands of miles hiked, I have forged a deep connection with that rugged landscape. The vibrations of the unforgiving ancient rock have reverberated up through the soles of my boots and shaped the person I am today.

On my first backpacking trip in the Grand Canyon, during the winter break from college in 2002, I visited Horseshoe Mesa. The adventure resonated with me because it was real, not something I read in a book or stared at through a museum display. It stirred my curiosity of the natural world and gave me landmarks in my quest for knowledge.

I discovered rocks of more textures and colors than I had ever experienced. I can remember an outcropping of particularly colorful pebbles stopping me dead in my tracks. I crouched down to riffle through them. Giggling at their brilliance, I lifted a few towards the sun, gasping as they sparkled. These rough gemstones were unlike any other rocks I had experienced. These stones were raw, full of the mystery of creation; they were mystical.

Along with gemstones, I explored artifacts on location. The cobblestone rip-rap on the hike down seemed to be in perfect condition, some 110 years and thousands of copper ore-carrying mule trains later. How, I wondered, was that even possible? I remember looking at the stone walls and chimney in the miner's cabin. I explored the artifacts scattered about the Last Chance Copper Mine. I marveled at the skill and effort it took to build these things. What was life like for a miner at Grand Canyon, I wondered, and what would drive a person to go to such effort to live here?

Something within me was coming alive as I immersed myself with history and nature. I went spelunking in the Cave of the Domes. I watched as the waters of Page Spring trickled down maidenhair fern into my water bottle, and I enjoyed the cool water from deep within the earth. I tasted wild mint. That night, I watched the last bit of the sun's golden rays kiss the tips of Vishnu Temple and Wotan's Throne. As I lay in my sleeping bag, breathing the crisp desert air, the immensity of pure black blew my mind, and I was introduced to the Milky Way. The sky sparkled like the rocks I had examined that day. I giggled once again when I was unable to pick out the constellations I had learned in science class—the stars were just too numerous.

Dawn came and we packed up. I groaned as I hoisted the heavy pack. I felt ripples of thunder under my feet with each step, and my body shook, not used to the weight and terrain. As I made my way up the trail, I felt like the canyon was playing a trick on me. Each switchback seemed to be steeper than the last. When I was sure I'd reached the top, the trail kept going.

"This is crazy," I muttered to myself.

I was certain this would be the last time I'd put myself through this kind of physical torture. When I finally made it out, I turned around and peered back into the deep abyss. A rush of accomplishment and wonder swept over me. A cheer of joy burst forth. I wanted everyone to know that I was special; I had just hiked the Grand Canyon.

My mind often returned to Horseshoe Mesa after that first hike. Long after the pains of accomplishment left my screaming calves, I daydreamed of the magic of being submersed in a nature so expansive, and a smile would come to my lips. After just one night, I formed a connection with that wild landscape, and I began to relate with those miners and understand what might drive a person to make a living at the Grand Canyon.

I went back to college, and my studies led me deep into the Southwest. I decided to work towards becoming a hiking guide. Consequently, it didn't take long for my boots to be reunited with the rocky canyon trails. After graduation, I moved to Flagstaff, hooked up with a hiking outfitter, and decided to stick around awhile. A few hikes later, I became a Grand Canyon backpacking guide.

Sometime before my second season as a guide, I grasped this motto that I relate to hiking in the canyon: the harder the effort, the greater the reward. I wonder if those sparkly rocks and miners' artifacts would have made such an impact on me had it not been for the strenuous hike down to Horseshoe Mesa and back. It seemed as I continued hiking the canyon that the more challenging the hike, the greater the prize: whether it be a spectacular sunset, a ruin with handprints still cast in the mortar, a hanging garden of ferns and monkey flower, a herd of bighorn sheep, or a personal breakthrough of some sort. The vibrancy of this motto rang loud after one particularly challenging adventure.

It had been a sunny easy-going early spring hike through the "gem series." This route took me from South Bass to Hermit Trail on the south side of the Colorado River. Most of the hike is on the Tonto Trail, meandering around points that overlook the river and back through drainages with names like Sapphire, Turquoise, and Ruby.

On the last night of the hike, my hiking partner and I were camped up on Yuma Point, just west of Hermit Trail. We had finished our beans and rice, and were discussing how relaxing the hike had been. We recalled all the sunbathing we had done. It was nice to have such an easy personal trip before the beginning of the backpacking guiding season. I remember feeling the fullness of privilege, like I held some secret ticket because I hiked the canyon a lot. The view from Yuma lent itself to these feelings: we were perched on a throne atop the Redwall Limestone, with expansive views east and west. Clouds in the western sky gave way to a magnificent sunset: bands of magenta here, rays of yellow and orange there, a perfect ending to the trip.

Shortly after we fell asleep, a spring storm came roaring in. Our tarp was ripped off of us, and the rain came down in sheets. My hiking partner got drenched. We attempted to put the tarp back up, but it proved impossible, and our campsite had become a pool. The storm did not show any signs of letting up. Completely unprotected, we had no choice but to move camp. We packed up our wet gear and headed for Dripping Springs,

In that first stretch, I was certain one of us was going to fall to our deaths. The now-slick trail leaned towards a five-hundred-foot drop into the Redwall narrows of upper Hermit Creek. With each step, our boots oozed towards the abyss. We carefully placed one foot in front of the other, bracing ourselves with hiking poles jammed into the earth, trying not to imagine the drop-off that existed just outside the circle of light emitted by our headlamps. One step at a time, we inched our way forward, through the downpour and roaring wind, pausing every so often to make sure we were both still present.

Once we made it to the Dripping Springs junction, we realized we were too wet to set up another camp. And anyway, the overhang at the spring wouldn't offer much in the way of protection from the rain. So we continued on, shivering as the rain turned to snow.

Having been in the backcountry for over a week, we didn't know this spring storm would become a blizzard. By the time we reached the Coconino Sandstone, we were post-holing in knee-deep drifts. Flakes the size of silver dollars were falling on us. I strained to stay present while the physical exhaustion and the cold dug deep into my bones. Meanwhile, my hiking partner was showing signs of hypothermia. I felt like it would be up to me to get us safe and warm after we reached the top. My mind churned as we trudged upward, preparing itself for what could be next. Would my car start? If not, could we get into one of the buildings at Hermit's Rest or cram into the port-o-potty at the trailhead? Was that even safe? If the truck *did* start, what would road conditions be like? What if the truck got stuck on the way to Flagstaff? Could we survive out on the side of the road? What would that look like? In an effort to keep calm and grounded, I remembered how much I loved playing in the snow. I worked at seeing the beauty of the flakes and the rounded forms of boulders under the blanket that covered the trail. I dug deep inside as my boots dug deep into snow, crunching their way up towards the rim.

When we got to the top, we found that the rain had left a thick layer of ice on the vehicle, and the truck's doors were both frozen shut. Without pausing, I took my hiking pole and attacked the ice with the sharp end. Having stopped hiking, my partner was turning blue. It didn't take long before I broke through, and the door opened. Mercifully, the truck started up, and I carefully navigated through 18 inches of freshly fallen snow to South Rim Village, where I hoped a friend and fellow guide was home. Still revved on the adrenaline that won't take no for an answer, I banged on the door so loudly that it woke the neighbors. The door soon opened, and I let out a deep exhalation. We ended the night with a hot shower, soup, and a warm bed.

The next day, I couldn't shake the conversation we had on Yuma Point about how easy the hike had been. I was disappointed in my attitude that I was somehow special for being a more experienced canyon hiker: a lesson in humility can be bittersweet. I continued to reflect upon my experience during the drive back to Flagstaff. The pinon-juniper forest was nestled under a blanket of sparkling fresh snow. I had overcome one of the most physically and mentally trying experiences of my life, and it felt great to be alive—that moment was the reward for the challenge.

The cycle of dealing with fear on the trail is something that I revisit often enough. Once, I was traversing my way across a talus ledge dotted with cat-claw acacia. It was a slippery slope of shale that led to a break in the schist and down to the cool oasis of Phantom Creek. Below this 30-foot talus ledge was a 200-foot drop-off. I started in, and with each step the earth gave way beneath me. I would slide for a few feet before regaining control. A few steps into this predicament, I was past the point of no return. "Crap," I thought, "I should have taken the route off the nose instead."

It was one of those moments when the hiker has to have impeccable timing. Movement too fast might create too much forward momentum and project me into the void. But if I moved too slowly, I would be making too much downward progress, not enough horizontal progress, and also slide into the void. I had no choice but to take a deep breath and just keep moving. With each foot placement, I anticipated the erosion, and predicted how much time I had to make the next calculated move. I felt like I could accurately judge the behavior of the shale under my boot. This gave me confidence, and I made my way across. My next obstacle was to get through a grove of cat-claw acacia. Usually, I would barge through their mischievous branches and cuss as their claws grabbed my clothes and tore at my flesh. Not today. I stopped for a moment to analyze the behavior of each branch. I wound myself around and through the direction of growth. I moved within the space they created. Fear at the top of this traverse had heightened my senses, and that had created profound awareness. When I reached the creek, I baptized my entire body in its cool forgiving waters.

The canyon, its plants, rocks, water, animals, and I are now members of a community; they are my buddies. One morning when I lived and worked at Phantom Ranch, I was meditating on a beach of the Colorado River. I was going through a tough change in my personal life, and was using water to clear my head. My mind's eye was focusing on the movement of air above the river. It seemed to swirl in a pattern that mimicked the waves. My gaze moved over to the willows that lined the banks. The ones whose feet were still in the water were growing in an intriguing arc-shape, instead of erect like the ones on the beach. Algae and other materials had collected at the tops of these wading trees. The weight had bent them and kept the tops forever under water, bouncing along in the current. Instead of succumbing to the water and drowning, these willows continued to send new shoots skyward from curved boughs. They had adapted and were thriving under this structural deviation. I realized that I could mimic the willows. I dug my feet into the wet sand. I too could adapt myself to thrive under changes in my life, could happily bounce along with the current. After meditating on this a bit, the heavy feeling I had been carrying around was released and swept away in the churning water and air.

It is moments like these, when I observe and reflect upon my surroundings, that lead me to exciting discoveries, and I can piece together elements of the natural history of a place. The ponderosa forest of Powell Plateau feels different from that of the surrounding forests on the North Rim. It is an old-growth forest, and fire was not suppressed here. This ancient character gives it a different sort of feeling; it is a trickster. I discovered this personality on a volunteer patrol trip to Dutton Point, on the plateau's eastern thumb. As I hiked out towards the point, I found myself caught up in thickets of New Mexican locust, clawing and high-stepping my way up and over ravines and through grassy meadows. The forest confused my sense of direction and tried to lead me deeper into the wilderness, away from my target. I laughed along with its trickery. As I hiked deeper into this wilderness, I kept getting the sense that if I stopped to listen, I could learn a lot. The plateau is a sacred teacher.

At the base of a giant ponderosa, I sat down to rest and soak in my surroundings. I contemplated the layers of rock that crumbled into the chasm below, and the immensity of my view. I then came back to observe the ancient forest. Thickets of Gambel oak and New Mexican locust gathered here and there, creating a maze of plants that covered the plateau. Towering ponderosa with fire-blackened bark stood proud and wise with age. Meanwhile, groupings of the younger ponderosa saplings waited to see who would survive the next lightning fire. Yarrow, with its white flower heads, bright red penstemon, tiny yellow asters, and grasses of all sorts emerged from the shallow mat of the pine needles that carpeted the loamy soil of the forest. The grasses were swaying to and fro in the gentle breeze, seed-heads empty. A wasp traveled though the lupine, pollinating the sweet purple blooms and gathering nectar. A group of vibrant red dragonflies zoomed past. I heard the chirping of a Steller's jay. The dragonflies disappeared. A squirrel investigated fallen cones for seeds before retreating home to a ponderosa snag. The smell of sweet pine filled the air. I pondered my role in this dance of existence, and settled with the deep realization that everything, truly, is connected.

A couple months after that trip to Powell Plateau, I visited a slick-rock escarpment on the north side of the Colorado River. One morning I became a participant in the great symphony of the canyon. The sunrise from my vantage point was a spectacle to see. Light cascaded outwards, caressing and dancing along the sheer cliffs, expansive flats, dramatic highs and lows of the canyon's layers. As the waves of light mingled, the play of light and shadow that unfolded before my eyes thrilled me. I closed my eyes. Currents of air caught the tendrils of my wavy hair and brought the scent of dry earth and brush to my nostrils. I let myself go, to be caught by the undulating waves of slick-rock that held me like a drop of water on a sponge. I danced and maintained equilibrium on the brink of absorption. My breath undulated with the pulse of the canyon. In my mind's eye, I saw the chocolate-velvet sinuosity of the Colorado River, planked by the towering cliffs of Powell Plateau. There was Yuma Point, and

Horseshoe Mesa covered in a blue haze off in the distance: friends who have taught me many lessons as I crept along those ridges, each step forging a connection through my body to my mind, my heart, and my soul.

II

Problems

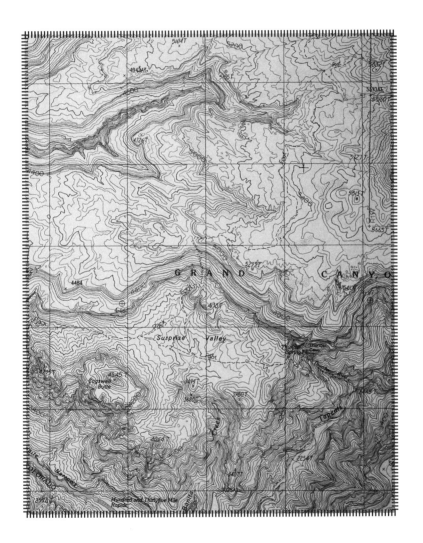

Sparks
by
Nathaniel Brodie

A National Park Service ranger found the man's discarded backpack a little ways off-trail. The following day, a half-mile south under a large overhanging boulder, another ranger discovered a stash of food, including a can of tuna fish, which the man had crushed open with a rock, as though in a frenzy to drink the juices. The boulder was between a series of dendritic drainages that merged into a small canyon, which in turn ran less than two miles into the Colorado River.

I figured the hiker was a fool who either overestimated his abilities or underestimated the Grand Canyon or both, and if he was dead—which seemed likely, as he was reported missing Tuesday and we flew in Friday—well, then he had died a fool's death, as had the five or six a year in the six years I worked on the trail crew in the canyon.

But then Cullen and I split from the others and slid down several slopes covered with scree, down past the boulder shading the snack cache, down into the narrow canyon, and in the dry stream gravel, I saw the first footprint. I followed with my eyes the wavering line of tracks down canyon, and something settled over me, something that still settles in fits and starts of memory and meaning.

I watched the change take hold of Cullen as well. Cullen had come to work on trails right out of college; he was young, baby-faced, and shy in the face of the rough-and-tumble camaraderie that characterized a trail crew. Four years later, he was a confident and wiry desert rat, who had logged more time hiking and climbing in the canyon than almost anyone I knew. Cullen swings between hummingbird-like exuberance and sullen lethargy. When he is down, he is way down, but on this search, he was up, way up, his blue eyes sparks above the red earth, his forearms rippling in knots and cords as he scrambled up boulders. When Cullen climbs, he dances along the rock, seemingly more at ease with being alive in the world on vertical rock than on level ground.

Once in the canyon, on the tracks, away from the helicopter and the others, he grew calm, more reflective, as I have often seen him become on a high route, working through a difficult move.

We followed the tracks. We pushed through branches broken by the man's passage and stepped on boulders still smudged with sand once stuck to his shoes. We'd lose the trail in the boulder fields and move slowly, stopping to scan the walls, the shaded recesses . . . and then the prints would appear in a sand patch, always down canyon, always toward the river. The days between our passings had slumped the track's edges into mere pressure spots, indents, nudges.

The heat was staggering. It was easily 105 degrees in the shade, but there was little shade. The air scorched the lungs. Heat waves warped the light to writhe around my shadow. The few patches of prickly pear had desiccated to flaccid, blanched pads, parched and partly skeletal. The antelope ground squirrels had slipped into hypnotic trances of inactivity called "aestivation." Lizards crawled atop a rock, did a few half-hearted pushups, and retreated. The heat was not general: In pockets of purple shale or near-black mudstone, it was as though we were wading through the heat, and I had to resist the urge to pantomime swimming. I had five quarts of water and doubted it would be enough to last the length of the three-mile canyon. I tried to breathe through my nose.

I stopped once and called his name. I thought he was dead, but I called out. No echo. The heat, or the pressing rock walls, absorbed the call. The natural world is a mirror of moods, reflecting one's joy, claustrophobia, pain. But always, at the core, is indifference. I had cut my hand on a sharp stone and wiped the blood on a rock, thinking, *unforgiving*, but even as I thought it, I knew the word didn't apply to mute stone or catclaw acacia, that the word hung unspoken in the air, dissipating in the sun, its little truths having nothing to impart to stone or thorn. There is nothing to forgive, nothing to do the forgiving. Every way I turned, every indication from the raw surroundings reinforced what I already knew: Life here is hard and not to be taken for granted. Perhaps especially hard for pale, mostly hairless, upright primates, no matter our brain-size or will. But hard regardless—I've seen deer and sheep dead before their times in these canyons. I called out again. Silence. A fly would buzz then stop, and the heat, the silence, hissed in the ears. Cullen called from down canyon, and I continued following the two pairs of intermingled tracks.

Not two weeks before the search, Cullen and a mutual friend, Matt, attempted to climb a Grand Canyon formation known as Newton Butte. They are both skilled and experienced rock climbers and mountaineers, and as Newton was not a technical climb, they hadn't brought ropes. They scrambled up a series of natural ramps and small cliff faces until, at a certain point, they deemed their chosen route unsafe and turned around. As Matt was navigating a tricky descent, the large rock he was using as a handhold peeled off the wall. He plunged 20 feet, bounced off a rock ledge, fell an additional 20-some feet, and finally landed on a large rock, shattering one of his feet. They were a few thousand feet below the rim of the canyon; at least three miles by trail. The sun was setting. Cullen climbed down to Matt, left him with his warm clothes, headlamp, and cigarettes, and set off, up the dangerously exposed, skinny-as-a-sheep-trail path known as the Shoshone Point Route. He then hiked a mile and a half to the road, called dispatch, and within three hours was leading a search-and-rescue medic back down the route in the dark. The medic later told me that, on the way down, she felt the wind rising out of the black night and realized it was coming from 400 feet of exposed cliff. They eventually reached Matt, shot him full of morphine, and in the morning attached him, with the medic, to a line hanging from a helicopter. Cullen, for the fourth time in 12 hours, made his lonely way along the Shoshone Point Route. Later, he would tell me of the "instant and everlasting connection" that sparked between him and Matt in the seconds Matt plummeted past him, out of sight, seemingly to his death, before yelling up that he was alive.

The peculiar realities of this search were stitching similar bonds between Cullen and me, hiking closely together now, as it was between the man somewhere down canyon and us.

Almost immediately, the dry streambed plunged off a rock shelf. It wasn't a huge drop, maybe 30 feet, but sheer, and I scouted the steep bank of scree to the right of the pour-off. There was sheep sign and sign of something else, something heavier. I knew it was his path, because I was looking and because I have traced my own faint paths back when ledges failed or turned to cliffs. I knew because my work on the National Park Service trail crew—the hiking, the daily use of pick, shovel and rockbar—has made me intimate with the nature of disturbance in these desert soils: the broken crust, the scuffed rock. We avoided the pour-off as he had done.

Despite the pressing walls, the heat, the tracks, my eyes were caught by rocks and shells. In certain sections of the canyon, we crossed bedrock that had shattered into thousands of crystalline shards, all clouded reds and translucent pinks, speckled and marred by intrusive veins of dissimilar rock. I held them to the light and pocketed the more brilliant. Dried millipede husks and flat, dime-sized snail shells glinted amidst the red shale slopes. I picked them up, and they powdered at my touch.

My job on the trail crew entails drilling holes into boulders in order to split them into workable blocks. We use a large, gas-powered rock drill, which rattles and chatters, hammering as it drills, necessitating double ear protection—earmuffs over earplugs. The world, suddenly muted, comes alive in unfamiliar ways. I'll notice a single oak leaf, hung from a spider's strand, spinning wildly, without a single other leaf moving. I'll notice, on the flat surface of the rock I am drilling, minute sand grains popping like splattering oil to the vibrations of the drill; the muscle power of a raven's tail-feathers angled when banking; the liquid slide of clouds over the canyon's vertical relief. All these phenomena stand out in near silence and acute visual clarity, and strike in me an almost nostalgic chord, like waking in a strange place and not knowing where I am or like the detached contentment of a lucid dream. So it was then, in that canyon, following the dead man's tracks, amidst the stones and shells. Some ineffable light, glancing off of them, caught me, held me.

Part of the surreal nature of the day, besides the stones and shells, the pressing walls, the heat and tracks, was that the standard geology of the Grand Canyon—a geology I have looked at and worked with for years—was warped and awry. The particular section of the Grand Canyon in which the man had gone hiking had long ago been rent by a series of enormous landslides, perhaps a dozen in all, the biggest landslide complex in the entire Grand Canyon. The streambed beneath our feet carved through the rubble of these slides. The canyon's distinctive sedimentary layers were present and recognizable, but rather than layered striations, all was rubble, upturned and askew.

The evening was long, but dusk in the confines of a canyon within a canyon is brief. Cullen and I lay our sleeping pads over a stretch of sand broken by the man's footprints and ate our freeze-dried meals in near silence. What we could see of the sky between the narrow canyon walls was veiled in clouds. Occasionally, a muffled star shone through. We didn't talk about the clouds, about how sleeping in a sandy wash in a narrow canyon in monsoon season was a tempting of fate. But it was on my mind, and I knew it was on Cullen's. I slept fitfully, in and out of dreams, bothered by the mosquitoes, the heat, the grit on my bare skin. I awoke in predawn to a rising nasal whistle, a "toweeeep" shriek, and only minutes later, hearing the "hoo, hoo-hoo," did I recognize the owl screech and call. I lay on my pad and watched the bats swoop and twitch in the soft spreading light.

I have done many dangerous things. I did many of them at this man's age: 19 years, the threshold of manhood. It was an age at which I found it inescapably important to challenge and prove myself. These challenges, predominately set against some natural form, some cliff or swell or slope, were more than a thrill. They represented everything I had come to love in this life—a furious and absolute presence in the moment, a unique natural phenomenon that sharpened the edge of life. I had, in large part, constructed myself as an insouciant individual, free to throw myself into such lovely risks. Yet, there came a time when this inner fire, this absolute need, waned. Falling in love had an integral role in the waning, as perhaps did the simple act of surviving long enough to age. I realized life is ever a series of challenges and hurdles to meet and overcome, and most of them are far more grave and life-affirming than the symbolic challenges of my own making. Certainly, I was beginning to suspect I would never be fully satisfied with my challenges—there would always be a bigger rapid, a harder climb. But perhaps the man-boy Cullen and I sought wasn't seeking to test himself, and my dawn thoughts were just my idle projections of my past against another's possible death. Most likely, he was just in over his head: no more, no less.

By the time we were up and hiking, the sun was sliding down the western slope like a guillotine. It was five days after he should have emerged. The first traffic on my park service radio concerned flying in a cadaver-sniffing dog.

Within 10 minutes of scrambling down canyon, we came to another pour-off. The bedrock streambed funneled between two cliff walls and abruptly ended, continuing a good 120 vertical feet below where we stood. I lay my belly on the burnished red floor and inched my head over the drop. The pour-off was overhung—I could look straight down at the rocky streambed below and crane my neck to see the cliff wall concaving under me. I suddenly remembered how, the night before we flew in to search, Matt, with his cast foot propped on a pillow and his eyes alternating between musing vacancy and sparkling intoxication, had told me he'd been praying a lot those last few weeks.

I made my way along the slope to the left of the pour-off, seeing if the man could have avoided the drop and continued down canyon. If not, there was no point in going over the edge. There was scant space on the steep slope between the sheer cliff above and the sheer cliff below—any misstep and I would have slid over the lip. The only person we knew to have ever hiked this canyon had described the rock as "manky." We didn't know what the word meant, but we didn't have to ask: We knew how the canyon's once-solid rock had weathered into rotten choss. I stretched out each foot and scraped the manky scree to form a foothold before stepping into it; the loosened shale skittered into freefall. I stopped every so often and scanned the slope for similar tracks but saw nothing, perhaps because I was so carefully attending to my own footing. I made the traverse—certain the man-boy could have done the same—and returned to the pour-off. Cullen, watching my slow progress, had already pulled out our gear and set up the rappel.

I was accustomed to the heat but was ripe with sweat. The littlest things—fumbling with the radio battery, a slip of the foot—and the sweat sprang out all at once, coating my bare torso. I was happy to have it, for I knew there were only so many layers of sweat and that, in time, it would grow thicker, ranker, and eventually stop. I knew sweat was effective only if it evaporated, and I noticed the beads and sheets didn't seem to be evaporating, just runneling down my skin. I also knew the instant irritation at the little nothings that cued some of my sweat flushes signaled the first stages of heat exhaustion.

We put on our climbing harnesses and clipped ourselves to the rope, which was actually two 150-foot ropes tied together and attached to the anchor. The anchor consisted of webbing and cordelette tied around a large rock, which was perched on the lip of the fall. One after the other, we stepped backward off the edge, leaning back into the void. Our feet touched the vertical wall for two steps, then the wall curved away from us, and we hung, twisting slightly in midair. Cullen zipped down, the rope whirring through his harness clip. I played the rope slowly out of my tight-clenched fist, enjoying the vertigo that blossomed and pressed my stomach.

About 100 yards downstream, we came across a single footprint in a spill of sand. We sat for a while in the last of the shade and watched the track change with the rolling sun. The shadows marking the cupped earth seeped into the sand, and the bleached track all but disappeared.

The night Matt fell, a number of us had gathered to eat dinner—indeed, Matt's car pulled up, and we cheered, only to have Cullen rush out and tell us what had happened—and talk turned to the canyon and how many of us believed it was, in a way, its own entity, an eminent force with a penchant for the occasional bitch slap. Most opined that this punishment was meted out toward those lacking the requisite respect, those who underestimated or abused the canyon, but others argued that the canyon had more than a little Old Testament wrath and would lash even devotees: hence, the handhold that gave on poor Matt. But I don't believe in a conscious or concerned force, be it the canyon or God. Nor do I believe that one can trace an effect back to a singular cause, be it a slight or a mistake.

As part of my job, I've spent countless hours clearing landslides from the trail. I have studied them in books and studied their scars on distant slopes, and though I resist the notion of simplistic causality, I understand the appeal to fixate inevitably on the split-second of initial action, that moment when the slightest tic can trigger collapse: one more degree of heat, one more night of freezing temperatures, one last carbonic acid molecule bonding with one last calcium carbonate molecule, one final grain of rock at last succumbing to gravity—so that millions of years of quiescence end with a crack and shudder of tumbling rock and dust.

Nobody knows the exact sequence of events that sparked the complex of landslides we wound through or even the time frame in which they occurred—whether as a sustained and gradual (albeit geologically quick) slumping or a more typical crash-and-boom collapse. We know many probable causes: the saturation and lubrication of an underlying shale strata, the exposure of that shale by the incision of the Colorado River, the significantly wetter climate. We know the result: a few million years ago, a 2-by-8-kilometer section of the Grand Canyon's rim broke off, slumping into the space the river had removed—an event so large that many geologists don't call it a landslide but "bedrock land slippage." We know this, but a more exact sequence, a more detailed geomorphic anatomy has yet to emerge, if it ever will.

Nor will we ever know the exact sequence of events that led to this man's journey down this canyon. We know he called his dad before he left and told him when he should return. We know where he parked his car, where he left his backpack, where he ate a snack. We know his brain flooded his skin with sweat, just as it flooded his capillaries with blood seeking temperatures cooler than his core. But the air that pressed against his skin was hotter even than his spiked core temperatures. It is likely that his head hurt, a heavy clenching of the mind. Perhaps the strange veil fell across his vision—a sparking of sunspots, his sight marred by floating, psychedelic dust motes. With all his blood pressing against his skin, less blood went to his muscles and brain. His brain had already begun to malfunction—dehydration, like inebriation, allowed bad decisions: abandoning his backpack, leaving the trail, striking off down an unknown canyon. His body, unable to dissipate the heat, began to cramp, stiffen, stumble. His stomach heaved with nausea. His world spun. He tore off his pants. His body became a furnace—at 104 degrees, his life was threatened. At 106 degrees, brain death began. He slipped into a coma.

We know where he died.

After edging past the last pour-off, he hiked downstream. The canyon walls opened into spread-out hills, with an open view of the Colorado River corridor barely a quarter-mile away. The river—water, life—

was right there. Perhaps, then, he had hope, though that last pour-off was surely still lodged in his mind like a thorn. And then the open canyon, almost a valley, swung to the south, and suddenly the strata shifted into the banded purple-brown Tapeats sandstone, and there, after all that, so close, so scared, alone, crazed, he scrambled down a series of bedrock ledges, hoping that what he saw wasn't what he saw, and peered off the lip of his life.

On a boulder at the lip of the final, undescendable pour-off was the dead man in the silent heat. He was draped across the boulder on his belly. He was naked below the waist, and his skin was burnt near black. It was as though he had fallen from a height onto the boulder. It was as though someone or something had placed him on the boulder. There were liquid stains on the boulder and bedrock ledge beneath his head. Maybe he died while bent over the boulder and throwing up; maybe he stood and fainted forward and died, and, in death, his swelling body's liquid ran out of his mouth. What sticks with me, more than the liquid stains, the red-black skin of his bare legs, was the twist in his left knee, the way the muscles and tendons and ligaments skewed and slackened in death.

After some time regarding the dead boy, I studied the rock he died on: a water-smoothed boulder of Temple Butte limestone. I thought of how billions of ancient sea organisms died, piled up on the sea floor, were covered by silt and sediment, and, after hundreds of millions of years of pressured weight and heat and uplift and erosion, became this boulder now squatting at this cliff lip, serving as a cradle for death. I thought of how, in a millennium or two, the boulder will be pushed off toward the river and of how it will crumble in time and make its way as silt to the ocean floor. I thought of how this man-boy's body, a body like a potsherd in the dust, a ruin, now with other, still-animated men's bodies moving about it, not touching it, would be taken out of this canyon, in a bag attached to a helicopter, and buried in real soil with grass on top. I looked at the body, and I looked up at the implacable face of the distant slopes, the pockets of beauty I had become accustomed to, pockets my ancestors had to learn to find beautiful, and past them, I looked into the white-blue sky, the spark of the sun in cold space.

If I seek some connection between cold space, the violent creation of this certain section of the Grand Canyon and the violent death that then lay before me—I stretch. There is no literal connection. It was an easy place to die, and a man died. But some tenuous connection stretches between me and these forces and events. On the map of the Grand Canyon above my desk, I catch myself, months later and hundreds of miles away, searching for that small stem of a canyon. I hold the crystals I found that day in my hand; I smell the sulfuric tinges of the heat they once held. I peer into their clouded transparencies and know that, like the canyon's rock walls, his death is but a screen upon which I project my own shifting thoughts: He was a fool—he was like me—and to ask what his death "meant" is as useless as attempting to point to a single cause or to presume I could find an answer lurking within the clouded crystal.

Yet, I ask. And I realize, in fragmented answer, that the man-boy, like death itself, had moved from abstraction to intimate stranger and back again, and it was never him moving, but me, just as I still move between the need to challenge myself and a more general contentedness. The old challenges and the man-boy remind me that I most appreciate living when touched by death. This still holds true, though I have learned to attempt courage, grace and satisfaction outside of wanton disregard for danger. I've learned to seek beauty and meaning in the sparks of life rather than in death.

The George Steck Memorial Toenail Trip
by
Bob Bordasch

One of my earliest off-trail backpacks in Grand Canyon ended up in near disaster, with the lives of a couple of people in real danger. I learned a lot from that experience. With that in mind, I thought it might be useful to recount the experience here.

The hike took place in early October, 1990, soon after George Steck's first book, *Grand Canyon Loop Hikes I*, was published. Although I had been an avid backpacker since I was 13, I had previously done only one short off-trail hike in Grand Canyon—along the river from Tapeats Creek to Deer Creek. I used the one-sentence description in Butchart's book, *Grand Canyon Treks*, which said, "It is not hard to follow the bench east beyond Granite Narrows and then go down to the riverbank." And it turned out not to be difficult, although it was a little harder than we expected. So, when Steck's book came out, I probably didn't take his "warnings" as seriously as I should have.

After reading Steck, I was so thoroughly excited about doing one of his loops that I aggressively tried to recruit a group of backpackers to do the Tapeats Creek-Kanab Creek loop. I ended up with a group of eight—four men and four women, one being my wife, Kathey. None of them had any Grand Canyon experience. We were all in our 30s and early 40s. I distributed copies of the route description, as well as Steck's "Comments and Caveats" chapter. I held a meeting in which gear, food, and water were discussed, as well as route details. I emphasized the importance of wearing sturdy hiking boots because of the steep, off-trail nature of the route. In retrospect, I should have limited the trip to only those individuals who were extremely strong hikers, and serious about doing the trip without any cajoling on my part.

We camped at Indian Hollow Campground the night before the hike. We drank beer and partied until 10 or 11 PM. People were slow getting up the next morning, and none of my coaxing had much effect.

I remember being somewhat dismayed that some people were cooking bacon and eggs, and taking their time doing it. We finally got going at 9 AM, about two hours later than I had planned. Everyone was told to carry at least four liters of water. I later found out that a couple of people thought that was too heavy and not necessary, and pared it down to three liters. Clearly, I should have been much more forceful in getting everyone up and on the trail by seven. And I should have checked to make sure everyone had enough water.

Once we turned off the Thunder River Trail and onto the Esplanade, the pace slowed way down. It seemed there was always someone who had to fiddle with something—adjust their pack, get a snack or a drink, remove a layer of clothing, reorganize gear, adjust boots, etc. And they always wanted to know which way to go, even though I pointed out a distant object and told them to head for that. They wanted to know if they should go to the left or right of the large boulder up ahead. At that point I started to get a little worried that not only were some of them not taking this hike seriously enough, perhaps some of them shouldn't even be doing this hike. Despite growing misgivings, I urged them on.

Our first rest stop was at Ghost Rock. As we sat in the cool shade, one of the women in our group, Catherine, mentioned that she had always had a problem with heat. *Yikes,* I thought, *great time to be telling me this.* I also noticed that several in our group had ignored my footgear warning and were wearing lightweight trail running shoes because they were "more comfortable." We had gone no more than 200 yards past Ghost Rock when Catherine collapsed backwards on her pack. The heat was, apparently, already causing her to feel faint. She drank some water, put a wet bandana on her head, and seemed to feel better. We went on.

We got to Cranberry Spring in mid-afternoon and managed to collect a little water (perhaps two or three liters total) before we moved on. I was really pushing them hard at this point. It was late afternoon by the time we got to the point overlooking the river. I realized that there was no way we would make it to Deer Creek before dark, so I decided that we should set up camp right there. Since we only had a few liters of water left, two of us hiked back to Cranberry Spring. We spent almost two hours collecting water from the drips.

I can't remember exactly how much we got, but I think it was only seven or eight liters. With our headlamps we hiked back to our camp to join the others for dinner.

Feeling rested and optimistic, we headed out early the next morning with a little more than one liter of water each. We reached the top of the Redwall chutes soon enough, but which chute was the correct one? There were no ducks or cairns, no footprints, no sign of humans anywhere. I remembered Steck saying that you can't see the bottom of the chute from the top, so that you might think you are off-route. Steck also said that he once went too far and found a chute that was much harder than the correct one, and ended up going back a ways. So I was expecting something that looked very difficult. This led us to try a couple of dead-end chutes before we found the correct one. The wrong chutes were very steep and ended in huge drop offs. This futile exploration took a lot of time and energy. It was late morning by the time we found the correct chute, and it was getting very hot. We made it down without much difficulty, but people were moving very slowly. By the time we exited the lower end of the chute and climbed up and onto the talus slope, it was already early afternoon. And now it was seriously hot.

For those not familiar with this route, the talus slope, in my opinion, is physically the most demanding part of the route. It is about a thousand vertical feet, and very steep. Steck describes it as being at or above the angle of repose.

Once we began our descent of the talus slope, the situation deteriorated quickly. The slope faced due south with little or no shade, and the rocks were sizzling hot. Two of the women, Kathey and Catherine, were having a very difficult time hiking without falling. At this point people were starting to go into survival mode. Kathey and Catherine took off their packs, and Kathey's fell over and tumbled about 100 feet down the slope. Luckily nothing was damaged. Before we were even half way down, all of us were out of water and scattered all over the place. We were all getting seriously dehydrated. I was near the back of our group trying to help some of the slower people who eventually became so discouraged that they ditched their packs. At first, I shuttled up and down the talus carrying abandoned packs, but after a couple of trips I realized that I couldn't make much progress that way and was just getting more and more dehydrated myself. The four of us who were together decided to take some essentials out of our packs and make a run to Deer Creek for water. We yelled down to the others to explain that we were abandoning our packs. I remember being kind of astonished that I could hardly think clearly about what items I should take with me in my day pack. I probably spent 10 or 15 minutes pondering the matter. My mind was just a blank. It was like, *oh yeah, I guess I need water bottles*. After another minute I would think, *oh yeah, I guess I need some food and a flashlight*. Three of the people up ahead didn't bother to take anything at all. One of the stronger hikers was way ahead and out of earshot, and he kept on going with his pack.

Near the bottom of the talus, Catherine was having serious problems. We found her lying on a hot rock in the sun. I urged her to get up and continue on to where I could see some shade. She told us to just leave her there and that she would be fine. I got her up on her feet and literally dragged her along by the back of her pants, wobbling like a puppet, towards the shade. She was dangerously dehydrated, but not yet suffering from heat stroke. When we got to the shade, a small cave-like structure made from the rubble, we had her lie down on a cool, shady rock and remove some of her clothes. At that point I was with Kathey, Catherine, and Rob. I knew that the four others were below us somewhere, but I didn't know their condition.

After about 30 minutes I decided to continue on to Deer Creek to fetch water. Kathey agreed to stay with Catherine. I expected Rob to come with me, but when he tried to stand up, he immediately started retching. He was obviously in no condition to hike. The three of them later told me that they actually "wrote notes" to their families, using sharp rocks to scratch letters into the overhanging rocks, just in case they didn't make in back alive.

I gathered all the water bottles we had (not very many), and started out again in the sun and heat. There is a deep, steep-walled ravine to cross before you get to the flat terrain, where there is a dry lake bed. When I emerged from the ravine, I saw a huge boulder in the distance and headed for it. When I got to the boulder, I found Brian lying in the shade and feeling very ill. He mumbled that he couldn't continue. He said that three others had gone ahead to Deer Creek and that one of them, Tom, still had his pack. At the lake bed, I ran into two people who had already made it down to Deer Creek and were now coming back with water for the others. Unfortunately, most of our water bottles were still in the packs that we abandoned on the talus slope, so they only had about three liters of water between them. I drank almost half a liter and continued on. I remember getting to Deer Creek and literally falling face down into it to drink. I was intending to drink it all.

It didn't take long to fully recover. As I was filling my bottles, I met Tina, who had managed to get to Deer Creek with the two who had returned with water. She said that she was just too weak to hike back. I finished filling my bottles and rushed back up the slope. It was late afternoon and the temperature was dropping. The water and the cooler temperatures had revived the stranded ones enough to continue. I encountered them just beyond the dry lake bed. They were still dehydrated, but doing much better. They gulped down the water that I brought, and we all continued on to Deer Creek. It was almost dark. We only had three flashlights among the seven of us, but we managed to get down without incident.

We spent the night at Deer Creek without much food and only one sleeping bag between us. But we were ecstatic to be alive and next to the sound of running water. It was a long, cold night. The next morning we hiked back up to retrieve our packs. Ravens had opened some of the zippers and stolen what food and shiny objects they could find. There was a lot of cheering as a couple of the stronger hikers shuttled abandoned packs down to their grateful owners. When we returned to our camp at the creek, there was a nasty note from a park ranger, who was pretty irate that we had started in illegal campfire. Our perspective was quite different; we were just happy that we had survived to read the note.

We decided not to continue on with Steck's loop. Instead, we spent two days relaxing and rejuvenating at Deer Creek. About half the group had badly damaged toenails from wearing inadequate footwear on the long, steep descent. Eventually, quite a few toenails turned black and fell off. It was suggested that we officially christen our hike "The George Steck Memorial Toenail Trip." We still refer to it this way many years later.

A number of things contributed to the near disaster, most of them being my fault. Here is my summary list of the major contributors:

1. I was not a strong enough leader.

2. We should have gotten a much earlier start on the first day.

3. Some of the people should not have been on this hike.

4. I should not have done an unfamiliar off-trail route with such a large group.

5. Cranberry Spring is not large enough to provide water for eight hikers.

6. The temperatures were above normal for that time of year.

7. I should have paid more attention to the details of Steck's route description.

The following spring I attempted the hike again, but this time with just one other strong hiker who had some Grand Canyon experience. I was so concerned with water and running out of daylight that we left at first light with about five liters each. We found a huge pothole near Ghost Rock, drank all we could, and refilled our bottles. We managed to get to Deer Creek by early afternoon, although we were both very tired, and over the next five days continued on to finish Steck's loop without any serious problems.

Freedom and Risk
by
Nic Korte

1. Bedtime Stories and Life Lessons

I don't remember much from my youth. But when I was nine or ten, growing up in Illinois, I watched a TV show called "Four Winds to Adventure," and have vivid memories of boats tossed by a muddy and raging Colorado River. Going there didn't occur to me because with my family's work schedule and finances, the Grand Canyon was as accessible as the moon. And yet, my first view of the Grand Canyon, when I was twenty-five, felt like a homecoming. Or as John Denver sang, "coming home to a place I'd never been before."

Two other students and I had driven all night, slept for 3-4 hours in a forest service campground in Williams and then drove in early to obtain a permit for the Grandview Trail. It was Memorial Day weekend. How hot was it near the first of June that early 1970s weekend? Really hot, but I lived in Tucson. It was ok. But the first view. What can prepare you for it? The writer Joseph Wood Krutch captured my feelings as he described a young cat's first encounter with catnip: "Can such things be? Indubitably they can. He flung himself down and he wallowed."

The canyon became an obsession. I just walked around my home and counted the books I have purchased (and read) about the Grand Canyon—more than 40. Until I began thinking about this essay, I didn't realize how pervasive the canyon has been in my life. When my children were small and asked for a bedtime story, I frequently described John Wesley Powell's canyon voyages. I would opine how the courage of Powell and his men was greater than today's astronauts—no support team, no practice, poor equipment and actually entering the unknown. Now, there's little in my life not represented by the canyon. Mostly, there is freedom. I felt trapped growing up—trapped in a small town where Mom knew at 7 AM Saturday morning which girl I sat with at the Friday night football game. Trapped also by a conservative religious upbringing, complete with the eyes drawn on the blackboard when the nun left the room. "He is watching you!" The first time I walked up to Hermit Rapids, it was populated by a mixed-gender group of skinny-dippers. Could such things be? In Illinois, I was threatened at gunpoint by an angry farmer for straying over a property line when hunting rabbits. The West had hundreds of square miles of public land—Grand Canyon National Park (which is not the entire Grand Canyon) has nearly 2,000 square miles. This was unimaginable freedom.

The canyon also represents the possibility of overcoming fear. I came of canyon-age when the great Harvey Butchart's first book had just been published. The Park Service sold them, but they were hidden behind the counter, not to be displayed. A friend had told me to ask for one. I still have it, complete with the type-written note the Park Service had inserted: "WARNING: THE SUPERINTENDENT OF GRAND CANYON NATIONAL PARK HAS DETERMINED THAT HIKING IN MANY PARTS OF THE GRAND CANYON CAN BE DANGEROUS TO YOUR HEALTH. *All of us who are privileged to work at Grand Canyon National Park are fans of Harvey Butchart. . . . He has over forty years experience hiking and climbing. In his excellent booklet, 'Grand Canyon Treks,' Dr. Butchart is very graphic in his warnings about the dangers of heat and dehydration. He is less explicit in his descriptions of Inner Canyon routes. When he speaks of 'rather precarious footing,' he is speaking of routes that are impossible for most of us. Many of the routes pioneered by Dr. Butchart are accessible only to . . . expert mountaineers and . . . experts in desert survival. Few of us possess . . . these skills to the degree demanded by the Grand Canyon."* The Park Service also provided a guide to *Inner Canyon Hiking.* Here's a sample of the rhetoric within: "a 1/3 mile section of rock slides in the Supai formation should not be underrated . . . the connecting trail at this point is faint to non-existent . . . the trail is vague but never totally missing for long . . . the east side contains two dangerous sections where the trail has washed away . . . The trail, or what remains of it, . . . is illogical . . . even experienced cautious hikers could get hurt without much trouble."

Well, you get the idea. Combined with these warnings and rhetoric, an acquaintance of mine, an extremely fit and strong hiker, had recently died in a snowstorm on the Tanner Trail. He now has his own paragraph in the book *Over the Edge: Death in the Grand Canyon.* So I didn't just admire the canyon; I feared it. Now, thirty-some years later, I realize the canyon taught me that life's fears and obstacles often represent the possibility of accomplishment. Such was the case with an early companion who was an experienced Grand Canyon backpacker, despite having such poor eyesight he was unable to drive a car. I learned from him how poor eyesight has both its advantages (he couldn't see the weevils in the breakfast cereal, so he didn't go hungry as I did) and its torments (he couldn't get a view of the naked females at Hermit Rapids).

And so the people of my life became much intertwined with my canyon experiences. A decade or so later, my wife and I took our son and daughter, then 9 and 11, on the Boucher-Hermit Loop. I can still see them dancing on the jelly-like "quick-mud" at the mouth of Boucher Creek and, later that night, trying to save "Fred," the prickly pear pad one of them had knocked off, by re-planting it carefully on the Tonto. I've since done trips with one or the other of my children as their schedules allowed.

My daughter and I made some winter trips. Once we ascended the Tanner Trail covered with more than a foot of fresh snow. This was the same trail, the same time of year, the same type of snowstorm in which my acquaintance had died. I had told her the story the night before, and now here we were in a similar situation. But we had each other, and we considered our options. We only walked when the fog gave us a ceiling of a few tens of feet. We knew we could reach 75 Mile Saddle even without the trail. That part was simple. "Don't climb the buttes on your right and don't fall in the canyon on your left." At 75 Mile Saddle, we intended to camp if the visibility was no better, but the fog lifted a bit more and even with the snow, we carefully negotiated the steep ascent and climbed out.

My son was available at the opposite time of the year. Once, he badly sprained his ankle at Sapphire Canyon. We were nearly 20 miles from either the South Bass or Hermit's Rest trailheads, precisely in the middle of a hike referred to in one guidebook as "no man's land." We had hired someone to drive us to the South Bass Trailhead. It was late May, and we learned later Phoenix set an all-time high that day with temperatures above 110 degrees. Now, as I looked at the anxiety and pain in my son's eyes, I recalled our driver's negative shake of the head regarding our plans. He left us with both a "good luck," and "I don't go down there this time of year." At least there was a trickle of water in Sapphire Canyon, but would I have to go for help? Would it be better to hike to the river and flag down a raft, which I could probably do in a half day with some climbing and route-finding, or would it be better to hike out to Hermit's Rest, which I couldn't do in a day? We sweated out the heat for several hours; I took most of the weight from Adam's pack. I loaded up with four and a half gallons of water in case we couldn't make the next water source. We rigged up two walking sticks, and he hobbled—not doing badly going level or uphill but suffering plenty on rough and downhill terrain. He did well enough to make Boucher Creek the next morning, and we were able to finish the hike.

My daughter and son have embraced more challenges and experienced more of life's difficulties at a younger age than I did. Both have probably managed better than I would have. I wonder how much their experiences backpacking in the canyon and elsewhere are responsible for their resilience. Will they look back someday and see their experiences in the canyon in the same light as I do mine?

Eventually, my canyon experiences encompassed more of my family and friends. My younger brother and I were not friends as children. As many rivalrous siblings do, however, we came to respect and value each other more and more. I moved away. He stayed. I worked hard to maintain my physical condition. He didn't. Then, for a variety of reasons, sometime in his forties he made as thorough a change of eating and exercise habits as I've seen. I always returned to my hometown for an annual event that included a race. One summer in the late nineties, I was amazed. My brother was running with me. He couldn't have done that at 25, and here he was doing it at 46. "Let's go backpacking," I said. He took his first backpacking trip, the Tanner Trail to the Little Colorado and back, at 47. I especially recall two incidents from that trip. Did we really want to do the 12-mile all-day hike from Palisade Creek to the Little Colorado and back? Brad had already endured an all-day plane flight, a long-drive, a hike with 60+ pounds. (No, I wasn't trying to kill him. The heavy packs allowed us to dry camp and cache food and water for the hike out.) When it was time for the long day-hike, I said, "Lead on." I could sense his determination from his initial forceful strides and knew we were going to the Little Colorado. The second thing I recall from that trip is my brother looking back at Chuar Butte from 75 Mile Saddle as we rested before the final ascent, and saying, "If someone told me I could walk that far and back, I would never have believed it. "That statement wasn't just his thanks to me for introducing him to the canyon, but more an acknowledgement of his own strength and ability to change his life and make it stick. I don't know many people who have done that. He's not just my brother; he's one of my heroes.

I also took my sister and her husband on the latter's first backpack trip. It was my time to learn or at least re-learn something. Both of them reminded me, both verbally and by example, not to forget to have fun. I looked for the trail and described the rocks and plants. They looked for places to jump into the creek. Soon, there I was in my late fifties jumping out of a tree and swinging out on a rope over a four-foot waterfall to drop into a deep pool on Havasu Creek. It was a blast. I'm sure I've missed many such opportunities in the past. Maybe I won't miss the next one.

Finally, there was the giddiness of a friend who accompanied us to Havasu. She was so excited on the way out, not because she was happy to leave, but because of what she had accomplished. "More than thirty years ago my first serious boyfriend came here," she said. "He wouldn't take me. He said I couldn't do it." This comment was poignant because her long-time marriage had recently dissolved, and this trip was one of many demonstrations of her renewed self-confidence.

Freedom, possibilities, accomplishment, relationships. These are among the reasons I return to the canyon. But when I consider further what brings me back, my answer is more complex. Recently, when a friend suggested I give a talk to a local conservation organization, I declined. Not because I don't enjoy speaking to groups—I love it, just give me an audience. But what could I say about the canyon that wouldn't be trite? Eventually, I came to a word that sums up why I re-turn—*time*. Doesn't everyone talk about time as a reason to return? My career as a geoscientist brings me back because the canyon connects me with "deep time"—a hint of realization of millions of years. As I write this, my most recent hike was along the Clear Creek Trail where the Great Unconformity is vividly shown as "islands in a Cambrian Sea." But my sense of deep time in the canyon isn't geoscientific as much as it is spiritual. I sense the vast age of the earth and the brevity of my own life span. I wish everyone on earth could place their hands on that gap of time. Could we then gaze at one another with compassion for our brief and often difficult lives and recognize that we do, indeed, all of us, belong to the same family of man? But there's more to it than a sense of time and brotherhood. Currently, I'm waiting again to hear from the Park Service on a permit request for next spring. But really, why go back so often? I can actually see a Great Unconformity just a few miles from my home in Western Colorado.

George Steck, in his book *Grand Canyon Loops,* discusses his reasons for returning. Initially, he quotes Harvey Butchart as saying being "first" was most important, with aesthetics "near the end" of his list. Steck's own list, paraphrased, looks like this:

The physical and mental challenge

The glorification of essentials (such as water)

The magnificent contradictions of the canyon; it is made up of ancient oceans, but there isn't much water to be found

The pure unity of a group under stress

The appearance of wildness

"And then there is the beauty; and don't forget the fun."

I asked myself if Steck's list captured my feelings. Is it the physical challenges? I've experienced the wilting sickness caused by the heat. I was at Tapeats Rapid, light-headed and nauseous when a river party's thermometer read 120 degrees. For several hours I sweated and napped and finally fell into a late-afternoon deep and reviving sleep before I could go on. I've waited under a rock reading a book from ten thirty in the morning until four, in early June, and then hiked until nearly ten at night. I've also hiked out in a blinding snowstorm to find our car nothing but a white lump. Those experiences were meaningful and give me stories to tell, but I would have preferred clear skies and cool weather.

I am surprised Steck and Butchart give wildlife and plants only a casual mention. I find my photographs are full of shrubs and trees growing in a spare crack, or of a shade-loving, cool-season plant growing in an odd corner where the conditions are just right. I have photographs of flowering plants in January and of flowers blooming in full sun on a southwest-facing dune in early June, when nearby rocks were hot to the touch at ten in the evening. Favorite memories include sitting on a Redwall cliff one January as the sun set and looking back to the west at a full-curl bighorn ram silhouetted against the sky. Another time my wife and I watched a beautiful male wood duck playing in Deer Creek falls. Playing? I'm not being anthropomorphic. The duck landed in the plunge pool and sat there bouncing up and down in the waves churned by the falling water. Then he paddled against the current to the middle of the pool right in front of the falls. He'd tire after awhile and ride the swift current back alongside the canyon wall into a small eddy. Then he'd swim farther back, leap into the air and land in front of the falls once again and take another ride in the waves to the back of the pool. We counted at least six repetitions.

Some wildlife memories are commonplace except for their ability to evoke the feelings of *that place, where I was.* The morning my son was resting his badly sprained ankle, I headed down Sapphire Canyon looking for a walking stick. I saw an ash-throated flycatcher hunting in the top of a mesquite. It was finding some caterpillars, but every so often it would stop and rest—opening its bill wide to dissipate heat, its throat quivering. My remembrance of that flycatcher brings back all the heat and anxiety of that day.

Condors sailing, mice chewing through my tent as I slept, bald eagles gliding along the river with their shadows against the opposite wall, ringtails running off with food while flashing their bright green eyes in our lights, a cream-colored California Bat flapping just over a sunset-illuminated pool at Bass Camp, mergansers and goldeneyes sailing so fast and low they seemed part of the rapids, a rock squirrel chewing through my brother's pack, a herd of deer gamboling across the Tonto, ravens pulling on my tent's zippers, a six-inch desert-spiny lizard gobbling insects as I lay nauseous under the same bush—I could go on for thousands of words.

Nature is free here, and while I'm here, it is also mine. So it is that the word that best sums my reasons for returning to the canyon is *possession.* Possessing memories is my driving force. To have "been there" is my special feeling. I own the bighorn on the rim near Cardenas Butte silhouetted against a setting January sun. I own the wood duck playing in Deer Creek falls. I have ownership in Little Nankoweap, Scotty's Hollow, Vasey's Paradise, the Slide of Susurrus, and Elves Chasm. The names roll off my tongue as in a poem: Grandview, Zoroaster, Havasu, Serpentine. Then there is Hance, Bass, Boucher, Dox, Dutton; names of those who were there first. Some of their history I now possess. I can't describe it any other way.

Conversely, each spot that is blank on my memory map represents something I want. For years, I desired the "gem canyons" on the West Tonto Trail: Serpentine, Emerald, Quartz, Ruby, Jade, Jasper, Turquoise, Sapphire, Agate, Slate, and Topaz. I finally hiked that nearly 30-mile stretch which has something like eleven "vees" where the trail seems so close across each side canyon, but then disappears back into a deep cleft far from the river. I'll return as long as there are more memories to possess, which I guess is as long as my own life and strength endures. So, I'm inspired by a couple doing the so-called "Freefall Route" in their seventies and by Steck and Butchart hiking the canyon into their seventies and, more recently, by the man celebrating his eightieth birthday year with more than a hundred rim-to-rim hikes.

All this is why the canyon symbolizes so much of my life. It represents both the possibility and feelings of accomplishment. I've hiked all of those scary trails the Park Service warned about. I know that many of those warnings were overstated—at least relative to my caution and eventual experience. Yet I can still connect with those early, fearful feelings. I've hiked the abandoned trails listed in the Park Service's booklet, plus a number of routes not in guidebooks other than those of Butchart and his ilk. I've had to bring some rope along and use it—all of which speaks to the possibilities of my entire life. The canyon remains the symbol of the vastness of time, the vastness of experience, the realm of possibilities and of freedom.

2. Something Happened

If only there didn't need to be a Part 2. Unfortunately, Part 1 is no longer my entire story. I can't rewrite it either. I like it, but I'm no longer the same person.

Something happened.

Some months after writing Part 1, I planned a trip with my daughter and son-in-law to visit Deer Creek and Thunder River. This was going to be my fourth trip to those locations, so I wanted to add something different. I came up with the idea of visiting Tapeats Cave and Spring—a major source of water to Tapeats Creek. We would continue on and do a cross-country exit at Crazy Jug Point.

I gathered numerous trip reports. I looked over maps and talked to people who had hiked the area. We knew what we were doing. The trip had gone very well. My son-in-law Ryan, who is an expert climber, and my daughter Ann, an experienced climber in her own right, were great companions. Ryan brought some gear so we could do the little rappel (no longer permitted) into Deer Creek narrows. We slid around in the chutes and pools. It was a blast. But two days later, it all came down. We hiked over to Thunder River, spent a nice evening there, and hiked up Tapeats Creek the following day. It was a fun hike, requiring some wading, some hoisting of packs—lots of places, in retrospect, where someone could fall and break an ankle, or a leg, or an arm. The hike took longer than expected.

When we came to the spring branch emanating from Tapeats Cave, we dropped our packs and everything but water bottles and some food for lunch (I emphasize "everything"—a mistake that was nearly fatal), and headed to the spring. The route again was slow, in the creek, over rocky ravines, etc. As we had been doing all day, we followed a trail-of-use toward this side canyon's head. Ann and Ryan had been leading the entire trip. We were hungry and it was after our usual lunchtime. Ann needed a snack. She stopped, had trouble retrieving a granola bar, and asked Ryan for help. I said, "I'll go ahead and look." I followed a faint path to the head of the canyon. I don't have any particular recollection of anything dangerous. I reached a cliff and soon realized we couldn't continue west. I looked south and headed down the slope I was on and came to a lesser cliff—maybe 15-20 feet. Obviously, this wasn't the way, so I headed back. By this time, Ann and Ryan were coming along. I yelled to them. "We are too high." Ryan nodded and pointed down into some trees as the way to go. So I hurried to meet them. Perhaps I hurried too much.

Here is what I remember: I came to a ravine full of rock. In my mind this was only about three steps across. I had crossed this ravine just moments before. This time, I was a dozen feet or so lower on the slope—still tens of feet above the cliff. Most of the rocks didn't look like they would support my weight. I've crossed a lot of talus and that's essentially what this was. I stopped and looked for a rock that would support me. I saw what I took to be a big block of Redwall—a chunk of limestone. That's a good way to cross talus. Step on rocks heavy enough to support your weight. I recall pushing with one foot. The rock was solid—until I put all my weight on it. As it moved, so did the nearby rocks. I recall yelling "No, no, no, no" as I looked up and saw eight or ten feet of the slope above me collapsing. Although I can put together a few snapshots of disconnected intervening memories, what I recall next is waking up in the intensive care unit in the Flagstaff Hospital. It was five days later. I remember saying to the nurse, "This isn't a nightmare, is it?"

Here then is what my daughter and son-in-law had to say in separate emails to their friends a few days afterwards. Ryan is a Fireman/ EMT and Ann is a rehabilitation therapist. Without their training, I would not have survived. It is also important to note that this was after mid-October when river trips are infrequent.

ANN: On the morning of Oct. 19th, we awoke around 7:30 and broke camp. Our plan was to head up Tapeats Creek north of the junction with Thunder River and explore a side canyon with a cave that held the spring that feeds Tapeats Creek. . . . Ryan mentioned we might want headlamps because there was a cave at the end. So, as an afterthought, all three of us took headlamps. Unfortunately, none of us brought a first aid kit or any warm clothes. . . . After some rough scrambling and route-finding, I needed a snack. My dad decided to go on ahead while Ryan stayed with me. . . . We looked across and saw my dad had gone too high and had missed the route down. . . . We yelled to him that he needed to come back toward us and he yelled back that he had already figured that out. Ryan and I were directly across the canyon from him. We both watched as he tested a large piece of Redwall and it appeared to hold. He then put a little more weight on it and it pulled right off the hillside taking the ground around with it including the area above where he was standing. We heard him yell "No, no, no, no" as he tumbled sideways down the slope and then disappeared over the edge of a vertical embankment. Everything was silent after that except for my screaming. Ryan jumped over the boulders separating us from where my dad landed and ran to the bottom of the embankment, and I sat down right where I was and slid down the hillside to get there as fast as I could. I kept screaming to Ryan, "Is my dad okay?" and he finally answered that he didn't know. Moments later as I was climbing over the last boulder to get to them I heard my dad's voice and got a little hope back. Seeing the fall, I honestly could not imagine that he could have survived.

RYAN: *The route was difficult. . . . Once we realized we were a hun-dred feet above the mouth of the cave, we started to descend. In the process a large rock (medium or suitcase-sized) moved when Nic tested its integrity. That test released the rock and part of the hillside above, causing Nic to roll down a 40-degree slope for at least 30 feet and then over an approximately 20-foot cliff into a dry stream bed with large boulders.*

The crazy part is it was the same terrain, slope, and condition for the whole hike up. It was one of those things where nine times out of ten it's okay; however, the tenth time the rock and ground gave way. Nic landed in the best spot possible, but his condition was really BAD!

(Time 1325) My assessment (less than1 minute from the fall) wasn't good. Nic wasn't breathing well. He was unconscious and bleeding from the front and back of his head and his left side was badly damaged. Within a few minutes, he regained consciousness and was able to follow my com-mands and requests. After about five minutes, I left Ann with her dad and went to go get help. First, I had to decide which way to go.Up to the car (15 miles + 4,000 feet up and maybe find the Park Ranger we had seen 3 days before) or down to the Colorado River (10 miles - 2,000 feet down without knowing if anyone was there). I decided for the river, because we had seen a river trip the day before while hiking to Thunder River.

As I left for my backpack and ran through the creek, through cactus, trees and bushes, I kept thinking, we don't need two injured people and my pain is temporary compared to Nic's. After an hour (1440) from leaving, I had about five rough miles down and was back to where we started our day. I left a detailed note at the campsite and continued down canyon. I was back on trails, which meant I could make better time and possibly see people that could help. This is a very busy area in summer, but I met no one. I proceeded to the Colorado River. At (1540), I was at the Colorado River. No one was in sight. I kind of lost it a little, alone, dehydrated, hun-gry, and with the thought of my wife watching her father die. But I moti-vated quickly and wrote a note for help and headed upstream to a known river camp at Mile 133. A half hour later (1610) I was cliffed-out with the river and canyon and I could not see any boats, so I turned around and decided to head downstream. About forty minutes later (1650), as I was approaching Deer Creek Falls, I was on a steep trail above the river when I saw boats. "Help, Help, Help!" was all I could get out, but I was still a mile or more away and maybe a thousand feet above. I just powered the climb and in minutes I was yelling to the rafting party. This was at River Mile 136 which is also the narrowest part of the canyon (Of course!). I left the cliff area and proceeded to Deer Creek Falls. By (1740) I was at the river level with the rafting party, but they had trouble getting satellite reception and could not reach Park Service or 911. At this point the emotional roller coaster was back because I knew my family would be staying the night and I had failed to reach help in time. By 1810, I had finally spoken to NPS 911 and was told a helicopter and paramedic would be launched from Park Headquarters. As great as it was that a paramedic was on the way, I knew there was no way they would be able to evacuate Nic that night. I knew that NPS helicopters have to be grounded within an hour of sunset and there was not time to find him and do the rescue.

ANN: My dad was in severe pain and I tried to reposition him several times, but it was very difficult, given that he landed in a boulder field and could not tolerate his leg being moved. I cut off the straps of the daypack I carried and tried to splint his wrist against his chest, using a rock to position his hand and half of his broken trekking pole. I was at least able to make his arm more comfortable, but I could not do anything for his leg, and what I began to suspect was a pelvic fracture. I constantly monitored his vitals, which gave me a little piece of mind as they remained relatively stable.

We were in a very narrow canyon, and as we lost the sun my dad started to shiver. I remembered seeing on a survival show on TV that you could use vegetation for insulation, so I spent the next couple hours cutting down every bit of grass and every tree limb nearby and covering him with it. I think initially he thought I was crazy, and then at one point when I stopped to check his pulse, he told me he thought it wouldn't hurt if I cut a little more vegetation.

As the hours passed, I became more and more terrified. I was worried that Ryan might have gotten hurt rushing out for help or that he just wasn't able to find anyone. My dad was becoming so cold that I climbed under the vegetation with him and tried to lie over his chest. He just kept shivering and his vital signs were weakening.

At 6:30 PM I thought I heard a helicopter and I jolted up. I grabbed my headlamp and turned on the flashing mode and ran to the highest rock I could find nearby. The paramedic later said they only spotted us on the first pass because of the flashing light. I still don't know what made me think to do that when it wasn't even dark.

The helicopter circled back one more time, and I was positive they saw me; I had dad lift his hand out of the vegetation and wave so they could see him and know he was alive. I told him it would be over soon, and they'd get him out, and we wouldn't have to spend the night. Then the helicopter went back down canyon, and I didn't see it or hear it for awhile. About 7:00 it came back again, and we thought they were dropping something out of the window, but neither of us could see where it went. Then I watched as the helicopter turned and went down the other canyon, clearly leaving for the night. I was sure that they had dropped someone off to help us, but I yelled and yelled and no one answered.

As time passed and no one came, I started to think they weren't coming. My dad said, "I might not make it through the night," and then he told me he loved me and he was proud of me and that I had done the best I could and I shouldn't feel bad. I told him not to talk like that and made him promise that he would stay with me that night no matter what. About 15 minutes later, I heard a whistle. I jumped up and started yelling, and some-one answered me. I kept yelling, trying to direct him to us. About 8:45, an NPS paramedic named Brandon Torres climbed over a boulder to us. He told me it had taken him two hours to get to us from where the helicopter had been able to drop him off.

His calm demeanor and positive attitude put both Dad and I more at ease. Within a few minutes he had gotten the history and started an IV and given Dad his first dose of morphine. I helped Brandon splint my dad's arm and leg, and then we rolled him to get a vacu-splint (a larger pad filled with bean bag filling that can have the air sucked out to make it rigid like a backboard) under him. Then we moved him to a flatter area with fewer rocks. After Dad was a little more comfortable I sat down a little ways away and sobbed uncontrollably. It felt good to be able to let all that emo-tion out, especially since I knew my dad was in good hands. At that point I felt reasonably sure that he was going to make it.

I can't say enough about how wonderful Brandon was to us. Hiking that terrain in the dark with all that gear was heroic. His being there and the way he interacted with us gave me hope.

RYAN: At least I knew help was on the way. I just lay down on the sand and cried. I was lucky. The rafting party (mostly nurses) welcomed me and took great care of me. We talked about the accident, and they kept me positive because we all knew the chance that Nic would live through the *night with such major trauma was not good. I slept some but I just kept replaying the accident, the noise, and second-guessing my decision-making. By morning, I was an emotional wreck thinking that Nic had probably died from his injuries. At (0700) I got satellite reception and was talking to NPS dispatch and heard the park ranger in the background say that the patient was stable and waiting for the helicopter. They informed me that Ann would hike to a spot where they could land, and they would pick her up and come to the river for me. When the helicopter landed around 11 AM, Ann jumped out and we hugged, and she told me she thought her dad was going to make it. Meanwhile, the rafting party was cheering. Under other circumstances a helicopter ride through the Grand Canyon would have been spectacular, but I don't think either of us saw the scenery.*

Ryan had worked for the NPS in Alaska, and he was an experienced emergency responder. His decision to leave in the first five minutes, literally grabbing Ann by the shoulders, telling her she was in charge of me and saying, "I have to go now!" saved my life. His mad run through that rugged terrain, that far, that fast, was remarkable. Only those who have been there can realize the extent, difficulty, and speed of his journey. Similarly, Ann knew what she should and should not do for me. She kept me warm and in the safest positions possible. I now know what an effort it was for her to appear calm to me, even as my vital signs weakened. And, then there was Brandon Torres. He visited me later in the hospital. "Just a park ranger," is how he described himself. Yet he hiked with a heavy load more than two hours in the dark on the same kind of rough terrain that nearly claimed my life. Ann and Ryan each received life-saving awards from the American Red Cross. All of us wrote the Grand Canyon NPS requesting commendations for Brandon and the NPS team.

My pelvis was separated and had multiple fractures. I had multiple broken and dislocated ribs, a fractured sacrum, a collapsed lung, and a badly shattered wrist and femur (somehow my femoral artery was not severed). All this was on my left side. I did not learn until later that my right humerus had sheared off soft tissue in my shoulder socket. Somewhere in all of this or in the contortions needed with rehab, I also damaged my left knee. Miraculously, no internal organs were damaged. Two surgeons worked on me for three long days. I spent a month in the hospital. Over the next two years, I had shoulder and knee surgery and six wrist surgeries—having to wear various splints and being in various phases of recovery most of the time.

Every day I deal with the aftermath. Because of my metal femur, pinned hip and chained pelvis, I'm no longer a runner—something I greatly miss. My wrist and shoulder surgeons tell me that their "fixes" are only temporary. I go to physical and muscle therapists two to three times most months.[1] My personal exercise routine is now about seventeen hours per week—down from approximately twice that for much of the first two years post-accident. I have needed, and still need, all of this to maintain most of my flexibility and to address pain from the injuries. A frustrating aspect of this experience is the difficulty living up to everyone's expectations. "Oh, you are all healed now," is something I hear frequently. I'm doing well, but it is a new normal. Instead of running I use a stair-climber and an elliptical machine, and it remains difficult to let go of the longing for the flexibility and confidence I once had.

This past spring, Ryan, Ann and I completed our first trip together since the accident. We had a great time in the South Bass area, climbing Mt Huethawali, exploring Copper Canyon and Huxley Terrace. I have done seven post-accident, multi-night backpack trips in the Grand Canyon. Those, and an eleven-night river trip from Lee's Ferry through Lava Falls, have relieved much of the bad memory. But it is different. I'm less confident. What I miss most is the physical prowess I once felt and the satisfaction it gave me when I finished a trip. Now, much of what I feel is relief.

Nonetheless, the Grand Canyon's beauty and the story it tells through the exposed geology are as fascinating as ever. I have seen so much of the canyon, that almost every sight triggers a wonderful memory. The family and friends I have introduced to the canyon continue to visit. I know our shared experiences in the Grand Canyon have enriched their lives. What happened to me wasn't the canyon's fault. It is mine, because I enjoyed the freedom to be there and also took the risk.

1. Regarding his recovery from the accident, Nic states, "I heartily endorse the Institute of Physical Art (www.instituteofphysicalart.com) and their training of Functional Manual Physical Therapists (FMPTs). They are a breed apart from other physical therapists and when surgeons told me I would limp or have chronic pain; the FMPTs told me it didn't have to be that way, and they were right."

About Water
by
Dillon Metcalfe

I am standing on the balls of my feet. My hands are holding fast to small holds to keep my upper body from pulling out and away into the abyss below. Under the heels of my tennis shoes are four hundred feet of empty space. My backpack, full of fifteen pounds of water, hinders my movements, but is absolutely essential to survival in this arid furnace of a canyon. A drop of sweat falls from the chin strap of my helmet, spreading out on the limestone and evaporating instantly. Some words from a Kid Cudi song run through my head: "If I fall, if I die, least I lived it to the fullest. If I fall, if I die, know I lived and missed some bullets."

This morning, I camped at Phantom Creek, where crystal clear water flowed in abundance, collecting in emerald pools deep enough to swim in. At times like that, I feel that the Grand Canyon is a nurturing womb. Birds chirp, insects buzz, and frogs sing their exuberance in the wet world. Deep in the bowels of the canyon, water flows, life flourishes, and thoughts are happy and carefree.

Then I decided to climb. As I picked my way slowly up the alternating cliffs and slopes, the canyon transformed into the open maw of an immense demon. Climbing became a tense dare. I felt the desire to climb the buttes and mesas, to stand on the very tip of one of the pointed fangs of the demon. A hot wind belched forth from the depths of the canyon, and I closed my eyes so they didn't dry out.

I moved through the scary section. Looking back at the traverse, I estimate that I climbed 120 vertical feet of crumbly Redwall Limestone. After that I traversed across a long ledge that was pretty easy, except for one spot with a four-inch-wide foothold, with a sheer cliff below. One of the old-timey canyon explorers named George Steck had written about this route in 1989. He had described it as "easier than I expected. Nowhere was there the gut-wrenching feeling of exposure. . . . Even on the traverse ledge, which—except in one place—was quite like a highway, I had no feeling of the possibility of a fall—the 400 feet to the bottom was not a concern."

George Steck is crazy. How could he publish something so terrifying and dangerous in a guidebook, and call it a route?

Now, I am up on the Supai saddle between Shiva Temple and Isis Temple. Isis Temple is my goal for today. To the south, it looms over a thousand feet high. I think that I might be able to find a way up through the mazelike layers of Supai, and then simply walk up the broken-looking Coconino Sandstone that caps the summit. It looks long and hot. I choose not to think about the return trip just now, when I will have to re-negotiate the narrow Redwall ledge and then downclimb the two vertical sections.

At the saddle, I rest and look at my map, which tells me nothing about how to climb Isis. I peer out from behind my mirrored sunglasses and under the brim of my tattered visor. From here, it seems as though I will have to sidehill around to the south of the summit. There is no semblance of a trail through the crumbling Supai. The talus ends abruptly at the lip of the Redwall that surrounds Isis, and it is at least a six-hundred-foot drop on all sides. I decide to travel close to this edge.

I would never listen to music while hiking. It seems stupid to deprive myself of a major sense when senses are what keep me alive. But even though I don't have headphones in my ears, that does not mean that I don't have tunes running through my head. "If I fall, if I die, least I lived it to the fullest . . ."

I begin my horizontal, counter-clockwise march across the Supai. As it turns out, the edge of the Redwall is only occasionally the best place to walk. It is better to take advantage of the intermittent horizontal ledges of the Supai that present themselves. While choosing my route through the talus, my mind wanders, and I begin to think about my surroundings in academic terms. I think about the age of the Supai layer that I am walking through—285 million years, the age of the canyon itself—six million years, and the age of myself—26 years. I think about the boundaries of the canyon, how it is 277 miles long, 10 miles wide, 1 mile deep, and so much bigger than any number can suggest. This is what I love most about the canyon: its dimensions lie somewhere beyond the limits of my comprehension. From the summit of every butte, I can always see how much more there is for me to know and discover. The summits and the river are where the great and powerful canyon shows itself. The side canyons and springs are where the magical little mysteries are sheltered. The whole presents a magnificent story like none other ever told.

A misstep causes a basketball-sized boulder to begin rolling. I am very near the Redwall edge here. I calmly step away from the rolling boulder, and don't look back to see where it stops to rest. I hear it roll once, twice, three times, and then it is silent. I assume it has stopped. I take a few more steps, and my thoughts have time to wander again before I hear a loud crash echoing off the valley walls below. I estimate that the heavy boulder took about five seconds to fall the full height of the Redwall to the Muav Limestone below. "If I fall, if I die, least I lived it to the fullest. If I fall, if I die, know I lived and missed some bullets."

A juniper tree provides a rare place to stop. I have been on the move now since dawn. It is only ten thirty, and the temperature must already be in the mid-nineties. It is hard to think with the sun beating down on the top of my head with such ferocity. Under the scant shade of the juniper, I empty my backpack and examine my water supply. Five liters have already disappeared. That leaves me with one. It is time to turn around. I look up at the summit, no nearer than when I began sidehilling two hours ago.

"Another time, Isis," I say aloud. These are the first words I have heard spoken in two days. The action causes my mouth to dry, and I resolve to not waste any more words—and water—until I am back at my shady poolside haven at Phantom Canyon.

I turn around and walk back the way I came. I walk, and walk, and walk.

At one o'clock, the heat is debilitating. I spot an alcove in the Manakacha layer of Supai above me. I scramble up to it and the welcome shade that it offers. I begin to think about my situation.

The thought of reversing the Redwall route of the morning causes me to shake. Downclimbing is harder than upclimbing. I pull out the map to search for other options. The contour lines reveal that the Redwall break leading down from the saddle is much steeper on the north side, which is the way I came up. It seems like the south side is gentler. I stand up to take a look at it from where I am, careful not to step out of the shade. It looks more mellow, but there is no telling for sure until I am in it. I return to the map and search for sources of water.

If I descend the Redwall break on the south side, it will deliver me onto the Tonto. Easy walking, but exposed to the afternoon sun with nowhere to hide. I use the string on my compass to measure the distance I would need to walk to get all the way around the base of Isis and back to its eastern saddle with Cheops Pyramid. From the summit, Isis Temple sprawls across the landscape in an alternating series of descending ridges, separated by deep ravines between the ridgelines. On the map, these ridgelines are like arms reaching through the inner Grand Canyon. I will need to round six arms of Isis on the way to the saddle with Cheops. From there I know I can get down to Phantom Creek, and the water that flows there.

The string tells me six miles. Six miles across the Tonto, on a summer afternoon, with one liter of water. I know that it is not enough. It is too much to ask a body to walk that far, in the present conditions, with so little water. So stupid. I recline against a boulder in the shade of the cave and hang my head in my hands.

I wait in the cave for two hours, until the late afternoon arrives and the temperature dips into the nineties. While I wait, I nap, read every printed word of material I have available, and pore over the map for other possibilities. I find none. I read a passage from George Steck, which I hope does not foretell my future: "There is no easy way out of Outlet Canyon, but in the fall of 1975 a young man came over Shiva Saddle from Dragon Creek, took a wrong turn, ran out of water and tried to find an easy way in. He got part way through the Redwall someplace in Outlet by jumping. He reached water but he fractured his skull and broke both of his legs in the process—one had a compound fracture as I remember. His body was found several days later. This is what can easily happen if you forget the injunction always to explore *from* water and not *to* water."

I read this and know that I am not following Steck's advice. I am hiking a route that I have not hiked before and hoping that I will be able to get to water this way. So stupid. The words to the song float through my head again, and now the words have a threatening clarity: "If I fall, if I die, least I lived it to the fullest. If I fall, if I die, know I lived and missed some bullets."

I pack up and begin walking. I have waited hours for this time of day, and my margin for error is thin. The sun is going down. While this makes it cooler, it will also make navigation through the many small cliffs and ledges very difficult. If it gets too dark, navigation will be impossible. I have a very long way to go.

I pick my way down the south side of the Redwall break and am surprised to find that it is very easy. I only need to use my hands in one spot. Right away, it seems, I am out on the Tonto and into the direct sun. Only small, pointy plants grow here. Blackbrush, prickly pear, agave, yucca, and withered bunchgrasses. Every organism jealously guards its moisture on the Tonto. None have any spare drops for me. A bead of sweat runs down my cheek. I catch it with my finger and reclaim it. My march begins.

I use every trick I know to keep my water. I pop up the collar of my shirt to keep the sun off of my neck, and unroll my long sleeves to do the same for my arms. I strive to breathe only through my nose, despite the hard work of off-trail hiking. I put the hose of my water bladder away to avoid the temptation to sip at it, and resolve to only let myself drink every time I round an arm of Isis. I decide to pee into a water bottle, having heard a rumor once that this could be used as an emergency source of fluid. *Just in case*, I think to myself.

As I work my way southeast, I think about how foolishly I have behaved. This morning, I committed to a difficult route that I felt uncomfortable reversing. I should have stopped at the top and re-assessed immediately. Instead, I chose to attempt another long and exposed climb before considering where my next water was coming from. Now, I am going against the advice of an experienced Grand Canyon explorer, exploring *to* water and hoping I will find it. I can already feel the desperation creeping into my drying tissues. I am thirsty.

The liquid left in my water bladder diminishes each time I round an arm of the temple. It is difficult not to be greedy with water at these stops. I swirl it around in my mouth each time I sip, relishing the pure taste. Despite this small supplement, I grow more and more dehydrated the farther I walk. The canyon shadows stretch longer, and I welcome the relief they offer. I no longer have the coherence to recognize that long shadows mean my time is growing short. Soon, I will be stranded on the Tonto overnight with no water.

I begin to think of the water in my bladder as something more precious than Gollum's Ring. It is such a small amount and yet so important. I begin to chase lizards that cross my path, hungering for the moisture contained in their tubular bodies. I envision tearing off one of their heads and slurping out their blood and organs. They always scurry into the safety of a dagger-like agave. I continue to march.

At the ridge of one arm, I stop and sip at the tube. I hear the telltale bubbling sound that means it is almost empty. "Never drink your last drop" is a mantra I have used before, but I have never been this desperate. I pull out the map while sitting under a lone juniper. I sit very still and analyze my projected route. I see that there are three rough miles left to go. I allow myself a single spoken word, despite the moisture that it will waste: "Doom."

In and out of another drainage I go. It has been forty minutes since my last break and my last sip of water, but I will not allow myself the luxury of either now. I think about all the times I have stood naked outside the shower, just waiting for the water to run the right temperature. I think I would give one of my toes for that amount of wasted water. The color of the canyon walls turns a deep red hue.

At the next ridge, I cannot think about anything but the last drop in my water bladder. I pull out the hose and drain it dry. I have gone against my mantra and drunk my last drop. If not for this time, then what for? I think about how much water is present in this canyon, and how inaccessible it seems. I think about how a household in Las Vegas will use 250 gallons of water a day, one in Phoenix 140 a day, and one on the Hopi reservation maybe twenty. I have used two today and am ready to do anything for another pint. I am amazed at how so little can mean so much.

I round the last ridge and peer into the back of the drainage on the other side of it. It is gloomy in the early evening light. The sun has set, but I still have enough light to see that this last drainage is a steep, rugged scramble along a slide of Redwall debris. On the far side, I can see the saddle between Cheops and Isis. From there, there is a sheep trail that I can take down into Phantom Creek, where my pools and salvation lie. It looks like a long way.

In the back of the drainage, I look at the steep climb ahead. It is almost too dark to see my footing, but I can see the route up to the saddle. No cliffs. My tongue is thick in the back of my throat. I pull out the last drop of moisture that I still carry: the bottle that I urinated in hours ago, the last time that I peed. I unscrew the cap and hold it for a moment. The words to the song that have been stuck in my head all day float half-heartedly through my head. The record is now a broken one. "If I fall, if I die . . ." I hold my breath and take a quick swig. I swallow immediately, trying not to taste.

The sour urine puckers the back of my throat and feels grotesque in my belly. I cough and pour the rest out. It does not feel like a nourishing source of hydration. As I empty the metal bottle onto the ground, I am able to see in the evening gloom that the urine is dark as apple juice. Maybe if I had saved urine from earlier in the morning, when I had been hydrated, it would have been effective, but not this stuff. It is pure ammonia.

Climbing the slope, I trip on easy ground. I wind back and forth. My stomach hurts. The taste of a livestock stable sours my breath and my lolling tongue. It is the taste of stupidity. It is the taste of inexperience. It is the taste of looming desiccation and expiration at the hands of a brutally beautiful landscape. It is the taste of reckless behavior inspired by desperation. I think about other ends I would pursue in order to drink. I think of the young hiker in George Steck's story, who jumped down a side canyon to get to water and broke his legs and skull. I think of Margaret Bradley, the marathon runner the rim rangers tell everyone about, who died the same way only a couple of years ago. Those two are among the ranks of dozens. I wonder if I am creating a similar story this night.

I make the top of the ridge, and have the good sense to put on my headlamp for the descent along the sheep trail. When I turn it on, the stars in the sky dim as my pupils adjust to the new light source. I came this way before, two days ago, when climbing Cheops Pyramid. No more unknowns to frighten me. No more fear of impossible, off-trail, night-time navigation. With a featherweight, empty backpack, I begin a semi-controlled fall down into Phantom Canyon. I fool myself into believing that I am running.

"It is a good thing I have run so much in the canyon," I think. "I have prepared for this." My constant stumbling and weaving across the trail, however, betray the truth.

Halfway down the slope, I can smell the water, and the riparian vegetation that depends on it. It is the sweetest thing I can imagine. Images of its smooth, flowing surface fill my mind, and I can see little of the rocky trail that my feet are just barely navigating. I trip, and catch myself on a large rock with my hands.

I am close now. All my senses except taste are full of the knowledge of water being close. I can even see my headlamp reflect on the surface now and then, although the creek is still a hundred feet below. I can hear it running over small waterfalls at the base of my pool. It is there. It doesn't matter what happens now. I could fall and break my leg and still be able to drag myself to the edge of the creek and drink deeply. It is the only thing that matters.

I don't bother stripping off my clothes. I don't jump, but rather fall in, face forward and arms outstretched, like a child returning to its mother after a long absence. I flop into the pool with a splash, and in the darkness open my eyes. I am completely immersed in the thing that I have sought for so long. I am surrounded by music and laughter and dancing and life. I float to the surface, and there gulp down so much creek water that I begin to sink. I climb out and lay on my back, looking at the stars. Every few seconds I lean over and drink deeply from the creek, the source of all life, and in whose absence non-life is the rule. Cottonwood leaves rustle over my head. Frogs sing. Bats seek to eat humming and chirping insects. There is no place in my mind for pop tunes now. Only the sweet music of the creek and all the life it supports. I think of how much life can be supported by so little water. I will never let the shower run down the drain again.

A Day Off-Trail
(or, How to Almost Die in the Grand Canyon)
by
David G. Zucconi

I felt very alone, standing on the Tonto Plateau overlooking Bright Angel Canyon. I could see a speck of color far below, the brightly-colored backpack of one of the two friends I had left more than an hour before, and I was reflecting on how one could have a considerable change of heart from the time you say you're going to do something, to when you actually do it . . .

My co-hikers Jack and Doc shared my long-time enthusiasm for the Grand Canyon, each of us having walked its trails for a number of years. On this trek in early March, 1983, we planned to follow an old cattle route that ascended from the Bright Angel creekbed to the North Tonto Plateau, via a break in the otherwise sheer Tapeats layer, and thence south and west along the plateau to some vague point where we could descend to Phantom Creek. From there we would follow Phantom out to Bright Angel Creek and the North Kaibab Trail. The route had been loosely described in a popular trail guide of the times and although information was scant, we were confident that our collective savvy would see us through for the overnight, off-trail walk.

The adventure was planned to begin on our second day in the canyon. After a first night at Bright Angel Campground, we lugged our packs along the North Kaibab Trail to a point where we could see the break in the Tapeats. It was an absolutely gorgeous day, so we decided to leave our packs and side-bar to Ribbon Falls where we lingered to enjoy its graceful beauty a little longer then intended. By the time we returned to our packs, daylight was fading; we had hoped to be on top of the Tonto for dinner, so we launched ourselves and our packs, replete with water for the night and the next day, up the first slope. Scrambling up a faint trail marked with sheep tracks, we soon lost the trail to scree; we weighed the difficulty of the climb against the amount of daylight left, and decided to abandon the attempt to the oncoming night.

As we ate dinner by flashlight, my hiking partners indicated their reluctance to resume our itinerary the next day; they preferred to return to Bright Angel Campground via the Kaibab Trail. I listened, but voiced no agreement. Later in the evening, I mulled over the prospect of doing the trek alone, completing it in one day instead of two, so that I would be back on schedule at the campground the following evening. I was well-aware that solo hiking in the canyon (or elsewhere) was not the smartest thing to do; still, I berated myself for not having the courage to "go it alone" and follow through on the original plan. So I decided to do it. My decision lacked the enthusiasm that characterized our carefree map-gazing of months ago; in fact, I felt a little bit scared. The reality that this off-trail, drainage-hopping trek would be attempted without the moral support of my hiking buddies was a sobering one. Already, my viewpoint was changing.

Following a very restless night, I emerged at the crack of dawn with a determination that was more like resignation. By the time I had packed my gear and finished a hasty breakfast of granola bars and coffee, Jack and Doc were stirring. It was 7 AM when I somewhat nervously predicted that I would rendezvous with them that night—"See you for cocktails this evening," and all that sort of thing—as I headed for the talus slopes.

The route was clear insofar as to where I would have to climb through the break in the Tapeats layer—that sheer strata of sandstone that underlies the Tonto Plateau and effectively blocks access up or down except where it has been breached by earth forces. The looseness and steep grade of the route posed a degree of concern as I cut from the top of the first rise into a slight drainage, then up the other side to reach the final slope leading to the plateau. Never considered a daredevil, and seldom feeling at ease with unstable footing and great heights, I found myself experiencing relief as well as a sense of isolation when I finally stood atop and considered the route I had just followed. My companions were barely visible to my eye, but I could see a speck of orange representing Jack's Kelty. I waved several times on the presumption that they were watching with Doc's binoculars, then set off to follow this non-trail under the combined guidance of terrain features and sheep tracks.

My trek in and out of numerous drainages throughout that morning and afternoon, and my subsequent descent off the Tonto into Phantom Canyon, was made comprehensible with the aid of a detailed topo published by the National Geographic Society in 1978. Printed on a larger scale than most topographical maps, and in considerably more detail, the map helped me stay oriented all of the time that I was on the plateau. This was a matter of paramount importance to me; if I didn't know where I was at all times, I might be at a loss at to where I should climb down off the Tonto. Sheep tracks were abundant and often helpful, and several times I trusted to their direction rather than resorting to my own judgment of the contours; invariably, the tracks were right. It was interesting to note that bighorn sheep—like people—appear to follow the path of least resistance when going from one point to another (i.e., heading a drainage as opposed to going down one side and up the other).

As I worked my way into and out of drainages, trying to find a happy medium between distance and elevation, I found that bushwacking on the Tonto Plateau required much more concentration with each footstep than I had imagined. On a maintained trail, or just a well-walked one, there is seldom concern about tripping on stones or walking into the sharp spines of agave or hedgehog. Here, however, it was necessary to pick my way at nearly every footstep; when I failed to do so, I paid a price. A moment's distraction, looking for a landmark on my map, earned me a sharp stab from spines that seemed to grow EVERYWHERE on this plateau (the fact that I was wearing canvas sneakers didn't help, either). Another moment of inattention resulted in a stumble over some boulders and a cut hand. I learned from these painful lessons, but as I continued hiking, I grew increasingly leg-weary and sometimes less mindful of the lessons I had just learned.

The beauty of that warm day with blue skies and no hint of rain was marred by the buzz of helicopters and aircraft conducting their aerial tours over the Inner Gorge. Their droning led me to consider the paradox of my situation: I was not far, in terms of distance, from people, campsites, and air traffic, yet I was totally isolated by the place and circumstance of my trek. I exulted in the exclusivity of my situation, with not another soul in sight or likely to be; at the same time, I lamented the absence of a companion or two to share the moment.

I lunched briefly in one shallow drainage, found a trickle of water in another to replenish my supply, and took a mid-afternoon break at a third site. By the time I had rounded Johnson Point and negotiated the long canyon of Buddha's Cloister, I was tired and freely admitting it to myself. The spring was gone from my step, and I had ceased to care about taking photographs—an unusual attitude for a happy-snapper like myself. At Sturdevant Point I encountered the unique "oasis" that is characterized by cottonwood trees, desert yucca and waist-high grass. Visible from the South Rim (after recent rains), this spot appears as a small patch of green amidst the brown, high up on the plateau just below the point. Evidence of mountain sheep were everywhere—tracks, pellets, flattened grass. I could easily see how this would be a favorite resting place for them. I considered the sight of this oasis in a somewhat detached fashion, however, since I was now only concerned with finding the route that would conduct me off the plateau and down into Phantom Canyon.

Up to this point, it had been my hope that the route would intersect with Phantom Canyon at a place where I could easily climb down into the creek bed. Now, after several consultations with my map, and after noting the manner in which the terrain was laid out, I decided that my most probable course of descent should be in the drainage between Buddha Cloister and Schellbach Butte; this required a certain optimism that those smooth spaces between the 100-foot contours of my map did not conceal pour-offs and other precarious obstacles to downward progress. As it turned out, my chosen path of descent would in no way have accommodated the herds of cattle, pre-1900s vintage, that are alleged to have followed this route.

I worked my way down into this drainage with a minimal amount of scrambling and stopped to rest in a shady spot. After what turned out to be a brief nap, I trudged on down canyon. A trickle of water in the streambed soon led to a waterfall, where a clamor of amphibian calls had me wondering what those "ducks" were doing below the waterfall. (I was really, really getting tired.) The fall's height of perhaps 15-20 feet, and its sheer drop, caused me to consider the situation for a moment before I proceeded, pack and all, over the edge. ("I don't give a rat's noodle; I'm too tired to stop now!") This elegant feat of foolish abandon required a rock climb down the east side of the fall. At another time, and in the company of more sensible people, I would probably have declined this scramble, declaring it too steep, too high, too risky, and returned the way I had come. But I was already too far along in the day to accept that wiser option; my prime motivation now was just to keep moving ahead, regardless of obstacles. I remember being a little surprised at my own boldness as I began my hand-over-hand descent, ignoring the fact that some parts of the wall were more than vertical as I hung out over space. During the descent, I heard the chorus of frogs congregated in the pool at the fall's base, oblivious to all except the promised bliss of springtime nuptials. It almost made me feel ignored. (Shouldn't my present danger be sensed and respected by all creatures in the vicinity?) When I reached the base of the falls, I felt pretty good about what I had just accomplished; at the same time, I found myself desperately hoping that this frightening experience would prove to be the hardest, and the last, I would encounter on the remainder of my bushwhack.

It was not too much further downstream before I reached the intersection with Phantom Creek and felt a wave of relief for having reached this particular milestone in the trek. I was sufficiently renewed in spirit that I even walked back to the waterfall, camera in hand, to take a few photographs.

After I returned to Phantom Creek, I spent more time walking in water than not. The banks, where they existed, were crowded with boulders and vegetation—more difficult to walk on than in the bed itself. There were frequent pools to bypass, ranging in depth from a couple of feet to five feet or so. In an effort to keep my outer clothes dry, I stripped down to my skivvies and put my clothes inside my pack, informing myself that I was at least half-way to emulating Colin Fletcher as he hiked, nude, in *The Man Who Walked Through Time*. I certainly was not worried that I would encounter anyone else as I slogged along in my drenched skivvies and waterlogged sneakers—there could only be one fool on this misadventure today!

Bypassing some of the deeper pools of Phantom required a measure of deliberate climbing along some fairly smooth rock walls that offered only the barest of holds. Although a slip, in most cases, would have resulted in little more than a drenching for my pack and me, I was motivated by the challenge of returning to camp both unscathed and un-dunked! Hands and feet were not enough for wall-scaling at times, and I would "tripod"—using my hiking stick (these were pre-trekking-pole days) as a long extension of my arm; this permitted me to reach across to the opposite side of a pool while my feet and other arm were braced against the canyon wall, and thereby I walked the sloped and shallow edge of the pool. At other times, an ungraceful leap into the shallowest portion of a pool was my only recourse to evade the deeper part. For a while, I thought myself pretty lucky. Then, I encountered the BIG pool. . . .

Mechanically, my exhausted legs had raced the oncoming darkness that was filling the canyon. I had met all obstacles up to that point and had even acquired an air of overconfidence, but mixed with that hubris was a solid measure of fatigue that deprives one of sound judgment. Now, as I contemplated the obstacle that confronted me, it was obvious that this pool—some 20-25 feet wide and at least 30-40 feet long to the point where it disappeared around a bend of the canyon wall—was well over my head in depth; worse, the encompassing walls were much smoother than what I had encountered up to that point. It seemed inevitable that I was going to get wet, so I sealed my shirt, pants and wallet in a large plastic bag that I stowed inside my pack, shrugged my shoulders, and began the attempt.

I didn't have to go far before I ran out of any kind of hold and dropped like a rocket, almost with predetermined resignation, into the creek's waters. I was right about it being over my head; my pack and I were totally submerged and I was not touching bottom! Kicking vigorously, I surfaced, grasping for whatever slight irregularities might be found in the canyon wall as I flailed my legs to keep my head above water. Unfortunately, my pack had tilted sideways and the left shoulder strap seemed to be pulling me backwards and down. I submerged, resurfaced again, and this time found a slight depression in the wall to stabilize my position in the water. I remember that my breathing was very heavy, no doubt a result of exertion and panic, and I was hoping that I could float myself alongside the wall by using a succession of handholds. So smooth was that wall, however, that it was impossible for my wet hands to grasp anything. Instead of waiting until I fully caught my breath before attempting another move, I yielded to panic and launched myself along the wall in desperation to find a handhold. There was none, and I went under again. When I resurfaced, I could find no purchase whatsoever, and a major concern was racing through my mind (i.e., "is this the way I die?"). Wildly, I kicked my legs and kept reaching for the unseen. It was during this moment of desperate foreboding that I saw—and realized—that my outstretched left hand was not responding to the urgency in my mind; it was reaching and clawing with only a fraction of the effort that my mind was commanding. It struck me that exhaustion, numbness from the cold water, and sheer panic were acting in concert; desperation of effort was about to be my permanent undoing if I didn't find an alternative action soon!

All at once it dawned on me to jettison my pack and swim to a safe landing before my exhaustion was complete. Fortunately, I was able to disengage my hip belt and shoulder straps without complications. I then noticed that, without the attached weight of my body, my pack was floating, thanks to the bladder effect of the sealed plastic bag with my clothes. I quickly grasped the bottom posts of the pack, one in each hand, and kicked and propelled myself forward (similar in fashion to a water event described by Fletcher), around the bend in the canyon wall and to "shore"—a natural dam caused by an earth slide into the creek bed. That sloughed mass of dirt and rocks had created my "pool from hell," but never have I felt so grateful to be alive as when my feet touched its dirt and mud!

The exhilaration that accompanies survival was immediately lost to the cold, shivering sensation that next visited me, and for the second time in minutes, I was grateful that I had placed my outer clothes in a plastic sack. After putting these on, I set about to assess the rest of my pack's contents and found everything thoroughly wet—down sleeping bag, camera, tent, extra clothing, food—everything. Darkness was overcoming the daylight, so as rapidly as possible I wrung out everything as much as I could and repacked. Perhaps fatigue had an effect on my ability to estimate, but I swore that that pack now had the heft and feel of a 75-lb load. (It was closer to 50 when I had set out that morning.) Wearily, very wearily, I continued on downstream, hoping that I would be able to return to Bright Angel Campground before total dark set in. It seemed that I was covering miles and miles of creek, trudging on with no other determination than to "get home." There were more pools to climb around and riffles to negotiate, but I was now unfazed by these minor obstacles; I only hoped, quite fervently, that there would be no more big pools or waterfalls. I was within perhaps a mile of the junction with Bright Angel Creek when I noted shoe-prints in the mud of the creek bank. This was cause for optimism, I thought; surely there would be no more serious impediments between there and Bright Angel Creek, and I would have clear sailing the rest of the way to the campground. Although partially true, this last piece of Phantom Creek was no piece of cake, and comfortable stretches of walking were few and far between, right on down to the confluence.

Darkness became an even more serious concern as I guessed my way between barely discernible boulders in the creek bed, and I debated the possibility of camping on a small patch of bank and completing my trek with daylight's return. This was not a good option; the idea of camping with wet clothes, wet sleeping bag and wet matches did not appeal, especially to someone already exhausted and chilled (and evening lows were expected to be in the 40s). Also, there remained a hint of that wanton sense of adventure, a challenge if you will, that was urging me to doggedly keep lifting one foot in front of the other, against any better judgment about the hazard of hiking in the dark between wet rocks and boulders. I occasionally glanced up, watching the last vestige of daylight slowly disappear between the parapets towering darkly above. At one point I thought I felt a warm breeze rushing at me from down-canyon; dare I hope that this was a harbinger of the confluence? After what seemed like an eternity of rock-hopping, the smaller flow of Phantom Creek yielded to the larger and much more forceful surge of Bright Angel Creek. It was fully dark as I negotiated the thigh-deep waters of the Bright Angel in order to reach the Kaibab Trail on its east bank. This I did as slowly and deliberately as possible, to avoid the consequences of a slip in that fast, dark current.

Once on the other side and heading south along the Kaibab, I felt safe and "home free;" the unknown was behind me. Although exhausted, I could enjoy the luxury of self-admiration, as well as the comforting thought that camp and my companions were only a mile beyond this point. As I wearily trudged that final mile, sporadically employing the assistance of my failing penlight but relying on the good quality of the trail along this stretch, I wavered between the euphoria that comes with achievement and the frightening reality of what unhappily might have been. My one day off-trail had opened up a whole new viewpoint to me, one that I would think about often in the days and years to come.

Night Hike, South Kaibab
by
Kristi Rugg

10:37 PM. Shoes tightened, straps clipped on my pack, hiking poles in hand, water bladder filled, headlamp secured upon my baseball cap—everything is ready.

At the brink of adventure and struggle, I stand with my two hiking partners—my thoughts and the world which surrounds me. The canyon seems distant for the moment, as I am absorbed in the day's events, the journey ahead, the constant to-do list. I am in every moment but this one.

For the past eight days I have been working as an interpretive ranger at Phantom Ranch, the backcountry ranger station hidden in the deepest depths of Grand Canyon. It has been a tough tour of duty— the canyon floor reaches 130°F midday in the June sun, we had spent four days without fresh water, and each day brought new challenges as hikers, mule riders, and river runners arrived at Phantom with a variety of medical troubles, resulting in an average of 30 contacts a day. A cardiac patient had consumed my afternoon and evening hours, delaying my departure until this late at night.

Nothing is taken for granted in the canyon—she does not discriminate. A young, fit river runner doubled over in pain from kidney stones, an older, semi-conscious woman violently vomiting, and many in between have all fallen victim to her. Cuts, blisters, twisted ankles, fire ant bites, scorpion stings, heat exhaustion, dehydration, hyponatremia… the list goes on, and that list has my mind spinning.

Though I've already worked 15 hours, I know I must hike out tonight. Tomorrow, the forecast is 125°F in the sun, which will make the 7.2-mile, 5,000-foot climb deathly dangerous. The cooler temperatures, full moon, clear night skies, fresh air, and time to decompress have convinced me to start the long slog out now. It's still over 90°F, but as I ascend from the canyon floor to the South Rim, the temperatures will descend dramatically, and I have several layers tucked into my pack to prepare for just that.

Before me lies the Black Bridge at the base of South Kaibab Trail, disappearing on the far side into the mouth of a lightless tunnel. With a deep breath, I make my way onto it. The upper lip of the inner canyon is brightly lit by a spotlight moon. But here at the heart of the canyon with its toweringly steep walls, the bridge, the river, and I are left in the dark. The bridge seems to sway slightly as the river crashes blindly below, although perhaps that is just the adrenaline surging through my body as my shoes move upon the worn wooden boards that run along its spine. I let my fingers rhythmically bounce over the chain-link sides, and my heartbeat keeps time.

I stop halfway across. Above me, long cables stretch upward and grasp onto rock nearly half the earth's age. The silhouette of spires, buttes, and mesas are backlit by tiny specks of light. I can only identify partial constellations. Below, the Colorado River roars by, unseen and calming in its constant pulse. The Milky Way points my way out, and with a smile, I continue. Slowly my inner monologue is silenced. My presence matters not, but the canyon's presence is my whole reason for existing here. Deep within the bowels of the earth, I let go—I let go of replaying medicals over the last eight days, of sore muscles, of the long to-do list that awaits me at the top, of work, stress, fear, of life outside of this moment.

At the end of the corralled bridge path, I pause at the mouth of the abyss. Blasted right through the igneous and metamorphic basement rocks, the tunnel at the base of South Kaibab Trail is my first obstacle of trust. It is wider than my wingspan by the length of a hiking pole, and just tall enough that a mule rider need not duck to pass through. Its length is tricky to calculate in the dark. I've hiked this trail before, and in my mind I know every step I must take. I wait for my eyes to adjust, but this is the kind of inky darkness that light cannot invade. The roaring Colorado echoes off the walls, silencing the beating of my heart. Hot air blasts through the passage, quickly drying my sweat. The tunnel reeks of hikers and beasts of burden who have rested in its sheltered shade.

When a few moments have passed and the blindness has not lessened, I proceed slowly, relying on my hiking poles and a slower step for safe travel. Each time my foot gratefully grips solid ground, connecting me back to the inner gorge, I move forward. In the dark, the mind runs wild—mountain lions creep in the shadows, ready to disembowel me if I so much as glance in their direction. The headlamp upon my brow remains unused though, because I know this enveloping blackness will soon be broken by the full moon's glare. The tunnel turns slightly and I can make out the whitish-gray light that emanates from the opening on the far side. Exiting, I feel a small sense of relief. None of the garish creatures my mind created in the two minutes of darkness swooped down to consume my soul. Silly, perhaps, but in the darkness nightmares are real.

With another deep breath, I set my eyes forward and begin the steep and steady climb. There is no warm up for South Kaibab. The trail scars its way through craggy walls of midnight-shade Vishnu Schist, scored by deep-flowing veins of Zoroaster Granite. These walls are hard, radiating the heat of the long-gone sun. The scent of creosote and cottonwood waft up from Phantom Creek, a strange perfume that mixes with the stench of mule urine puddled against the water-barred steps and spheres of mule scat dotting the trail, which at times force me to pull the neck of my shirt up and over my nose. Elsewhere, these smells would either go unnoticed or be met with heavily perfumed deodorizers. Here, you become part of the smell, your own sweat and salt mixing into the fray.

The moon's beams have not yet invaded the trail, but there is enough ambient light to continue hiking without the callous glare of a lamp. Up a few switchbacks, I stop for a moment at the trail split. To the right weaves the river trail, edging precariously along a nearly sheer wall high above the water. To the left, South Kaibab continues steadily upward. My heart thumping loudly in my chest longs to turn right and return to the bottom. But I am leaving, and somewhere in the far distance the promise of a hot shower and comfortable bed bid me to continue. For one last moment I watch as the moon first brushes across the river, leaving the peaks of the waves tipped in silver, while the ebbs remain void. The river's tumult is but a distant roll upon a large orchestral timpani.

Returning to the ever-ascending path, I allow my mind to wander and ponder the many mysteries of the canyon. Heat hangs heavy in the air, surprising for this late hour. I remove my hat to brush away the sweat, and I wet the cotton lining with water from the bite valve of my bladder pack. As I place the hat back on my head, cool streams drive down over my face and slip beneath the cotton collar of my shirt. The water carving its path is a welcome relief, and a renewed energy surges through my complaining legs. I marvel how just a little water refuels, and in this desert environment, it is the water by which we barely survive or thrive.

Shadowed by a large sandstone cliff, I am hidden from the South Rim. In the distance, I can see the first break in the inner canyon, where the bright moon's light now dances across the trail. Everything in perspective; when I step out into the light it seems too bright, and I pull the brim of my hat down securely over my eyes to block the glare. Without the harm of light pollution, the skies are illuminated with unparalleled fervor. Turning a corner, I pass by Train Wreck, an aptly named tumble of giant oblong rocks resembling boxcars strewn across the landscape. A week ago a pack mule lost his life at this very spot when he slipped off the side and down a scree slope. Imagining the echoing gunshot that ceased his suffering, I shudder slightly and bear forward with intent.

Each turn of the trail has a story, a memory, and a memory to make. Alone on a path that experiences thousands of footsteps a year, my imagination runs wild, reliving history and weaving tales—the Hydes, a couple on their honeymoon rafting the river, who after hiking up this trail to spend a few days in civilization returned to the river and were never seen again. And Eddie McKee, the second park naturalist, who in order to court Barbara Hastings would hike from the South to North Rims along these trails on his weekends. The stories go on.

Lactic acid burns through my calves and thighs, and the late hour creeps up and weighs heavily upon me. I yearn to close my eyes and allow the wind to lull me into a much-deserved rest. The trail turns sharply and steps up through a narrow side wash. I near Tipoff, a point where the inner gorge broadly opens at the Tonto Platform, and mentally calculate the distance yet to travel and the elevation to surmount. Leaning heavily on my hiking poles, I trudge forward. Up on the flat plateau, the heat that radiates from the inner canyon has dissipated, and for the first time I shiver.

With eyes trained on the trail as I climbed, studying every surface and rock under the moonlight, I had only been glimpsing the outlines of animals and insects dashing off the path in front of me. Now, breaking out of my tunnel vision, I notice the shadowed outline of a mule tie-off. With no mesas or buttes to block it, the moon seems nearly as bright as the noon-day sun, and everything is aglow. Suddenly, low on the horizon, a meteor burns its way through the sky, searing its path into my memory. Alone, aching, and losing the desire to continue, I looked up at the perfect moment. Immediately I brighten, and a smile breaks across my face. My pack feels instantly lighter, my muscles renewed, and with passion and energy reignited I ascend this graciously less steep section of trail.

Here, built upon shale, the trail is ground down to a fine, eggshell-colored dust that coats my shoes and fills the crevices between large boulders. The rhythmic drumming of nearby cicadas rubbing their wings together, the creaking of others in response, and every so often the sonic clicking of bats swooping through the air unseen—all are silenced by a whipping gust of wind.

At the base of the red and white switchbacks, I sit down for the first time since leaving the bottom. This steep serpentine section of the trail marks the halfway point. I find a smooth boulder on the trail's inside edge, unclip my pack, and set it down behind me as a pillow. Hours earlier, the sun super-heated this rock, but now as I feel every fiber of my exhausted being sink into the fallen limestone bench, I am met by a chill. My breath slows, and my heart follows suit, as I look into the night sky. I am lost among the stars, and find my eyes tracing patterns into their unordered existence.

For this moment I am one with the canyon.

III

Immersions

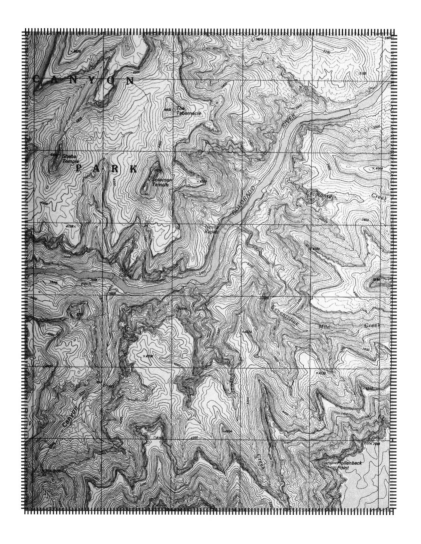

The Unnamed Side Canyon
by
Chris Propst

"Existence is beyond the power of words."
—Lao Tzu, *Tao Te Chi*, translated by Witter Bynner

I feel that exposure, empty space opening below on the right, molecules of air floating innocently, calling me downwards: the release of death is here, seductive, just below, down all the strata, in the sandstone rubble; launch out into that space and don't keep holding so tenaciously to the life of the brown earth.

1. Break time

Day Three on the Escalante Route, March 14, 2012: We're nestled into a nice, protected resting place, a third of the way through the "unnamed side canyon" on a scree slope—apparently this name is a kind of joke for Escalante veterans, belying its difficulty and its sometimes one-foot-wide trail ("one foot" being not a measurement in length, but rather the actual width of a general foot covered by hiking boot that someone might have on the end of their leg.)

We've made it up most of the elevation from last night's river camp, about 1,200 feet or so, and are about 20 minutes into a break. We're a bit tired from "commandoing" it from Cardenas, excited to make some horizontal miles at the beginning of the day, our legs recovered from the relentless downslope of the Tanner Trail.

I break off a piece of Powerbar, savoring its sticky firmness. I eat all the time down here, not being able to get enough, wanting salt and sugar and every bit of Powerbar or Cliff Bar, but forsaking Gu, those little packets of gelatinous-flavored sugar and caffeine sucked down by so many endurance athletes and Everest summiteers. At this point, only half way through our journey, I'm too holy to partake of the infernal substance though I'm eager to get a pack of Camels (despite not being much of a smoker), a Coke, a Reeses, some Gummy Bears, and maybe some Cheetos. I want to eat myself into a stupor and suck down that wonderful smoke through my nice, freshly exercised pink lungs to bring me to that happy spiritual place—relaxed but aware, anxiety-free.

The evening before, Kip, a veteran wanderer who knows enough to bring good reading material, lent me a well-worn copy of the *Tao Te Chi*. After twenty minutes by headlamp, the entire journey began to take a mystical turn for me. Lao Tzu teased me: "Those who know do not speak. Those who speak do not know." Drifting off to sleep, I asked what is it to *know?* What do I want to know? The sage's words wandered through my consciousness, waiting to be knocked speechless by the canyon.

I open the *Tao* again in our Roc's Aerie when our break turns too long, to section 26:

> *Gravity is the root of grace,*
> *The mainstay of all speed.*
> *A traveler of true means, whatever the day's pace,*
> *Remembers the provision-van*
> *And, however fine prospect be offered, is a man*
> *With a calm head.*

Amen brother. Lao Tzu tells me to keep track of my food and not go too fast. I swig some water; I would be an acolyte to him. By "gravity," I take the old Chinese mystic or his translator Witter Bynner to be playing word games. Gravity can mean "gravitas" or seriousness, or it could be to keep one's balance and a center of gravity. Gravity pushes on me, forcing me down by this big sandstone boulder that offers both shade and protection from a little hundred-foot plunge.

I hate to take long breaks, preferring the kind of slow mountaineer's pace that Lao Tzu ascribes to—step, breathe, catch your breath, and keep stepping another notch of elevation towards a summit or goal—not wanting to slow momentum or cool my body down too much. Usually, I try not to sit or lay down on breaks, having learned as a camp counselor years before that if I did, the kids would follow suit, and then good luck getting them back up on the trail again. Ignoring that lesson, Danny, Doug, Kip and I stretch the break out into lunch.

From our little citadel of rock, I can look out across the canyon to the 15 layers of Neapolitan ice cream. The river is there somewhere below, the cut of it clear in the black gash of what Kip tells me is "Vishnu basement rock." Close to me, the scree slope's contours enclose me with rusty ridges of chocolate brown and little green tufts of cheatgrass. Red rises above the river, then there's another grey-green layer of the Tonto, and further away, the iron of the Redwall, and other light green layers up to the yellowing top of the far rim.

Yes, I saw the description of this part of the trail from the Park Service, stating that "caution is indicated throughout this area as there are many places where you will want to avoid a misstep at all costs . . . traversing slopes that fall steeply away for hundreds of feet . . . the exposure may appear dramatic but truly is comfort hiking . . . the trail seems to traverse west forever." How, I wondered, could "dramatic exposure" be in the same sentence as "comfort hiking"? But like many hikers, I dismissed this description as being for the average hiker, to dissuade the unprepared or novice. I am no novice, I told myself. However, my pot belly and age counter my experience, along with a knee that an MRI showed needed surgery and a back that sometimes goes out.

2. Path

What does it mean to be a "seeker on the Path?" Because I grew up with a New Age mother, this question was never far from my mind.

Being on the path means you're headed in the right direction. It's not the primrose path necessarily, and you'd better be seeking while you're doing it, sniffing after various flowers, trying on certain philosophies, scrying the "Truth" (with a capital "T", but even a little "t" will do). The path in this esoteric way always seems to be paradoxical—it is itself the destination if you find the really wise philosopher (Tao Te Pooh?). So while you might fool yourself that the path might have a really good destination (water hole, Colorado River, Tonto Plateau overlook, parking lot after journey with big beer waiting for you, home again with family), heaven is right here on earth, in the form of this trail, this small space in the dirt we trod upon, putting print after waffle print into sienna dust.

At the very least, being a seeker usually means that nothing bad can happen to you. If Buddha can sit under a tree with a giant cobra for an umbrella and make heaven on earth, and this path is heaven, then I need not fear falling off of it, nor fear any rocks rolling down upon me: comforting thoughts, but you still have to concentrate to not stray too far, since rocks and tumbles do hurt.

If you are "on the path" in the Christian sense of the term, you are on the way to salvation, not straying from it to do too much sinning; in the Grand Canyon there's not much opportunity for that anyway. Down here, a sin would be forgetting to bring enough water. Another would be not being in shape for carrying a pack long distance. Dropping trash would be desecration of the highest order, worse than starting a fire (the rangers say no no no to that). Not saying hello to a fellow hiker would seem to deserve a life sentence, although that sin is annulled the closer you get to any busy trailhead. Another sin would be not paying attention to your hiking friends—is their gear all together, do they have enough water, what rock is it they're photographing? The most mortal sin would be passing through the Grandness without letting it touch you.

My mother died two years before this hike. She's often on my mind on the trip, and I sometimes pray to her when I come upon cliff edges that fall a thousand feet.

3. Pendulum

She gave me a pendulum and showed me how to use it as a kind of oracular divining tool, somewhat like a Ouija board. The particular one she gave me is a teardrop of polished wood perhaps an inch in diameter, looking like a carpenter's plumb-bob, attached to a simple brown string. You hold it by the string, letting the teardrop hang, and ask a yes/no question. If the pendulum swings clockwise, the answer is yes. If it swings counterclockwise, the answer is no. So what makes the pendulum swing one way or another? It could just be your own subconscious, making your hand move to create the answer you want. My mother believed it was universal resonations, or God speaking through the pendulum. If you asked questions of it, you had to be careful, because you had to listen to the answers. She said, "The goal is to become so good with the pendulum that you don't need the tool any longer. The answers will come if you're quiet enough and ask the right questions."

Here, the questions that come to me are how get myself and my team back to the rim again, how to be safe, how to exist in an ever present state without driving myself crazy, and how to not use up all my toilet paper before the end of the trip.

But there's other questions too that flicker into mind every now and then, like why did I depart from my notes at my mother's memorial and launch into anecdotes as if I were a comedian at open-mike night? How her VW van, which always broke down, had been waiting for her in heaven for 15 years. How we got stranded in the middle of summer in Iowa on the way to her father's memorial in Maine, and how she made friends with the mechanic's wife who gave us breakfasts and trips to zoos, and we watched their English sheepdogs getting stuck mating. Before that comedy, what was it that made me sit in my chair at the memorial, frozen by grief after walking through a hallway filled with pictures of her wedding night, painted raven totems on leather drums, and dream catchers she made herself, mementoes of her life now gone, crying for an hour, so overcome that my brothers were worried that I wouldn't be able to perform my part of our memorial?

4. Leaning into the Slope

Finally, the break is over and we shoulder our packs. "Okay for me to go?" I shout back to Kip. He waves me on nonchalantly, and I swallow some anxiety and push away from this safe place.

There's comfort in these steps. Whenever I find myself in a performance like a speech or a racquetball tournament, I'm always nervous before beginning, but once I do begin, I settle in. So too now, the muscles are working fine and the pack is not too heavy.

I find myself fixating on the path itself. This is not good, I tell myself, remembering my mother's driving lessons from when I was 15: "You can't just stare at the road," she said. "You'll get tunnel vision." She taught me that by moving your vision from side to side, you're better able to focus on the road or path, a paradox. Since she is my own personal sage, I take her advice and make sure to glance around.

Looking up, I see that we are about 300 feet from the top of the ridge. The slope steepens near the top, abuts against plump rock teeth that rise jagged and fat, ready to chomp us. Here and there a yucca or blackbrush dots the hillside. Everywhere, tumbles of rock like haphazard creek beds. The path itself is reddish brown, like someone had painted it fresh against the duller surrounding clay, then fired it in the kiln. In front of me, I can see the path in increments, until it turns around the bend.

The others take their time, and before they even start, I've lost them behind me, a good thirty feet below and a hundred yards back. Pausing, I wonder if I should wait. Yes, there's some safety in numbers, but I don't want to accidentally kick a rock onto them, since the path here still rises. Also, I'm in a rhythm and I don't want to interrupt it by being in the presence of others—one of my mother's gurus said meditating with a group of people would cause one to soak up their energy and perhaps be brainwashed. So I push on.

The path rises sharply another 100 feet or so, then levels off. I walk 20 or 30 of these vertical feet, then do the "power snort" that I learned on a trip to Mount Rainier a few years back: inhaling through my nostrils, exhaling forcefully through my mouth to keep from getting too winded. (Sounds counterintuitive, doesn't it? It may just be a psychological trick.)

The only sound is my own breath and the gravely steps of my boots on the path. I can't hear the others, and there are no birds here; I keep my pace steady, even when winded, trying to take slow steps, but find myself having to stop sometimes. I keep those breaks quick—allowing myself a 10-count for a few, then a 30-count. Towards the top of the rise, I stop counting and wait until my heart pounds less staccato.

Now the trail is following a lip along the top of a band of cliff, level until the next bend, perhaps 400 yards ahead of me. But will it alter course afterwards and head up to the teeth of the ridge? It seems that it wouldn't do something so illogical, that it will find the best way to our destination. Nevertheless, I ask myself—could I turn directly into this ridge and hike straight up? It would be grueling, more like a McKinley climb than canyoneering, but possible with lots of power snorts and rest steps.

While the break from the ascent is welcome, I find little relief from the exposure. I lean to the left, though I know it's not good for my balance. To my right, I feel a chasm. When I actively scan, I see that there are some spots where you might not suffer too badly if you fell—even if you didn't stick your landing like an Olympic gymnast. In other places, the grade is steep and that pack on your back would make you cork-screw downwards, and you wouldn't be able to stop your momentum. And then there are a few places that are much more rectum-tightening, where you'd plummet. I hurry past them, trying not to think of the splatter of bodies on canyon bottom, the smash of femur or the un-natural kinking of a neck. It's easier to just focus on my feet or hands, on the feel of the rock I'm leaning into.

It's probably getting close to noon, and the day is beginning to heat up. Yes, it's March and the morning was cool. Now, however, the sweat is pooling under my armpits and dripping onto my sunglasses.

Sometimes I rest-step, then breathe long, pause, then take an-other short step. The rest-steps keep my heart from pounding out of my chest, help me gather breath, and help me not overheat. Between breaths, I try to enter into the natural world all around me, as jagged and dusty as it is, to merge into the slope and the plummets: I try not to insert my needs and yearnings and unwelcome thoughts of the pile of composition papers to be graded or whether or not to coach my son's soccer team this summer. Another of Lao Tzu's poems, # 38, flickers through my mind:

> *Nature does not have to insist,*
> *Can blow for only half a morning,*
> *Rain for only half a day.*
> *And what are these winds and these rains but nature?*
> *If nature does not have to insist,*
> *Why should man?*

I've been walking a good twenty minutes—for over forty years in fact—but need to remember to keep that steady pace, not "insisting," just being there on the trail.

My mental image of the map tells me that I'm about half way through the traverse. I remember that I'm not alone on this journey and give myself a goal of making it to the next bend, where I can take a break and see how my fellow travelers are doing.

When I stop, I put my left hand on the side wall of the ridge to steady myself. The rock is dry and warm, sandy and crumbly. I shift my head slightly—I'm warm and feel sweat dripping down my chest.

Trying to take my pack off might unbalance me and send me down the slope. I can't turn enough to see clear behind, so I have to do a little maneuver: moving my left foot behind my right, then inching my left closer to the right—a pirouette with body leaning into the slope. I manage to jostle myself enough to be scared, imagining a backpack-over-tail cartwheel and careen. But my Mom didn't raise me and sacrifice to send me to college for me to end my life on a hiking trip: there's greater destiny than a death here.

To not be able to see behind me is like not being able to feel my future with my kids. This trail leads to the triumph of homecoming, but it also leads to our death if we stretch it out to the horizon. I think of my mother's funeral again, and Lao Tzu comes to visit, his robes brown with canyon sand, saying to "conduct your triumph like a funeral" (section 31). If one were to behave that way in this day and age, wouldn't that be odd? We'd rather do a touchdown dance, like our favorite quarterbacks doing their trademark poses: the Discount Double Check or Showing Your Superman Costume. Look at *me me me*, say these victors. He wants us to think about death in the middle of our new promotion or wedding, a kind of "Opposite Day" philosophy. Therefore, should I conduct my failures like celebrations? Treat the everyday like it's sublime? It's all getting a bit too deep, sucking me into my head and away from the trail's dirt.

I find myself on one of the wider bends and am finally able to look back quite a ways. There's a refreshing gust of wind, maybe five mph; I've sweat my shirt clear through. The rest of the guys don't come into view for another ten minutes or so, and when they do, they are about 400 yards back and 100 feet down. Perhaps they had a gear issue or didn't launch right after me, but they seem to be alright. My back protests against my stop, so I spin clumsily onto the trail and resume grinding out my steps.

What would happen if one of us took a bad step or tripped over one of the little rocks in the path and plunged over the side? It would complicate things greatly. Clearly, he would be injured. It would be difficult to down-climb to him. Would I have the energy to do so, and then would I have the skill to help him? The most likely scenario would be that we'd have to go for help, which would be a day or more away. It's better, I tell myself, to not visualize plunges or splats, to instead keep focused on the things that can be controlled—feeling my feet and breathing, adjusting my pack from time to time, tightening those shoulder straps until they hurt.

I look back at my fellow travelers and want to shout encouragement, imagining my strength and route-pioneering skill to be inspirational (yes, the heat did make me delusional).

Lao Tzu again straightens me out: "Knowing others is intelligence; knowing yourself is true wisdom. Mastering others is strength; mastering yourself is true power. If you realize that you have enough, you are truly rich." I need to let the others in my party go, not claiming to know them or their thoughts, to realize the delusion of my leadership, and to take mastery of these thoughts.

When I come close to the next bend, I think it's "the one" where we'll hit what the map shows is a saddle into the next little canyon to begin our descent back to the river and our next campsite. When I round it, though, I see that I haven't reached our goal. It was just an illusion, like a false peak; there's another bend ahead teasing me with its shapely curve. I had hoped to be able to give good news back to the troops, but instead have to keep trudging. The Colorado comes into view, blue and green against the rust and brown of the broken terraces. I polish the sweat from my glasses and take another plunge into the curve.

Ahead, there's a huge pillar of stone on the right side of the path, a monolith fallen from a higher layer, offering protection from the exposure. That's my goal, and I don't stop until I get there, then decide to make it my main break. It's a bit higher than me by about a head or two, wide enough on top for three people, and a different color than the rich chocolate of the trail, tan mixed with some olive green. Taking my pack off, I gulp down half a liter of wondrous water, eat half a Powerbar. Both actions seem a bit rash. Conservation is important when this traverse is only about at the half-way point of our day's hike, with unknown obstacles ahead. Already I am three bottles into my five bottles of water. But I trust the little pendulum in my head giving me nutritional advice, telling me that it won't get much more difficult than this today.

The trail curls outward toward the next bend, and I'm making progress. The bend bows hopefully, and there is a new wind cooling me. I pee here, a marker for the rest of the crew. It's a bit of every man for himself now, and though I see Danny in the distance, I don't wait for Doug and Kip.

5. Beyond

My feet scuffle dust, then I'm upon a saddle, a destination, able to look down on both sides and off in the distance toward the river. But where am I? The trail disappears near where the rack of rock breaks from the ridge above like the remnants of a stegosaurus' tail. I drop my pack amidst the boulders. I have a small feeling of giddiness, a flash of the map lines, although I can't remember them well, and I push the feeling down. Instead, I scan a long distance ahead into the cliff wall. Might the trail double back yet again? Am I going to have to make my way across *that*? My chief fear of the journey is just this—having to cross or climb something impossible, losing a foothold, freefalling into a dream where you don't hit the bottom. No path could be that stupid, I decide, swinging my inner pendulum to judge the rightness of my perspective, and then looking downwards.

I keen to feel that universal pulse, closing my eyes to the spin of the galaxy. There's a hum—the background sound of the universe, or perhaps simple tinnitus. A clockwise swirl moves from the top of my head through my torso and into my feet and downwards. The river cuts through rock, shows me a hopeful sign: a flotilla of little yellow rafts and red and blue kayaks going by. I want to yell to them, "Hello People!" but they are a thousand feet below and a mile or so away.

Fifty feet below, a cairn of stacked rocks shows me that my pendulum is swinging correctly. I feel a brotherhood with she or he who placed it there for me. The river shines below the path, beckoning with the churn of millions of gallons of hydration and coolness.

Only now do I celebrate, pumping my fist in the air like I have just won a wrestling match, though I remember I shouldn't celebrate my success too much.

Harder still is trying to compose myself as if I were at a funeral. I shimmy down to that cairn and place a bright white stone on its top. Then I see another one a good fifty feet below, and though I know I'll have to trudge back up to my pack, I go to it as well, and I make a little Stonehenge on the trail, adding another column of rock, the foundations of a supporting arch, working until I hear my companions' shouts of delight and the thumps of their packs in the dirt. I turn and make my way back to my pack, planting my feet firmly against the slope.

The Dead Deer at Yuma Point
by
Rick Jurgen

*"This is the most beautiful place in the world.
There are many such places."*
Edward Abbey

1. Descent

It's a quiet winter morning on the Boucher Trail. The towers on the
North Rim are lit up and glowing in the reddish early light. I sit inside
my tent, half-covered in my sleeping bag, sipping tea and remembering
yesterday. I arrived at the backcountry office at 12:30 PM, lunch time
for the rangers. I sat on the tailgate of my truck, waiting for them to
reopen. The day was partly sunny and warm for January. The sun was
a welcome sight after several weeks of the wettest weather in years for
this area. At last the storm track has shifted northward!

A large group of ravens was circling overhead, bachelor males I suppose, like me, sticking together for mutual protection. While watching
them I recalled how ravens would appear in pairs to Mele and me when
we hiked together in the canyon. She considered them to be her special
friends. Sitting there, at the last minute, I made new plans. I would
hike the Boucher Trail instead of the New Hance as I had intended.
At one o'clock, they opened the door to the BC office and I got my
permit. I asked for three nights in the Boucher use area.

I still needed to buy a couple of items, send out a check, and make
a few phone calls. By the time I got to the parking lot at the end of
West Rim Drive it was 3:00 PM, and less than three hours until dark.
I planned to walk down the Hermit Trail to the junction with the
Boucher Trail and then along the Boucher to Yuma Point. I expected
to camp at Yuma Point the first night.

I started down through the Kaibab layer. The switchbacks were a
little wet at first with patches of snow and fallen ice. I could see that

some slabs of ice still clung to the lip of the Kaibab cliff in spite of the warm weather. The next layer below, the Toroweap, was in the sunshine, and the trail was dry. I made good time in the Coconino layer on the dry switchbacks. I was nearing the area where Mele and I had seen some fossil tracks in the sandstone when we walked the Hermit to Bright Angel loop a few years earlier.

I noticed a pair of backpackers on the trail ahead, at the base of the next switchback. They were discussing something and pointing at the ground. They appeared to be in their forties. She was blonde, and he had short dark hair. They both wore khaki shorts. I realized, as I approached them, that they must be examining the fossil tracks. The woman was quite enthusiastic. I let her tell me about the tracks even though I knew about them:

"Look at this—you can see where he dragged his tail, and where his feet dug into the sand!"

She asked me how old I thought the tracks were.

"Permian."

"How old is that?"

"About 260 million years."

There were smaller tracks, too, some with finger-like claw prints. They resembled the tracks of a medium-sized lizard. She was on her knees, tracing the tracks in the petrified dune with her fingers. Looking over her shoulder, she said: "Maybe the big one was chasing the little one up the sand dune?" I wondered aloud whether anyone would be around to comment on our lifestyles in a few million years. Perhaps these reptiles had a more lasting impact on the Earth than most humans do.

Standing back up, she had more to tell me: "There's a dead deer at Yuma Point." They had camped at Yuma Point the previous night on a flat spot at the very end of the point. After supper, while wandering around, they found it.

"He was near the height of land, not far from the trail. A mountain lion got him!"

She told me that a piece of the deer had been eaten. When they got up the next morning, the deer had been moved.

"They came back during the night and dragged him fifty yards and ate half of him!"

"Did you see any tracks?"

"No, but we know it was a mountain lion."

I thanked her for the report and told them that I would watch out for it. I was skeptical about the cat part of the story. Maybe a deer dies of old age. Maybe coyotes come at night to scavenge it. As I rounded the switchback below them, she yelled down to me: "How old did you say those tracks were?"

"Two hundred and sixty million!"

"Thanks!"

The Coconino Sandstone was pale, almost white. Soon I was down to the level of the Hermit Shale, reddish brown, like the ancient mudflats that formed it. The shale forms a steep slope of loose, soft soil and rock that ends at a cliff. I walked on, past the turnoff to the Waldren Trail, to the Hermit and Boucher junction. I turned left on the Boucher. The Boucher Trail wound along the top of the cliff at the base of the muddy slope. I continued across the southern end of Hermit Gorge in the shade. In some places there was a drop of hundreds of feet just a few yards to my right. I could see down the gorge all the way to the main canyon and across it. I soon passed the Dripping Springs turnoff and was making good progress toward Yuma Point.

Now it was getting late. The sun had dropped below the South Rim, but the north side was still lit up with sunshine. The views were spectacular, astonishing. Except for those two backpackers, I had seen no one. I was less than a mile from Yuma Point when I came to a flat prominence jutting off to the right with several nice tent sites on it. It was late and the rumor of mountain lions and their prey was working on my mind. I decided to camp there instead of Yuma Point.

I have no vocabulary to capture the feeling of setting up a tent in the Grand Canyon and sitting down to cook dinner with no other human for miles around, while watching the sun set and the moon rise. Pictures don't do it justice either. Once you return to the teeming hive-cities of Rimworld, you slowly forget the feeling. You will need to keep coming back to recapture it. The relentless noise of the swarm covers the quiet sound of Earth in the rocks.

After I ate, I slipped into my down sleeping bag and thought about reading. I had an entertaining paperback novel in my backpack. The problem was that the book is fiction. How could I turn my mind to fiction with all this grand reality around me? At that moment, while lying on a bed of rocks whose pages tell the story of Earth, I couldn't care about the fantasies spun out of some writer's head.

For a time it was very quiet. The big moon began to climb higher and light up the canyon. The colors of the rocks and plants faded in the moonlight, but I could see objects clearly. I could even read the cover of my book. It wasn't exactly a black and white world, more like gold and tan, but two-tone, definitely.

The quiet was interrupted by a series of sounds: *Thud, thud, thud… boom!* I realized that a rock had tumbled down the Hermit Shale slope, flown off the cliff and crashed onto the rocks below. That type of sound was repeated, with variations, from time to time all evening. At one point there was a crash that shook the ground. I could feel the vibration as I lay in my tent. An echo rumbled up and down the canyon.

The unprecedented snows and rains this year had soaked the soil. During the warmth of the day, the soil had dried, hardened and shrunk. Now, in the dark, water was dripping and running from the cliffs, seeping and soaking and lubricating the soil. The earth was swelling and loosening, and rocks were breaking loose to tumble down the unstable slope. Thus the canyon grows larger by shedding pieces of itself. I poked my head out to look around. *I am on a flat spot, that's good*, I thought. I noticed a cluster of juniper trees and some car-sized boulders just uphill from me. I hoped I was protected from falling rocks. Where else could I go? This was home for now.

A bit later I heard new sounds, coming from the direction of Yuma Point toward me. I had heard that sound before, deer hoofs clattering over the shale rocks. Those deer were in a hurry and not concerned with being quiet. They quickly passed my tent and the sound faded— nervous deer. I thought about the cat. Is it on the trail? Am I prey? I considered that cats probably don't rip open tents, not like a bear would. A bear would tear into a log or a backpack just to see what was in it. A cat wouldn't do that. My mind told me that cats like to see their prey, study it. Besides, there is no cat anyway, just coyotes. My brain produced nice, reassuring thoughts.

I fell asleep wrapped in concentric protective layers, onion-like. Outermost was my nylon tent, then my sleeping bag—a fluffy bag full of feathers—and finally my warm, reassuring rationalizations. I woke once in the middle of the night to pee. I slipped my hiking shoes onto my bare feet and slid out into the moonlight in my underwear. The rest of my clothes were in a stuff sack forming my pillow. I watched my shadow move carefully in the moonlight. It was very quiet now. I peed into the shadows and said a little prayer, an excretory version of Grace: "Earth Mother, accept this gift of water, salt and minerals and use it to make a greener world." I usually forget to pray at mealtimes. Back in my sleeping bag, I was asleep at once.

Now it is morning. I awoke early, before the sun lifted above the rim, and started heating water on my little gas stove. My metal cup holds sixteen ounces. I put two teabags in it, one green and one black. Now I am sipping tea and reaching for my blue food bag. The tea is warming and healing, the best that I have ever had. Breakfast is a couple of granola bars, some dried fruit and a piece of cheese. It's peaceful and quiet, inside and out. No frightening predators lurk in the corner of my mind.

Packing up is a chore, like making your bed, only more complicated: Stuff sleeping bag into sack, roll up air mattress, pack up food bag, headlamp, first aid kit, personal accessories, stove, pan, gas, etc. It all goes into my internal frame pack. Eventually, I am ready to walk on. The sunlight is reaching me now. It's fairly warm, even here at over 5,000 feet in elevation.

As I start walking the Boucher Trail again, I can see the deer tracks in the soft soil between the slabs of shale—small tracks of does and yearlings. They are pointed away from my direction of travel. The trail soon gets rougher. It bends inward into small ravines and gullies full of fallen rocks, then climbs back out to the edge of the cliff. I turn left, descend, scramble over loose rocks, turn right, ascend, repeat. Progress is slow.

I traverse one side gully that lies below a huge, fresh white scar at the base of the Coconino cliff where an undermined slab has let go. Blocks of sandstone the size of pickup trucks have tumbled across the trail and lie scattered down to the top of the cliff. Smaller chunks of stone are strewn everywhere—pieces of shrapnel thrown off by the collisions of boulders. Junipers, agaves, and piñons lay smashed or ripped out of the soil. Timing is everything, so I try to hurry; I don't want to be in this gully when the next block of sandstone comes crashing down. Finally, the trail bends left and rises to the height of land at Yuma Point.

I begin the search for the dead deer. I am prepared to debunk the idea of a cat kill. First I scout around the flat part of the point. The surface is mostly "desert pavement," where the wind has blown away the loose dust and soil. What remains are bits and slabs of shale that the wind can't move. There are a pair of tent sites farther out on the point. I can see where the couple who told me about the deer had camped. There is no sign of a deer, but there are some human tracks in the few soft spots between the rocks. I turn left and walk back toward the trail.

On the west side of the point, close to the trail, there is a pale stripe across the ground twenty feet ahead, a line of whitish hair about four inches wide. The light-colored hair shows well against the brown shale background. It looks like belly hair from a deer. I follow the trail of hair east until it stops. The ground is hard here. There are no tracks, no blood, and no signs of struggle.

I turn and walk back along the deer-hair trail for about forty yards. It leads downhill to a little flat spot beneath a cluster of low junipers. An area about the size of a large mattress is totally covered with hair. There is an odd object on the ground at one end of the patch of hair. At first it reminds me of a pillow. I duck under the junipers and poke the object with my trekking pole—it's a stomach! The pale sack is still damp on the outside and packed full of greenery, like a bag of salad.

I look downhill, beyond the junipers. The soil is softer here. Stones are flipped over. I see scrape marks as if someone had dragged several parallel sticks along the ground. I follow the marks downhill. Now there are tracks in the soft earth—clawless, round, beautifully padded cat tracks the size of my fist. I look around nervously. Why are there no birds here? Shouldn't there be ravens? Again the thought: Am I prey? For a time I see nothing more. Then I notice something thirty feet farther down the hill—an antler, just visible behind a row of shrubs. I have found the deer, or what's left of him. There are four legs, at least the lower portions of them, attached to a skin that is twisted around and around, like a bath towel that has been wrung out. There is the neck, partially eaten on one side, and the head with its beautiful set of antlers. There is no sign of internal organs: liver, heart, lungs are all gone. It was a ten-point buck, a large and powerful animal.

I grasp the antlers and lift the head. There is no smell. The meat is fresh. The front of the head where the eyes should be is gone. The predator has chewed through the area between the antlers and the upper jaw. The skull is empty, the brain gone. I let go of the antlers, and the head flops to the ground. There is something shocking about the empty skull.

After forty million years of evolution and a lifetime of experience, this cat knew exactly what it wanted and how to get it. I picture the cat opening the head of a two-hundred-pound animal like a fat tourist cracking open a lobster claw in a seafood restaurant. I slap the right side of the neck, the only large part still intact. Unexpectedly, I feel a primitive urge. I want to take a knife, maybe a stone knife made of flint or chert, and cut a piece off the neck. I imagine how nice a chunk of meat would smell cooking over an open fire, impaled on a stick. Mele would have liked that too if she had been here to see this. I can almost hear the excitement in her voice. Then I put her out of my mind. I want to promote myself from potential prey to predator. I want to share in the cat's achievement, connect to a deeper and older place in my mind. I picture the joy of the ancients when they found a kill like this one. That neck would feed my family!

There is no horror now in this gruesome scene. I read what predator has written. The cat expressed itself in the medium most familiar to it. The picture is painted across the canyon soil in hair and bones and blood. The stomach, full of grass once destined to become deer flesh, is left behind. Deer meat is recycled into cat. There is no evil here, just the mastery of the artist at work, signed with clawless prints that say: "I was here, this is my work!"

I think about the deer. What did he know? He must have known where to find the best food and water and many other things. Did he have memories of close escapes? Did he remember his mates and his rivals? Did the lion know that particular deer? Did it watch it for days or weeks, waiting for the right opportunity?

The craving for venison passes quickly. In my pack is a blue stuff sack full of ramen noodles, mixed nuts, Snickers bars and other delights. I am moving on. I look up the slope toward the Coconino cliff.

Perhaps the cat is watching me. I wave. The trail leads away from Yuma Point towards White's Butte.

2. The River and Beyond

The trail through the Supai Formation is steep, verging on precipitous. I pick my way down carefully, past hundred-year-old juniper logs and pieces of iron bar that Boucher himself put in place to stabilize the treadway. Below is the top of Travertine Canyon and beyond that is White's Butte. I can see the shine of a bit of water running in Travertine. When I get there, I stop for a long rest, get out my water filter, and pump a liter into one of my plastic bottles. The water is sweet, not salty. It's melted snow that hasn't been mineralized. I eat and rest and start to think of Mele.

Her name was Marilyn. She got to be Mele when she worked in Hawaii for a time. I remembered something else: The Boucher Trail was supposed to be our next hike together! We had hiked the canyon together each winter for several years. Our last trip had been in the relatively easy Corridor, the Kaibab Trail to Cottonwood Campground. We did day hikes to Upper Ribbon Falls and the North Rim. She had just started chemotherapy then, and we thought it would be smarter to stay closer to rangers, emergency phones, and other hikers. The Boucher would have to wait. Unfortunately, she never got here.

It was actually the jasper that made me think of her. I am sitting near the top of the Redwall in an area with veins of jasper. Pieces of the reddish stone are scattered on the ground. During those days when we hiked the canyon together, Mele would find a piece of jasper on the trail, pick it up, and put it in her pocket. As she walked, she would find another piece that she liked better, pick it up and trade it for the one in her pocket; in that manner she kept temporarily borrowing pieces of jasper and then replacing them with new finds. Sometimes, when I hiked the canyon alone, I would pick up a tiny piece, perhaps the size of my thumbnail. Later I would mail it to her and tell her to bring it back out here to swap it for a better one. She always did.

The trail across White's Butte runs flat, a nice break from steep downhill. Soon I am scrambling off the west side of the butte, down through the Redwall. At one point I slip on the loose limestone pebbles and fall hard on my pack. It's hard to believe that mules once made this trip. The trail is equally steep in the Muav layer and finally starts to flatten out a bit in the Bright Angel Shale. I take a rest at the junction of the Tonto Trail and the Boucher. I am both elated at the beauty of the place and saddened because I can't be here with the one I had intended to share it with. Yet some part of her seems to be here with me.

I know I can make it to the river in an hour or so. I descend the winding switchbacks to the floor of Boucher Canyon. The remains of Boucher's cabin are here, four walls and a doorway. I wonder, was he lonely living here? Behind me is the entrance to his mine. The trail is just a route down the bed of the creek, a creek with a high water mark in the bushes on each side, showing how it recently flooded. A few hundred yards below the cabin I find a shredded tent, half buried in the sand and gravel. Why is it here? I try to pull it out. Maybe there is a name on it? The tent rips in my hands. It was obviously deposited here by the recent flood waters. I have to leave it.

The lower part of the canyon is much rougher. There is a bit of water running that has to be repeatedly crossed. The recent rains washed away most of the soft sand, leaving loose cobbles and rough boulders. Soon I am descending into the Vishnu Schist, the bedrock of the canyon, 1.7 billion years old. The rock is black and polished, with veins of white granite shooting through it like lightning bolts of stone. At times I have to work my way around cascades. The hard bedrock forms a steep-walled and sinuous canyon. I am in the shade, and a cool breeze is flowing up-canyon against my face. I can smell the river. I round one more bend and the chocolate-colored waves of Boucher Rapid appear. The clear stream of Boucher Creek tumbles into the brown river. On my left is a flat, narrow beach leading west to sand dunes that sweep up against the shiny, black schist. This will be my camp tonight.

There are fresh tracks in the sand—mice, a few lizards and something smaller, maybe a beetle. Near the river are the paw prints of a ringtail. It's good to see that the neighbors are all relatively small. While setting up the tent, I notice a light patch on the slope across the river. It's a bighorn sheep, a female, watching me. She looks over her shoulder at something. Gradually three more bighorns drift into view, one at a time. They browse on vegetation and occasionally pause to stare across the water at me. Once my tent is set up and I am in it, they ignore me completely and focus on their relentless chewing. I spend two hours in my tent watching them through my compact binoculars while cooking and eating a meal. I name them "The Girls." Mele would have certainly been brought to tears by the beauty of this scene. I struggle not to cry on her behalf.

The Girls slowly browse their way up the steep slope of the Vishnu Schist as dusk approaches. There is no sound but the roaring of Boucher Rapid. As the sky darkens, I lay in my tent peering across the boisterous muddy river in the dim light. A couple of stars show in the darkening sky. The moon rises above the Tapeats cliff, and I sleep.

I wake with no memories, at first light. I can recall no dreams. I didn't get up or even wake up once. I wonder where I was all that time, ten hours or more. It feels like I left and went somewhere and then came back. The last thing I can recall is seeing the moon rise. At once, before I even heat water for tea, I am thrown into an intense, almost overwhelming grief. My sense of loss is stronger by far than it has been anytime since the first few days after Mele died. I am almost paralyzed by it. I feel like I can't stay here and can't leave, either. My reality is so filled with grief that there is little room for anything else. I force myself to drink my tea and eat something. I slowly begin to pack up. I am afraid that if I don't move, I won't be able to move. I wonder how bad it can get.

The grief subsides a bit and I can feel something else, an odd sense of Mele's presence, as if she is somehow nearby. I wonder once again whether she is just out of reach, maybe in a parallel universe right in front of my nose, in a place of different natural laws or different dimensions. I put my hands out flat in front of me, as if to touch her. I am oddly detached from my body. I don't want to walk, but my legs want to; in fact, they want to wear shorts. I put my cutoffs on. I feel like I have no energy to move, but my legs assure me that they can do fine without me. I find that my arms are lifting my pack and putting it on my back. I know I lack the energy to do this, but my arms don't seem to care. I notice that I am moving; my legs are carrying me across the sand toward Boucher Creek. There are human footprints in the sand, pointing in the opposite direction—mine from yesterday. They look odd and unfamiliar. At the creek I turn right and start upstream. I remember "The Girls" across the river and stop to look for them. It's hard to focus; I seem to have tunnel vision. I don't see them. I guess they are gone.

Along the creek bed, my feet find their way past clear cascades of water and piles of loose boulders. The narrow canyon slides by, unseen. The wreckage of the abandoned tent moves past my feet and disappears behind me. I'm at Boucher's cabin again. My pack is on the ground, and my water filter is out. I drop the cap to my water bottle into the creek while trying to filter water. It begins to float away, and I watch helplessly for a minute. Then I stand up and go after it. I drink some of the water I have filtered. It's the best water I have ever tasted. I drink more; I am feeling better now, getting my senses back. A bird is singing. The water is filling me up, replacing something that was emptied out. After the two bottles are full, I thank old Boucher the Hermit for letting me use his place. This particular winter day is warm and sunny. I will walk up onto the Tonto Trail and look for a campsite where it turns right into Hermit Creek Canyon. The map shows a flat area there.

Compared to the Boucher, the Tonto is level and smooth. The rains have made the slopes lush, especially in the shady places. In some spots the greenery is as tall as my knees, and it is only late January. I have to slow down where the trail crosses Travertine Canyon. It is rough and rocky here. The sheets of travertine show how wet it once was. I try to imagine the landscape centuries ago in cooler times. I round the bend on the east side of Travertine Canyon, now looking straight down into Hermit Rapids, hundreds of feet below. It looks ferocious today. Large haystacks in many rows of waves are jumping up and sliding back and forth across the river. Upstream, I see part of Granite Rapid and downstream I see Boucher Rapid. My tunnel vision has cleared. The canyon appears sharp, clear and beautiful. Even the rocks on either side of the trail have unusual colors and a special sculptured quality. My destination for today is just ahead.

As expected, I find a flat plateau that forms a point jutting toward the river, just after the trail bends south into Hermit Creek Canyon. There are several obvious tent sites, but a short walk of a hundred yards or so brings me closer to the gorge and a nice little spot for my camp. My tent is thirty feet from the drop-off and right above Hermit Rapid. I can smell the river and hear it. If I were sleeping at the beach next to the rapid, I would be inhaling the muddy Colorado in airborne droplets.

From my tent I can see east to Zoroaster Temple and Desert View, west to the South Bass area, north to the North Rim and south to White's Butte, Yuma Point and the South Rim. A few feathery clouds have moved in. I pull out my journal and begin to write a running description of the sunset. One cloud looks like a hand with fingers reaching across the sky, then changes into a tree with branches reaching upward, and finally shifts into a giant squid with trailing tentacles, diving toward the horizon. Another cloud first resembles four horses galloping westward, but then morphs into two drifting elephants. The clouds gradually change color from white to pink to salmon to purple. Finally the sun goes down and the big moon rises.

Sleep doesn't come quickly. My mind wanders to thoughts of other sunsets and Mele. I read for hours. Now and then I take a short walk in the moonlight. It is light enough that I could easily hike up the trail. I even feel like doing it, but the tent is pitched and I am supposed to be sleeping. Orion the hunter shows himself feebly in the moonlight. Finally I am asleep and dreaming strange dreams about fishing with no bait, while wearing wool socks over my waders.

In the morning the tent is soggy with dew, my sleeping bag is damp on the outside, and I am very hungry. There is plenty of food left; I seem to have brought enough for two people. After I eat, I pack my damp gear and am on my way along the Tonto Trail to Hermit Creek Campground. An hour of walking brings me to a place where I can see empty campsites in the canyon below me. No one is camping at Hermit today. When I get to the creek, I filter enough water for the hike to Santa Maria Spring.

I walk from the campground, across the Tapeats, and up the Bright Angel Shale in a daydream. My mind is back in unnamed side canyons with Mele, looking for exotic agaves and the homes of the ancients. There was one side canyon that she nicknamed "Happy Valley," because it felt so familiar to her. There was the time we turned around to go back and found large, fresh cat tracks in the mud just a hundred yards behind us. Climbing the Redwall switchbacks, I once again notice the world beyond my eyeballs. I stop to take a long rest and a long look at the canyon, and the view snaps me back into the here and now. I am at the halfway point here between where I was and Rimworld.

The traverse through the Supai becomes tedious. The Hermit Trail has taken a beating. Rocks have fallen onto it, and pieces have fallen out of it. Cairns are missing. In one place there is a recent mudslide. I find myself off route a couple of times. Now and then I look up nervously, wondering when the next loose rock or slab of Supai sandstone is coming down. I keep thinking that Santa Maria Spring is just around the next bend, but when I reach each bend I see another bend farther on. Finally, I am at the spring.

It's time again for some food and more water. I filter a pint of the murky spring water. That should be enough for the remaining two miles. Water is everywhere. It's running down the trail, dripping off the sandstone, and flowing in every gully and ravine. I am beginning to feel the altitude. My pace will slow from here on. I pick up my now-heavy pack and start up the trail toward the Hermit Shale cliff.

After half a mile, the Boucher Trail enters from the right—the loop is finished. As I slowly reach the base of the Coconino, I look up and see ravens circling, way up high, above the rim. Oddly, I haven't seen or heard a raven inside the canyon on this entire trip. I am breathing hard with each step as I pass the fossil tracks again. Now I realize that it has been three days since I have talked to a living human. The sky is darkening. I make one half-breathless request of the clouds: "You can rain all you want, but just wait for an hour."

Finally, the Coconino switchbacks end. I catch my breath on the Toroweap traverse. I'm at 6,000 feet now. As I reach the base of the Kaibab layer, I see some very dark clouds approaching from the south. "OK, hold off for fifteen more minutes and then rain all you like!" I find a second wind in the Kaibab; maybe I'm "smelling the barn"? Still, there is no one on the trail. Finally I crest the Kaibab slope and start up through the woods to the parking lot. One last steep section and there is my truck. I get to the vehicle at 3:57 PM. At 4:02 PM it begins to rain.

The Edge Is What We Have
by
D. J. Lee

My father and I are at the bottom of the Grand Canyon stuffing energy bars and water bottles into our daypacks. I'm sitting on a rock while he squats beside his ballooning blue tent. Today's hike, to the confluence of the Colorado and the Little Colorado rivers, is just six and a half miles. It's late March, and although he's sixty and I'm forty, we're in fairly good shape. We'll easily make it back to camp in time for dinner.

This day hike is for my father. He's an amateur history buff, and he wants to see the salt quarry where the Hopi Indians built a stone cabin, which was used later by gold prospectors. This hike is also for me. My three brothers get to work with our father every day in the family plumbing business. Together, they lift half-ton hot water heaters through doorways, run thin copper pipe behind walls, drink coffee every morning in the shop, and eat hamburgers at noon in joints near whatever job they're on. Since I don't live close, I miss out. For once, it's just us, father and daughter, on the trail.

Four days earlier, just before my father, my mother, and I made our descent into the canyon, we stopped at the general store on the South Rim. If I wouldn't have been standing around while my mother tried to decide on postcards to send to my brothers, I may never have come across the book *Death in the Grand Canyon,* which chronicled all the ways the place could kill you. As I leaned against a shelf and skimmed the tales of people dying from dehydration, hypothermia, air crashes, freak mishaps, suicide, starvation, and flash floods, one story took my attention. In the 1960s, a man was found dead at the bottom of a steep ledge. Authorities concluded that he probably didn't have enough food and water, and no map, and because of that, he had lost his sense of judgment and thrown himself off a cliff. That's what bothered me about the story: if you were going on a hike in the Grand Canyon, why wouldn't you plan? For me, a backpack starts in my parents' kitchen, where my father gathers a sprawl of maps, hiking guides, history books, and to-do lists. Another thing that bothered me was the idea of falling from the edge. It seemed the worst possible way to die. Would your soul detach from your body as it went soaring through space? Or would it crash and crumble like your bones? But what really bothered me was the story's sensationalism. There had to be smaller, quieter experiences that were more meaningful because of their *lack* of drama. That was the kind of trip I wanted with my father.

I found him at the cash register, where he and my mother were buying T-shirts. He pulled out his credit card and laid it on the counter. "Can I see your ID?" said the cashier.

"Hey, if I were dealing in stolen credit cards, I wouldn't be making purchases like these." My father laughed. His laugh is of the loud and vigorous kind; it goes on longer than a normal person's laugh, and it often comes across as a challenge.

"Don't mind him," my mother said to the cashier. "We just got him out of the home." She pulled him aside and said, *Denny.*

We call him Denny—short for Dennis. The nickname must have started when my brothers joined the plumbing business twenty years earlier. They snap "Denny!" when he stomps around the shop after a dispatch worker takes down the wrong address or a customer doesn't pay. Our mother scolds him by barking "Denny!" when he acts out in public, like the time we were at the Arlington National Cemetery watching the ceremony at the Tomb of the Unknown Soldier. Hundreds of people were gathered on the lawn—a bunch of them were crying about things like nationalism, patriotism, and sacrifice—when a little boy slipped under the guard rope and approached a soldier, and Denny yelled, "Careful, kid, or he'll shoot you!" No one laughed. I knew what he was doing. He was trying to disrupt the sanctimoniousness of the occasion, because pomp and circumstance make him nervous. I also get uncomfortable when I feel forced into emotional responses. I was torn, as I often am, between feeling embarrassed by my father's extroversion and blessed that I come from such an exuberant forbearer. Because you can't have the enthusiastic Denny without the over-the-top version.

We're camped on a flat beach called Lava Rapids, along the Beamer Trail, where a prickly, black substance pokes up through the sand, making the area look like a piecrust with whiskers. After I finish filling my daypack, I go to step across the beach, and Denny bolts up and yanks me back. "Watch out!" he says, pointing to the prickly substance. "That's cryptobiotic. It's the layer of soil that holds the desert together. It takes a thousand years to grow and one second to destroy."

"Okay," I say. By now, I shouldn't be surprised by Denny's knowledge of the natural world, but oftentimes I am because his pro-Republican Party sympathies make him seem anti-environment. But that's Denny: He is a walking contradiction, and he doesn't care. We shrug on our packs, and my mother snaps our photo. Later, that's how I'll remember what we were wearing: Denny in khaki hiking clothes and a baseball cap covering his white hair, me in a peasant shirt embroidered with bright flowers and a bandana over my brown hair. We head off, the desert sun not yet peeping over the North Rim.

My parents raised us in a tiny house north of Seattle, where my bedroom window looked onto our front door. The window meant that I occupied the fork of my parents' marital problems. A couple of times a week, Denny stayed out drinking, and I was the first to hear him stumble up the walkway and slap his shoes off in the linoleum entry. When he went into their bedroom, he'd say, "I'm sorry," to which my mother would cry, "Why do you do this to me?"

One night, when I was about seven and they were in their late twenties, it was she who stood at my window, while my brothers and I hung out in the doorjamb. After fidgeting for a while, she walked to the kitchen, where she called one tavern after another, a tactic she often used. When a bartender picked up, she would ask for Denny, and if he came to the phone, she would put one of us on. "Mommy wants you to come home," we'd say. I liked telling my dad what to do, but I didn't mind acquiescing to my brothers. They sounded more innocent and were more effective.

That night, when we couldn't find Denny at the bars, my mom flew around the house locking everything. The only thing she didn't deadbolt was the kitchen window, an opening the size of the bathroom mirror. It would have been impossible to climb through anyway, because it was so far off the ground. She put us all to bed with extra care, reading stories until we fell asleep. I woke after a few hours to a clawing sound and came out to see Denny wedged in the window, his head, arms, and shoulders inside and the rest of his body presumably dangling outside.

My mother was leaning against a wall, her long black hair falling down her back, a hand cupping her mouth. I thought she was crying, but when I moved alongside her, I saw she was laughing, maybe at how ridiculous he looked, with his toothy, guilty grin; or maybe at the predicament, not just of the moment, but of their lives, two people not yet thirty with a bunch of kids and no money. She struggled with depression, he with alcoholism, but together they created a fresh, forward motion, and I think they often surprised themselves.

My mother slipped on one of Denny's jackets and took a chair outside for him to step on as he shimmied out the window. They came through the front door, poking each other in a teasing way.

Denny asks if I want to lead. When I say no, he takes off so fast that I have to run to keep up. The three previous days, on our hike into the Grand Canyon, we walked slowly because my mother was having trouble with her knees. I know Denny likes a fast pace, and now that it's just the two of us, I want him to stretch his legs. He's so much easier to be with when traveling a remote landscape than when surrounded by people in a restaurant, a shopping mall, or the family living room. There, he spews extremist dogma like "All ATV users should be thrown in prison," or "These days the U.S. is no different from Nazi Germany." But the vast open space of the canyon seems to absorb his intensity. Here, we don't talk politics. We don't even discuss the trail conditions or look at the map.

In fact, as we climb, neither of us speaks. We can afford the luxury of being lost in our thoughts because even though we're several hundred feet above the Colorado River now, the trail is wide, gradual, and easy. The air smells of sage and citrus from the barrel cactus in bloom as the cliff walls change from yellow to orange to purple green with each ray of morning light. On our way into the Grand Canyon on the Tanner Trail, because we could see so much at once, the immensity made me feel insignificant. But this day trip with Denny is intimate. If, as my daughter likes to say, the Grand Canyon is America's old vagina, then this trail is the smile on a young girl's lips.

When I was sixteen, Denny sat me down at the dining table, tapping his square fingers on the surface. "I want you to leave," he said. "You're not the only person in the family. You're causing everyone a lot of unhappiness." I had skipped so much school to drink and do drugs that I had failing grades. I was promiscuous, sometimes sneaking out my bedroom window at night to meet up with guys and then slipping back in just before dawn. I'd been arrested for shoplifting and breaking and entering, and—worst of all in Denny's eyes—I was having epic battles with my mother almost daily. "Every time one of your brothers has a birthday," he said, "you have a crisis."

"Fine!" I pushed away from the table and marched to my bedroom, but minutes later, standing at my closet, I regretted that I had been so cavalier. Part of me was thinking, *They'll be sorry!* But the other part knew that if I left, I would not be welcomed back. I had run away from home the previous year, and Denny had let me know that if I pulled that stunt again, he wouldn't come begging. Now he was *telling* me to leave.

As I was packing, I heard my mother say, "Dennis, she's our child. We can't put her out. That's not right." She worked on him for a few hours, long enough, anyway, so that he didn't make me go, but I knew that my place in the family was on shaky ground and that I had better turn things around.

Maybe Denny sensed the same thing. As I see it now, at least, he and I were on a similar trajectory. We were the family rebels, as selfish as we were driven, while my mother and brothers paid the price. Soon after his talk with me, Denny checked himself into an addiction treatment center. I was already away at college, and I remember the teary phone calls with my mother while I sat cross-legged against the wall of my dorm room. "I don't know what's going to happen," she would say, as if he might not come home, or as if she would not take him back if he did. "I couldn't go through this without your brothers," she'd say. At the time, I thought she was making me feel guilty for not being there, but now I see what she really meant. Because I was so demanding, and so much like Denny, she needed my brothers there as much as she needed me gone.

Denny came home all dried out, and after a few months of AA, he vowed never to drink again, a promise he kept for the simple reason, he will say, that he hated AA more than he liked drinking. I know, however, it's more than that: he quit to save himself. And us.

I often feel like this on a morning hike. A tiny voice inside is saying, *How did I make it from the frenzy of airports, office cubicles, and cellphones, of fighting with my daughter, cursing bad drivers, and complaining about my job, to this: quiet, and nature, and all my senses stimulated at once.* Up ahead, the trail climbs high above the river. I'm not worried. I've been all over the West with Denny and his hiking buddies: Cedar Mesa in Utah, the Sangre de Cristos in Colorado, the Sawtooths of Idaho, the Pacific Crest Trail in Washington, the Chilkoot in Alaska, the Earl Grey in Canada, and California's Death Valley. We've covered some tough terrain. No, I'm not worried.

Until we find ourselves on a precipice that we didn't foresee. In a matter of minutes, the trail has gone from an easy path winding around corners of a hillside to something unstable and alien. On one side is a rounded hill covered in loose rocks, totally unclimbable, butting up against the red, orange, and copper wall called the Palisades of the Desert. On the other side, a sheer cliff falls straight down hundreds of feet. "We must be on the wrong trail," Denny calls from his spot ahead, but he keeps walking forward. Wrong or right, I'm already registering that I'm on the scariest piece of real estate I've ever walked. That voice, it's now saying, *Focus on your footing. Don't look at the edge. Just plant your pole and step.*

And I do, like never before, every bit of my attention on bending one leg, swinging it forward, and placing it down. I'm telling myself that obviously somebody has worn a path along this cliff, and I'm surely just as capable.

But here is where everything changes.

I step on a loose piece of sandstone, and my foot slips. I stop, frozen, staring at the ground falling away under the tip of my boot. Down there—who knows how far?—six-hundred, eight-hundred, a thousand feet?—sits a raft, its bright yellow and red blazing against the brown of the riverbank. It looks like a child's bath toy, and the people on the beach are like twitching fleas. I wonder if they see me up here with no ropes or carabineers. Are they worried? Or are they thinking I look perfectly safe? *Wait*, I think. *Why am I fixating on those rafters at a time like this? I need to focus on the here and now.* But I can't. The story of the guy who fell from the edge to his death because he was unprepared skids across my mind, and then a memory intrudes from a time five years earlier, when I lived in London on a research grant for my job at a university and got so lonely that I flirted with thoughts of suicide. How careless I was then, to take life for granted! Here, I'm doing everything in my power to keep from dying.

I glance up. Denny has pitched himself against the bluff, right where the trail turns toward a draw. When I make it to that spot, I sit next to him, my boots planted solidly on the trail. Strange that I can hear the air moving right through my body and feel Denny breathing.

"Whoa," I say. "What should we do?"

"You stay here," he says. "I'll go around the corner and see what the trail's like ahead."

"I'll go," I say. "*You* stay."

"No, I'm older. I've raised my family. If something happens to me, well. You've got your whole life ahead of you."

"D*aaaaa*d." I remind him that he's a father, and a grandfather, and a great-grandfather; of how much time he spends with my brothers' kids, and my daughter; of how he tutored one grandkid through high school and kept another from turning to drugs.

"Well," he says, "I'm going." He seems to glow as he rounds the corner. The light has made everything blend and soften: pink rocks, red earth, milk chocolate river, and ochre sand.

"Oh, yeah, the trail widens out here," Denny calls. "It isn't so steep."

Hoisting myself up, I take one step, and another, and another until I'm around the corner. The path does widen, so I stop and look at Denny. He has already encountered another narrow patch on the edge, but he's going forward, and so I follow. We inch along until we're in the draw on a sturdy rock shelf, where we sit. Now, I'm hyper-aware of the slow, steady waves of normal consciousness replacing the *oh shit* thoughts of the previous thirty minutes.

"I think we should rest awhile," Denny says. "I just don't know about this trail. Some of it, mountain goats wouldn't even attempt." He squats and unzips his pack, breathing heavily through his nostrils, as he does when he's puzzling through a problem. "I forgot to count the draws," he says, unscrewing the cap on his water bottle and passing it to me. "Can you remember?"

"Let's see. Four, five? I don't remember." I hand Denny the map. We locate Carbon Creek Canyon, Peshlakai Point, and Temple Butte, features on both sides of the river, trying to figure out where we are. The map shows that we are on the right trail, and that it is exposed on two sections, but we can't decide if we've passed the two sections, or if we still have one to go.

"Damn the map," Denny says. "We have to solve this thing without it." Ahead, we see a giant slab jutting right out on a point. The slab will require us to make a hairpin turn so that our entire bodies—everything but our feet and our hands—will be hanging over the edge. "Some guys, they pitch their tents on sides of cliffs and think it's fun. We're not like that."

"No, we're not," I say.

We sit on the shelf for a long time—maybe an hour, or more. I write in my journal, and Denny lays his head back on a rock, closing his eyes. The canyon seems quieter now than it has since the day we descended. Even the wrens, which I have been tuned into all week, are silent. In this stillness, I gaze at the broad river glinting in the morning sun. Denny pops up, with a steady look in his eyes. "Let's turn back," he says.

I nod. I've already reached the same conclusion.

Back at camp, when we tell my mom what happened—"This was the closest I've ever been to dying," and "It's hard to explain how close"—I already feel the experience slipping into the realm of narrative. A week later, when I call my husband; six months later, when I talk about my "scariest hike" to a group of women I'm leading into the Eagle Cap Wilderness in Oregon; several years later, when I write up a version of the story and someone says, "Why did you put in that part about being suicidal in London," and I say, "Because, that's what I thought about when I was up there"; and even as I write *this,* I understand that narrative will never be enough to contain that experience. But it can point toward its meaning.

The hike didn't crystallize some long-missing father-daughter bond between Denny and me. That was already happening in the twenty years after we both straightened out our lives. The important thing was what happened after, when I fully realized this: that Denny and I had been on the precipice of the Grand Canyon, and of life, and we turned around.

Except, it is the moment before we turned around that comes back most clearly whenever I summon the experience. "Dad?" I say as we leave the shelf. "Don't worry about me, and I won't worry about you. If we both just pay attention to our own footing and balance, we'll be okay."

He starts walking, but I hang back. I don't want to arrive at camp just yet or return to the rim in a few days, or to my regular life. I want to stay here on the edge with Denny.

At Bottom a River
by
Rick Dean

From a time of growing up along the banks of the Missouri River, the notion slowly grew in me that if one could somehow get beneath all the surface features we encounter in the world—prairies and bluffs, dunes, oceans, cities, forests, deep blue-water springs, everything—at the bottom of it all there would be a river.

It may be, in a crude way of reckoning, that there are two kinds of people—those given to lakes and the others to rivers. People of the lake are ever-mindful of the dimension of depth residing within the arrangement of the world. They also hold to the belief that if one were to go deep enough, down through the topographical and intermediary layers, it is possible to hit bottom.

But growing up as I did along the river led me to suppose that even if I were able to work down through the layers, I still would not strike bedrock. At bottom there would not be anything like a fundamental foundation, but something forever passing, always coming and going.

The difference between people of the lake and people of the river is the age-old difference between Parmenides and Heraclitus, Plato and Hegel. Between fixed rock-solid substance and ideals on the one hand and unending change on the other. In our national history, it has been the difference between the stability of place and the restlessness of the frontier spirit, between established roots and a hope hungry for something better.

Coursing through the old rock at the bottom of the Grand Canyon, the river is the living cipher of the place.

Twenty three days after first venturing out onto Great Thumb Mesa, I am near the mouth of Red Canyon, sitting, for the first time, at the water's edge. The current laps lazily over my toes, agitates and swirls higher along the shoreline, soaking the seat of my walking shorts.

The day is sunny, just shy of hot, and the roar of Hance Rapids rides downriver on the back of an unbridled breeze. Running thick with the dust of Navajo Country's Painted Desert, the water is the shade of weak hot chocolate. One-half inch below the surface my fingers disappear. At one time the sediment whirling by could have been bits and pieces of Wyoming, Colorado, Utah, or grains of New Mexico from the San Juan basin. Before dams were raised upstream to act as settling basins, the flow through the canyon sometimes exceeded 100,000 cubic feet per second, with over half the volume comprised of sediment. Most of the sediment today comes from Utah's Paria or the Little Colorado, which is now in flood.

Sitting there on the bank, I wonder what the chances will be of working my way up the Little Colorado River and crossing over to the side of the Hopi Sipapu, which I have decided is a fitting place to end the hike. For that part of the journey still in front of me, the river will become the living, pulsating heart of the landscape. A stretch climbing up towards the head of Escalante Canyon, and on around the nameless canyon west of Cardenas, will steer me away, but only for a day. After that, either the water of the Colorado or its smaller tributary will be rolling nearby, until I retrace my steps back along the Beamer Trail to the foot of the Tanner, where I will begin the dry, sweaty climb up and out.

From the loose sand behind me I retrieve a pair of liners and sorry-looking socks stained with the red grit of the canyon. On the inside lip of my boot-uppers, padding has worn through the leather and now peeks out. Halfheartedly, I rise to my feet, then strain to hoist the pack onto my shoulders. The sap has gone out of me.

Climbing hands-over-head up the vertical slide at Papago, I feel something slip out of an unzipped back compartment. I glance over my shoulder in time to spy the half-gallon jug cartwheeling down the rockfall then splitting open like a ripe melon. Strands of water radiate outward, a winsome sight were it not for the need to descend and retrieve the shattered pieces.

Evening in a dry wash, east arm of Escalante Canyon. Crickets are chirping, their song rising up out of the dry earth, a disjointed chorus of monotonous strains. Earth music. Bats flutter and swoop in the twilight, playing a game of chicken around my ears.

While stooping to dig a hole for the evening deposit, I dislodge a scorpion from a crack beneath a rock. Its legs and tail flash the shade of harvest wheat, its segmented body limestone-gray with golden horizontal stripes. Out into the dying light of day it scuttles and disappears into the nearest slit. In no hurry, it will wait for the dark of night.

The scorpion is a beast with an attitude, which may explain why it draws my respect and annoys me at the same time. Scorpions have a metabolism so slow that some can go a year without eating. Exceedingly difficult to kill by natural means, they have been found to endure 120-degree temperatures and a two-day submergence in water. Once in Britain one was frozen for three weeks in a block of ice. When the block was thawed with a blow torch, the critter scurried across the counter top. Yes, a remarkable beast with a nasty reputation, but it is her scorpions that make the wild earth as rich as it is.

I offer this one a Franciscan blessing: *The lord bless and keep you, and grant you long undisturbed life . . . which you surely will not have should you stray into my sleeping bag this evening.*

I lay back to watch the muted light seep from the canyon. Two evenings before, in Grapevine Canyon, with the last light dispersed by a swirling mass of frothing cloud, the plaintive howls of coyotes shattered my evening ritual. Their feral yelps declared only their presence, not their location. Like a crooked preacher, the wild dog of the west is a survivor.

Thoroughly spent, I hook my waning attention to the passing of light and drift off into night's waiting arms, leaving the real work to the bats and scorpions and coyotes and whatever . . .

There are nights when in the hush of a cool desert, you awaken to feel the land cradling you. And slowly, as if by a passage of rebirth, you stir to a nascent awareness. The first sensation, even before you have fully gathered your senses, is of the land beneath you, the mute rock around you, the dome of boundless sky overhead. Any awareness of self cannot help but come later, as if you have sprouted from some windblown seed out of the maternal earth. Maybe nowhere else can the focus upon elemental priorities and fundamental connections be drawn into such sharp relief as in the desert.

The crickets have stopped. The icy white lamp of a half-moon hangs overhead, and the banks along the dry wash cast grey shadows over the lighter-shaded gravel at the bottom. I do not see the bats, but know that they are still at work. Maybe a quiver of breeze radiates out from their silent swoops. Perhaps I spy a dark waif trailing down through the starlight. There are many things, worlds in fact, too slight to pass through the brutish filter of human sensation.

Not a breath stirs. Only a settled silence too rich and full to disturb. My bladder can wait.

My camp is about a mile from the river. Now that I have dabbled my feet in its cold water, I feel it drawing me, its currents and undertows at the center of my world endowing the walk with whatever value it will come to hold.

My memory springs into flight with the bats. More and more of the trip is slipping into the past, becoming part of imagination and memory, a landscape of soul. I think of earlier that afternoon, the walk up 75 Mile Canyon.

At its lower end, this short canyon is a serpentine cut through sandstone, the eastern canyon's version of a small slot. Ten to fifteen feet wide, its bottom lingers in undisturbed shadow. A cold, clear strand of water cavorts along a polished gravel floor, plunges over ledges and collects in shallow pristine pools. Two high walls of slickrock, absent of plant life. A thin strip of deep blue sky overhead. It is a place of abstract simplicity, a winding, intimate artery through the bowels of rock, the kind of place which leads some to chant and draw down the moon, and others to contemplate the intractable silence of the rock, the play of running water.

The rock of 75 Mile Canyon is early Cambrian Sandstone, 550 million years old. The Vishnu Schist immediately below is over a billion years older. Nature, like her children, cloaks itself in mysteries, inconsistencies and unconformities. Neither end up being purely logical, thank god.

I break camp, gladly leaving the dry wash to the crickets, scorpion, bats, and all the other critters that slinked, scurried, and fluttered near my bag while I slept. Leaving as if I were never there.

These past few mornings it has been harder to get the kinks out of the engine. Invariably, the morning walk slumps into an exercise in lethargy, as if I were trudging through soft muck. But that is all right;

I am moving and the body still rules, this body which is matter, mind, me. No Cartesian "ghost in the machine" here.

Just before the sun peaks along the rim, muscles loosen. I draw on the last untapped store of fat and pick up the pace. More and more, the outlines of my ribs are defining themselves. There is less of me than when I entered the canyon. Descartes would not understand.

Tramping out of the side canyon just west of Cardenas Creek, I spy a small train of hikers strung out along the trail clinging to the far wall. Seven or eight brightly-colored shirts and packs bearing west. As distance closes, bodies can be attached to the colors, friendly smiling faces, most of them old and beautifully wrinkled, topped with large-brimmed hats, hands clasped around walking sticks. We stop and talk. Short, abbreviated biographies. Home towns. Our business in the canyon. Small talk, the marrow of life. As others straggle into the circle, I am asked to repeat myself. ". . . dropped into the canyon off Great Thumb a few weeks ago . . . over the Esplanade . . . down the Bass . . ." Two rounds, and I begin sounding like a 2 AM infomercial.

They are a jovial, spirited bunch belonging to a group following the teachings of the Peace Pilgrim. The Peace Pilgrim, as I discover, was an extraordinary woman who late in life decided that she would travel the country on foot sharing her message of peace and compassion with whomever listened. I try not to let it show, but I am more interested in the great distance she covered without need of property or possession than in her simple message that world peace begins with inner peace.

I find that the good disciples are generous of heart. They offer food and drink, but I waver, preferring not to take from someone who may hold a keen interest in conversion. Still, they are idealists and I like them. I tell them it would be nice if I could muster such optimism, but I am weighed down by too many existential philosophies. And then we part, heading off in our opposite directions.

After a few steps I turn and shout after them, "Should you decide to make camp down in Escalante Creek, watch out for scorpions. They are not always so respectful of high ideals, you know." And we all share a deep-cleansing laugh.

It is downhill now all the way to the river. Down the eastern side of the nameless side canyon. Dry, red, shaley country. Down below the rounded hump overlooking the Colorado, holding the foundation stones of an Anasazi ruin. Down past the once-fertile Unkar Delta on the north side, to the sand and willows along the water's edge. Ahhh, back to the river . . .

On a small ledge tucked into the bank beside the river, just past Tanner Camp, I sit reading, glancing up occasionally to ponder the sediment settling in the jug of water I drew a half-hour ago. Slow business. Maybe someday I'll give in and get a purifier, but water as muddy as this would only plug the filter.

Someone has left their pack on the ledge. I should not be here; the most private of properties in the backcountry, a pack stakes claim to the area immediately around it. But the ledge is shady and deserted, a cool out-of-the-way spot at the end of the trail just above the water. And even though it is early afternoon, I am finished for the day. Maybe later I will muster the ambition to wander off and look for a campsite. Maybe.

Just downstream at Tanner Camp voices rise up out of the willows, mingling with the hollow murmurings of the slack water curling just in front of me. The steady clamor of Tanner Rapids drones in the background. I lay my book aside, letting the sight and sound of water work its subtle magic, its soothing hypnosis.

Though the walk is still days short of wrapping up, I entertain a sense of having arrived. Nearly a month tramping through the canyon's upper reaches, through its cathedrals of rock, mute relics of time, has brought me here. Now within that same flow of time and space, place and self conspire to awaken a sense of belonging, a shallow rootedness in the long chain of natural events that have shaped and scoured the terrain. And at the bottom of it all runs the river whose waters haunt me with the notion that I shall live out my life caught between the stability of belonging to a place and a sense of homelessness.

A woman appears on the ledge to retrieve her pack. We exchange obligatory greetings. She is aloof, and I do not much blame her. Who am I to be sitting here so near her property? I play the penitent, but am really too spent and too comfortable to give a damn.

She is blond, earthy, and tan. Her face shows signs of time spent in the desert, wrinkles and folds, each one with a thousand stories attached.

Slinging her pack onto her shoulder she asks, "Where you coming from?"

"Since last night, or in the beginning?"

"Either."

"Last night, from Escalante. In the beginning, Great Thumb."

"Are you kidding?" she asks curiously. A grin slips over her face. She knows the place.

"No, I've been at it awhile."

So we talk, first about the place which has joined us in conversation, then a little about ourselves. Friends call her Ote, she tells me, short for Coyote. She lives in Flagstaff and has been rowing dories through the canyon for many years.

"It is what I do," she tells me. Her husband, also a boatman, manages the company now, and she has a teenage son who dwarfs her . . .

She leaves, and with nothing else to occupy me, I resume my vigil beside the river.

I douse my bandana, and then, after working my back into a cool slab of rock, drape it around my neck. Cold drips trickle down the small of my back . . . and the shadows grow longer here on the canyon floor with no foundation.

A lazy late afternoon, the latter half of April. One among millions. The date means little, indeed is swallowed up in canyon time. A nomadic breeze skims the surface of the river, brushes against my cheeks, and mingles with the cool scent of water to suck out what is left of the sagging ambition lingering in my limp frame. There is nothing better in the world, it seems to me at this moment, than to be sitting here on the banks of this river watching water that never rests.

Two women appear on the trail ending at the ledge. They are Ote's friends. One is an English professor from Salt Lake, the other, a gardener from Moab. They bring food and fresh water, and we talk. There are seven of them in their group, staying in the willows at Tanner Camp. A circle of seven women who gather annually to renew their connections, deepen their sense of self, and break free of the nonsense one encounters with our man-made constructions of the world.

By early evening I reach the conclusion that looking for a flat spot to spread out my bag might be within my ability after all. So I gather my belongings and trudge up to a rounded knoll overlooking the river, where before unloading and getting down to housekeeping, I soak up a view of the Colorado looping gracefully around the sandy tongue of a wide, flat bar on the north shore. Here at the bottom of the world the floor is fast sinking into shadow, and in the translucent light, the river's surface glistens with a silvery sheen. I glance up in the direction of the South Rim to where the Palisades, edge of the Painted Desert, pinch into the canyon.

After sunset I greet a procession of stars, and the changing of light. I munch on goodies the women brought to me throughout the afternoon—smoked sardines, cheese and crackers, chocolate, an orange—and am transported even nearer to the shores of paradise.

Late into the night wild shouts rise up out of the willows along the beach, followed by a loud splash . . . a shriek, then another *ker-plunk*. Sounds of renewal and release.

Earlier, some of the women had told me that in this last year one of their sisters had died, and that they would be holding a rite of remembrance this evening. Now awake, I wait for more. But that is all. The yawning silence of the desert returns, and the sound of the river running.

Claim Your Due:
A Backpacker's View of River-Runners
by
Rick Kempa

Backpackers fear rafters; there is no other way to put it. Our hiking permits warn us of them, along with "aggressive" ravens and "persistent" ring-tailed cats, and advise us on how to avoid them. They are the tamarisk invaders who crowd the banks; we are the willows, the supplanted native tribe. We have ventured "below the rim" (a phrase we are fond of) to trade noise for silence and society for solitude. The rafters' camp, with its big circle of lawn chairs and its boombox pumping New Age music into the air of afternoon and its nightly yodeling and strumming, agitates us.

Ours, we like to think, is the genuine adventure, theirs a glorified Disney ride. We have safely executed tens of thousands of conscious footsteps to get to the river; they have arrived here by sitting. We have skirted danger on trails that thread through cliffs or plunge down steep gravel slopes; theirs is a pseudo-danger, a jaunt through rapids whose every boulder is foreknown and often even named. The play that they sometimes indulge in—dousing each other with water cannons and buckets, talking like pirates, squealing like preschoolers—is annoying. "The Grand Canyon is no *playground!*" we sputter.

Most of all, we resent their opulence. The smell of cooked meat wafts through the willows to our little patch of beach and drives us crazy. If we creep close, we can hear the sizzle of the fry pan and the pop of can tops and grunts of gluttony. They have bacon and eggs, salami and three kinds of cheese, candy bars and pudding. We have chewy oatmeal, crushed crackers and slimy, flaccid cheddar, and, for dessert (if we are lucky), a wedge of dried fruit.

Our resentment is rooted in envy, and this makes us even madder, because we planned to leave all our Deadly Sins on the rim. We have been experiencing a net loss of calories, and our appetites are raging.

We would like to be invited to the feast, but don't know how to go about it. "Just do it, man," the stomach says. "I'm telling you, please." But we lost our social graces somewhere up in the cliffs, and the head dreads the interplay that is the price of eating. On a recent hike in the Nankoweap Basin, I came upon the outlying signs of a rafters' camp in a mesquite grove—the porto-potty, the first tents. Ahead of me I could hear the weird sounds of electronic fusion music. After three days alone, I could not bear such sudden society, so I plunged off-trail up-slope through the thickets, shredding my legs in the process, and traversed above them until, from the receding smell of hot dogs and the diminishing drumbeat, I knew it was safe to go back down.

The next evening was a different story. I was just starting the climb out, and my stomach sternly lectured me: "Listen, man. Now is not the time for shyness." A new rafting party was in residence—no techno-beat tonight. When I walked into their camp, the clamor of voices instantly ceased. Two dozen pairs of eyes were on me. I met the nearest set of eyes, nodded.

"Can we offer you some soup?" a voice cried out. A ruddy man down by the water had spoken. When I didn't immediately answer, because hot soup on a hot day did not appeal to me, he laughed. "Looks like I've got your interest."

I was actually more interested in the spread of crackers and cheese and meat. He saw my look and gestured. "Have at it. Our only rule is that you wash your hands first."

"I can do that," I said, and dropped my pack. When I fumbled with the contraption at the hand-washing station, he showed me how to operate it. While I ate, he and another man flanked me.

"So you're the leaders of this outfit?" I asked, between mouthfuls. One of them nodded toward the two immense rafts.

"Yeah, we're the bus drivers."

They were hikers too, they were quick to add, one from Moab, the other Flagstaff. We stood in silence while I ate, and soon they drifted away. A lanky woman joined me at the table.

"Tell me your name," she said, "so that I don't have to write 'that guy' in my journal."

Three pink-cheeked boys watched me hoist my pack. The bravest said, "So you're walking?"

"Sure am," I said.

Whatever the outcome, famine or feast, solitude or society, an encounter with rafters upsets the backpacker's equilibrium. Either way, a stomach ache is in store, if not from unquenched appetite than from a sudden engorgement. Either way, the spigot of language, which I have managed to reduce to a trickle, will be turned on full throttle. If I have shied away from them, I will spin fantasies of what I might have—*should* have—done instead: parried their questions with brilliant thrusts, disarmed them with terse, apt remarks. But if I have entered their camp, the aftermath will be worse. All through my evening's hike up Nankoweap Creek, I replayed the tapes of the encounter and found myself wanting. Busy as I was wolfing their food, I did not properly express my gratitude to the guides and coax from them the stories of their own hikes. And that woman who asked my name—clearly she was flirting. Why did I not ask for hers as well, for *my* journal? And those boys; why did I not take time to invite their unasked questions? It takes a good night's sleep for such hauntings to subside.

These, then, are the Backpacker's Rules of Conduct in Regards to River-Runners:

Control your impulses, for god's sake. Camp upwind of their kitchen. Live within your own sorry means.

When self-control fails you, proceed deliberately. Walk into their camp as if by chance, in full regalia—boots, backpack, staff. Suffer the sudden silence, the weight of all those eyes. You are an exotic species, like the bighorn sheep that perch on crags or the condors who ride the updrafts high above. You would do well to speak little; you are out of practice. Do not ask for anything, and they will ask you to stay.

Finally, and most importantly, claim your due. The unalterable rule of the river, known to boatman and backpacker alike, is this: Backpackers are entitled to free beer. It is the toll we exact for the disturbance we suffer, the gift they are duty-bound to give.

On a Tanner Canyon hike a while back, my buddy Bob was dosing on the beach when voices woke him. Three rafts were gliding by, accelerating on their approach to the rapids. Wasting no time, for the first two were already past our eddy and the last one broadside, he hustled to the water's edge.

"Cervesa?" he called out.

"What?" the man at the helm shouted back.

"Tecate?"

"WHAT?"

"BEER!"

"Are you a hiker or a rafter?" the man shouted.

"A hiker!" Bob declared.

"All right. OK." Gesturing downstream to where the delta of Tanner Creek curls out into a spit of sand, he said, "We'll meet you at the point. Hurry!"

Bob leapt to his bare feet and erupted into motion, flying over shrubs, goring himself on a root, arriving at the point just in time to effect the handoff from the woman in the prow, and off they shot into the rapids, and back he hobbled into camp, bleeding from a gash above his ankle, grinning and holding the gleaming can aloft. Dale's Pale Ale!

The rule, more simply stated, is this: Be like Bob. Over the decades, on beachfronts from the Confluence to Elves Chasm, I have garnered Heineken and Hamm's, Killian's Red and Coors Light, Polygamy Porter and PBR. Each, I swear, has been the best beer of my life, the memory of which, like old lovers, I will carry to my grave.

Are you a hiker or a rafter? That, to the river guides, is the question that matters. They need to know that you are not a jackal from some other rafting trip, a loser. The morning after I took to the brush in Nankoweap, I padded into the boat camp with an empty water bottle. Feeling a little lazy, I was hoping to spare myself the half-mile walk back to the creek. "Mind if I refill this?" I asked. It was a rhetorical question—of course they wouldn't—and I was already stepping toward the big ten-gallon thermos when a wiry, weathered dude—the guide, obviously—stepped in front of me.

"You know," he said gruffly, "It takes a lot of work to pump water from the river." When I didn't answer, he waved his hand and said, "But go ahead anyway."

His abruptness surprised and angered me. It was just water, for pete's sake. It's not like I was begging a slab of bacon.

Later, back on my own beachhead, I watched as, one by one, their yellow rafts appeared, five in all, spinning and gliding downstream.

Kayakers, one, two, three, flitted back and forth. The first pulled up alongside the lead raft way out there midstream, then cut cross-current in a straight line towards me.

"I have a present for you!" the helmeted, panting boy called out.

"Oh yeah?" I stood and walked to the shore. There in his lap was a 16-ounce can of Guinness Stout.

"Compliments of the guide."

I faced downstream toward the lead raft and raised the can overhead. It was, I understood, a gesture of apology on the guide's part for his earlier rudeness. He simply had not known I was on foot.

I chose four sturdy rocks and hauled them down to the river. I planted them in the sand in the shape of a square, where the water was about ten-inches deep, then wedged my Stout in the middle and lay a flat rock across the top. Kicking back, watching the wavelets lap against my cooler, I thought how they are not such a bad brood after all, these rafters. The guides are men and women of merit, gainfully employed. In another life, I could be one of them. The passengers could be having their canyon experience at the IMAX theatre in Tusayan, or in a helicopter with their noses pressed against thick glass. They could be shuffling along the paved trail at the rim, distancing themselves every few seconds with their camera lens. Instead, I admitted, they too are having an adventure. They are eating in the open air and sleeping on the ground; they are actually getting wet. Unlike this old curmudgeon, they are taking on the challenge to build community, make friends from strangers, with their waterguns and lawnchairs as props. I could even envision that, when my body gets too creaky for these crazy hikes—or maybe sometime sooner—I will come aboard.

IV
Pursuits

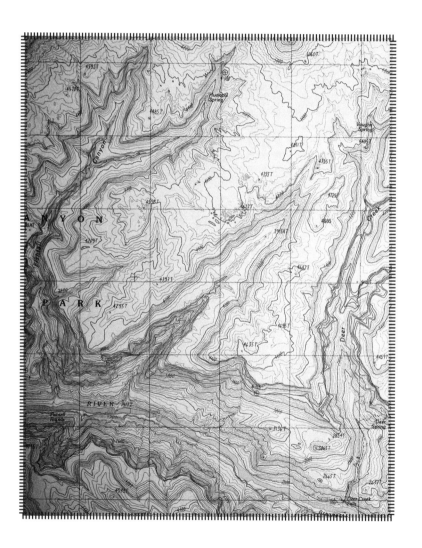

The Discovery of the Cranberry Canyon Route
by
Arnie Richards

Thursday, November 28, 1968

An icy wind cut through the junipers as we negotiated our way up the road through Zion National Park. Sunrise had set the sandstone cliffs ablaze with color, contrasting sharply with the deep blue sky. Soon we would be in Fredonia, Arizona, our jump-off point to Indian Hollow on the North Rim where we would begin our hike. I rubbed my eyes sleepily as we drove. We had been on the road all night since picking Dave up at the Greyhound Station in Bakersfield, and the fatigue was beginning to take its toll.

This was to be only my second backpacking trip into the Grand Canyon. The first, over a year and a half earlier, had been down the Thunder River Trail to Tapeats Creek, and then cross-country along the steep rocky taluses upriver to Stone Creek. That trip had remained etched in my memory as exciting, adventurous, and somewhat frightening—the taluses were steep, the rocks loose, and the footing unsure. I felt as though we were in a perpetual state of danger, and completing the endeavor had given me a profound sense of accomplishment.

The leader of that first trip had been Dave Mortenson, a friend of mine from high school. Dave's father, Brick Mortenson, had run the Colorado River with the well-known and accomplished boatman Pat Reilly, who was a pioneer of Grand Canyon boating from the late 1940s until the early 1960s. Brick and Pat had taken Dave on his first backpack trip into the canyon. At the time of my first hike, Dave was a freshman in college, and was beginning to show the leadership qualities that he would maintain throughout his life. He had organized and outfitted that trip completely on his own, and had led four rookies into the chasm and safely out again.

For this upcoming hike, Dave wanted to find an entirely new route to the river—a passage through the Redwall that probably no one had hiked before. Why? Precisely because no one had hiked it before, and we knew we could. Our teenage vitality and self-confidence dictated this. Our goal was Deer Creek, a beautiful perennial stream lined with cottonwoods and lying deep in Deer Creek Valley. One *can* reach Deer Creek by hiking down the Thunder River Trail and turning west at the bottom of the Redwall. But that route is 13 miles long, and it was Dave's desire to find a shorter route, somewhere off the Esplanade between Deer Creek and Mile 138.5 Canyon, which is the next tributary downstream. Such a route, if it existed, would shorten the hike from Indian Hollow to Deer Creek by several miles. As this was only my second trip into the canyon, and I had never even heard of Deer Creek, none of this meant anything to me. However, in my youthful exuberance, I'm sure I attached a lot more importance to the task than it deserved. We were not, after all, Lewis and Clark, and this was not the Great Northwest Passage, even though that's what it felt like at the time. The bottom line: I was very excited about what we were about to attempt. "We *shall* conquer the canyon."

Our party consisted of one other person besides Dave and me. Brian Collart was a sophomore at Los Angeles Valley College. His only prior experience in the canyon had been down to the Havasupai Reservation. I had known Brian since high school.

After a hearty breakfast at Ruby's Café in Kanab, we headed up the dirt road just south of Fredonia onto the Kaibab Plateau. We were driving my 1962 Chevy II Nova, which was strictly a street vehicle. On my first trip, we had driven Brick Mortenson's Toyota Landcruiser. Why I thought that my Chevy could handle the dirt road, I'm not sure, but we were willing to give it a try. I had had it serviced the day before the trip, and the mechanic had warned me that the ball joints were loose, and I was likely to have a serious accident if I didn't replace them. I didn't know what a ball joint was and figured he was just trying to fleece me, so I ignored his advice and made the drive. Turns out we had absolutely no problems, and reached Indian Hollow at mid-day. Our intended route would take us along the Thunder River Trail for approximately one mile, and then straight across the Esplanade toward the river, onto a "peninsula" of land lying between Deer Creek Canyon and Mile 138.5 Canyon. We would establish a base camp somewhere on this peninsula and spend the next couple of days looking for a way down to Deer Creek.

The Thunder River Trail runs west for ¾ mile along the rim just below the upper Kaibab Limestone cliffs until it reaches a slide which penetrates the Coconino Sandstone. Then it switchbacks down the slide before turning east for its long meander across the Esplanade. We left the trail about halfway down the slide and maneuvered generally south and onto the Esplanade. We moved slowly through the tortured sandstone landscape, stopping here and there to inspect overhangs for evidence of Indian occupancy; we didn't find much. The area between upper Deer Creek and upper Mile 138.5 was a little rough. The heads of the two canyons are close enough together that the erosion patterns seem to merge, breaking the area up into numerous side canyons and ravines. We walked for perhaps four hours before reaching an interesting little "depression" on the Esplanade. The depression lay about two miles north of the Redwall cliff at the end of the peninsula, and was about ¼ by ½ mile in size, encompassing the entire width of the peninsula. It sat about 20 feet below the Supai cap rock on either side of it, and was quite flat and smooth, with very few exposed rocks. It was a good place to establish our base camp.

A chilly wind blew across the Esplanade as we ate our dinner. We were all very tired after having driven all night and hiked all day. We hit our sleeping bags and were asleep by 6 PM.

Friday, November 29, 1968

The temperature dropped down to the mid-twenties during the night. Being poor college students (actually we were *destitute* college students), none of us owned a decent sleeping bag. We each had old beat-up polyfiber bags that were only good down to about 45 degrees, and none of us owned a tent. So shortly after midnight, after seven good hours of sleep, we all woke up shivering. Not only was it cold, but we were all suffering from the all-night-driver's version of jet lag (truck-lag?). It took two or three hours to drift back to sleep.

I re-awoke at first light, and watched the dawn turn into a sunrise. When the temperature had reached a tolerable level, I crawled out of my bag and started preparing for the day. Dave and Brian were content to stay in bed, so I took the opportunity to explore east of camp. I was able to descend the Supai in a small arroyo and walk out to the brink of the Redwall at the edge of Deer Creek Canyon. The view there was quite spectacular. The Supai talus had leveled off to horizontal at its junction with the vertical Redwall. The early morning shadows created the illusion that the gorge was a long deep pit. After a few pictures, I climbed the Supai back to camp in time to find Dave and Brian finally getting up. We enjoyed a nice breakfast and then started our exploration.

Number one on Dave's list of "Things to Try" was to explore the east side of the peninsula for a direct route into Deer Creek Canyon. We retraced my footsteps from earlier in the morning down to the talus below the Supai and began to work our way toward the Colorado. The talus, which started out level where we came off the Supai, steepened as we moved southward, eventually reaching an angle of 45°. About a mile down we encountered a steeply sloped amphitheater. At first we were reluctant to cross. Should one of us lose our footing, it was several hundred feet straight down to the canyon floor. So while Brian and I waited, Dave scaled the Supai cliff to the top of the peninsula to reconnoiter. Minutes later I became impatient and decided to try crossing the amphitheater anyway. It was much easier than it looked. Brian followed and a short time later we were yelling back and forth to Dave who was now 300 feet above us. We continued moving along the talus for about another half mile until Dave called down to inform us that the talus would soon peter out, eliminating this as a potential route to the bottom.

Brian and I backtracked to the amphitheater, climbed up to the peninsula, and hoofed back to camp for lunch. After our meal, Dave and Brian headed south across the top of the peninsula to check the south end for possible routes. I followed a few minutes later, but could not find either of them, so I continued along the peninsula in a southerly direction. The peninsula had a central "ridge" of Supai caprock, varying from 10 to 50 feet wide. There were several levels on either side of this ridge, each separated by about 10 feet of broken down cliff. The walk was very easy and I covered the two miles quickly. But I was totally unprepared for the view when I reached the end. Spectacular, incredible, beautiful, breath-taking, awe-inspiring: Though accurate, none of these adjectives were adequate. I was 2,500 feet above the river, and below me I could see about 15 miles of inner gorge. Upstream I could see almost to Stone Creek, downstream to Mile 140 Canyon.

Two thousand feet below me lay Deer Creek Valley, lined with golden cottonwoods. The approaching sunset had turned the cliffs into a myriad of red, orange, and golden hues. It was a very spiritual experience, and I sat there with my feet dangling over the edge for some time before getting up to continue my exploring.

Where I had been sitting, the Supai cliff ran parallel to the river. I noticed that to my right (west), the Supai jogged back toward the rim for maybe a couple hundred yards, before resuming its westward trend. Looking down, I saw that at the bottom of this jog lay a sizeable gash in the talus below the Redwall. The gash was a dry streambed which began as a steep chute at the top of the Redwall, and sloped very steeply to the river. Although the top of the chute was accessible from the talus between the Supai and the Redwall, it looked much too steep to hike down. From above it appeared to be a 60° or 70° incline, for a distance of perhaps 50 feet. Since none of us were rock-climbers, I did not think this chute would pan out.

The sun had just set and I hadn't carried a flashlight, so I figured I'd better start heading back to camp so as not to worry my companions. Even in the failing light, I was able to move quickly across the relatively flat peninsula. A quarter mile from camp I found Dave building a signal fire for me, so that I would be able to find the camp more easily. After he had chastised me for being out alone after dark (sorry, Dad), we headed back to camp, and dinner.

I spoke to Dave about the chute I had seen penetrating the Redwall. He had seen it as well. I expressed my doubts about being able to get through it. We decided that we would try to get down Mile 138.5 Canyon on Saturday, and if that didn't work, we would investigate the chute.

Naturally, when it got dark, it also got cold. Dave built a large campfire to keep us warm. It was so large that it spread to an adjacent bush and then to another. The local warming effect was quite pronounced, so we lit a number of nearby bushes on fire, which kept us comfortable for some time, and was entertaining besides. Years later, as I re-read this account, I realized how environmentally irresponsible we had been. In 1968, this part of the canyon—from Tapeats Creek to Kanab Canyon—was part of the Kaibab National Forest where fires of all kinds were permitted. We were neither in the National Park nor the

National Monument, so we weren't breaking any laws. Nevertheless, this was not a very respectful way to treat the fragile environment. An hour later we were in bed for the night.

Saturday, November 30, 1968

I awoke shivering again. The temperature had dropped to 24° by midnight, but clouds had moved in during the night, and it had "warmed up" to 30° by daybreak. It looked and felt like it was going to snow. After breakfast we began our decent into Mile 138.5 Canyon. This being Thanksgiving weekend, and the canyon at mile 138.5 being otherwise unnamed, I decided to call it "Cranberry Canyon." "Mile 138.5" is rather dull and clinical sounding, the kind of name that an aerospace engineer might give. "Cranberry Canyon" rolls off the tongue quite nicely, and is more romantic-sounding. For the uninitiated, there are no cranberries growing in Cranberry Canyon.

We descended the talus below the Supai and easily accessed the wash. As we walked downstream, we slowly began to penetrate into the Redwall Limestone. So far this had been easy. The cliff walls were maybe 100 feet high and the walking was trivial. Then suddenly, without warning, the wash made a sharp bend to the right and dropped ten feet over polished limestone into a twenty-foot plunge pool. Beyond that, it simply disappeared from sight, dropping perhaps 200 feet in a single fall, twisting and turning into the impenetrable depths. Many trips later, I would conclude that this was very typical of Redwall gorges.

Unable to proceed further, we climbed out of the gorge and onto the talus below the Supai. From here we decided to give the steep chute we had seen from the end of the peninsula a shot. Traveling along the talus to the end of the peninsula was easy. The lateral slope was gentle and there were only a couple of side washes that we needed to cross. We stopped for a rest at the end of the peninsula, on the edge of the talus overlooking Cranberry Creek. The view was outstanding.

However, at this point where the talus turned east and followed the Redwall, the lateral slope increased to 45° and I swear EVERY rock was loose. We stayed high on the talus, so that if any of us slipped, we would have the entire breadth of the slope to recover before reaching the brink. I think I must have lost my footing a hundred times in the next half mile. Finally we reached the chute at the top of the Redwall and stopped for lunch. I discovered to my dismay that I had left my lunch (which I had been carrying in a cloth bag) back at our rest stop on the point overlooking Cranberry. The others offered to share their lunches with me, but I opted to backtrack to the viewpoint and try to find mine. I looked all over, but couldn't seem to locate the rock on which I'd been sitting during our rest. I was perturbed by this, because it wasn't that large of an area; nevertheless, I could not find my lunch.

So I left "Lost Lunch Point," as Dave would later begin calling it, and worked my way back to the chute. Of course by the time I reached the others, they had finished their lunches so there was nothing left to share with me, and I would simply have to go hungry until dinnertime. Oddly enough, one year later I would "find" my lunch right where I had left it, the cloth bag all tattered and the food gone—presumably eaten by rodents.

The chute was quite a bit shorter and less steep than it appeared from the Esplanade. The steepest part was inclined only about 50°, and the chute was only about 30 feet long. It consisted of solid limestone with plenty of hand and footholds, and no loose rubble to give us any headaches. Dave proceeded down the chute with no problem, and I followed likewise. However, Brian had trouble. He couldn't seem to get enough traction on the limestone surface and felt like he was going to slip. None of us being rock-climbers, we hadn't brought any rope for situations such as this. Brian attempted several times, but each time backed off. Finally, he decided to wait for us at the top of the chute, while we proceeded to try to get through to the bottom.

Dave and I took off. Once through the steep part, the rest of the ravine was a piece of cake. The slope decreased to about 45°, and the ravine was filled with large boulders and rocks, creating what amounted to a giant staircase. We made it to the bottom of the Redwall in less than an hour.

From the base of the cliff, we exited the ravine and headed east across some hills which appeared to be the remains of a giant landslide. We crossed a small dry lake lying atop the landslide, went over one last hill, and down a 600-foot slope into Deer Creek Valley. Deer Creek Valley was originally called Surprise Valley, named by E. O.Beaman, who was a photographer on John Wesley Powell's second expedition through the canyon in 1872. Upon our arrival, we could instantly understand why he gave it that name. But somewhere along the line, a mapmaker's error placed the name "Surprise Valley" in the dry dull-looking desert hills between Deer Creek and Tapeats Creek. This is wrong and should be corrected.

But what an incredibly beautiful valley it was! The cottonwoods were a brilliant yellow-orange and the stream was gushing. By now I was pretty thirsty, and the water looked exquisitely refreshing. The excitement of having "conquered" the Redwall must have clouded my judgement, for as I reached the stream, I dropped to the ground and stuck my head completely in, drinking perhaps a quart of water in one long swig. When Dave arrived a few seconds behind me, my head was still completely submerged. No water ever tasted better.

We then walked to the foot of the valley and entered one of the most amazing little gorges I had ever seen. The stream had eroded the Tapeats Sandstone into a wonderfully serpentine gorge, sculpted, scalloped, and polished to a fine finish. The gorge was less than twenty feet wide, and cut a swath into the sandstone to a depth of 75 feet. The effect was that of an underground river. At its terminus, the creek spilled over a 100-foot fall into the Colorado.

This was a truly wonderful place, and I would have wished to stay longer. However, it was November and the sun would be setting early. As we began to climb out of the valley, I began to feel weak and tired. Perhaps it was from not having had any lunch. Perhaps it was from drinking too much water from the stream. It doesn't really matter—I was slowing down and running out of gas. By the time we reached our exit ravine, I was beginning to feel nauseous. The heaves came about halfway up the Redwall and again near the top. It was 5 PM and starting to get dark, and we weren't even on the talus yet. Dave called up to Brian, who had been waiting patiently all this time, to go back to camp and bring some food down. Brian took off while Dave and I continued our struggle up the ravine which we would later name "Starvation Gulch."

We managed to make it to the talus in reasonable time, and were halfway up Cranberry by the time twilight ended. We plodded along, periodically calling for Brian so that he wouldn't pass us in the dark. I felt like I was about to collapse. I heaved four more times along the talus before we climbed the final 400 feet to camp. Eventually we spotted Brian up on the Esplanade building signal fires. We called for him to stay where he was and proceeded to climb the Supai cliff in the dark, without flashlights. I'm not sure exactly how we did it. I DO know that at one point with Dave around a bend and out of sight, I heard a sizeable rock fall from where I thought Dave was.

"Dave?" I called.

No answer.

"DAVE?!?!?!"

"What?" he replied, nonchalantly.

"Don't DO that!" I said.

End of conversation.

We continued up the cliff. At times I felt like I would faint, and would have to stop and collect my senses. I walked like one of those creatures from *Night of the Living Dead*. Yet whenever I would come to a ledge or a cliff, I would grab what handholds I could find and claw my way up. We went up ledges that probably would have made me nervous had I been able to see what I was doing. At long last we were on the Esplanade. It was still ½ mile to camp, but over easy ground. I trudged the last several hundred yards to my sleeping bag and collapsed. There I lay for about 30 minutes without moving.

Finally, after a sufficient recovery period, I joined the others for some dinner. Dave had brought some brandy in a vanilla bottle. We tried to make hot toddies, but they were terrible. So we poured the brandy into the campfire and let it burn. I had brought a flare along for emergency signalling. We threw the flare into the fire and let it burn as well, casting a strange red glow over the camp. Finally, we were asleep.

Sunday, December 1, 1968

It had stayed "warm" all night long, never dropping below 40°, and we awoke to heavily overcast skies. Sometime during breakfast it began to snow. As we left camp and started for the rim, the snowfall increased, and a light breeze began to blow, giving the illusion of a blizzard. The Esplanade became transformed from a harsh desert stonescape to a winter fairyland. As we began climbing the rim-cliff, the clouds began to break up and a few shafts of sunlight streamed down onto the red and snow-white Esplanade. Despite yesterday's ordeal, I was feeling very good physically, and as we neared the end of the trail, I began to feel like a kid leaving Disneyland. The canyon was incredibly beautiful this morning, and I was feeling manly and proud, like we had really accomplished something important. I was not ready to leave yet. I longed to lie in the shade of the golden cottonwoods of Deer Creek, to drink from its sweet waters, to explore the depths of its incredible gorge. I did not want to go home, for I already was home.

Afterward

I arrived home at midmorning on Monday, after an 800-mile drive that took us from the North Rim to Dave's home in Fresno and then back to Los Angeles. The glow of this trip did not wear off for a long time. Dave and I planned our next trip—to Deer Creek—while driving across the desert. We would spend a full week there the following November.

I spent some time with Pat Reilly following this trip, showing him my pictures and describing the route we had found through the Redwall. Pat passed this information on to canyoneer Harvey Butchart who followed our footsteps some time afterward. Then, through word-of-mouth, other people began to use the route. I heard that George Billingsley took at least one party down Cranberry Canyon. I personally made four trips (including the discovery trip and a trip taken 40 years later), and Dave made seven. As of this writing, more than 45 years later, I have found that our whimsical naming of Cranberry Canyon has taken root. Both Harvey Butchart and George Steck used the name in their respective books on canyon hiking. Canyon regulars now refer to it as the "Cranberry Route." And the National Geographic Trails Illustrated map of the Grand Canyon officially designates the canyon that reaches the Colorado River at Mile 138.5 as "Cranberry Canyon." Maybe it was the Great Northwest Passage after all.

In Pursuit of Plants
by
Kate Watters

"It is certain in any case that life is quite disarmed by the gift to live so entirely in the present, to treasure with such eager care every flower by the wayside and the light that plays on every passing moment."
—Hermann Hesse, *Steppenwolf: A Novel*

There are endless ways to know plants. We have developed techniques to cultivate them as food, fiber, drink, and dyes. Plants beautify our immediate lives and gardens. If we are lucky, we may know them more specifically as rare specialists of continents, regions, soils, and geologic strata. We may also know them as weeds, as the unwanted or feared. I knew plants first as a gardener, turning soil to plant the seeds of sunflowers, squash, and red runner beans. After several seasons on the Grand Canyon trail crew exploring the varied topography with a chisel and sledgehammer, I grew curious to know more about the plants that prospered in such a rugged and inhospitable place. I laid down my shovel and began a journey to understand their world.

I have found that the discipline of botany is a terrestrial experience. I am grounded in work that connects me to the fate of a place. It seems that, like plants, humans too have specific places that we inhabit and distinct ways to adapt to (or more commonly, ignore) our surroundings.

Botany is a craft best learned by shadowing an experienced and patient mentor. After a rigorous semester at Northern Arizona University of textbooks and scrutinizing plants under the microscope, I was eager to try out my budding awareness of the Arizona flora in the field. I sought out agave specialist Wendy Hodgson from the Desert Botanical Garden in Phoenix. I first met Wendy when she gave a talk at the Arboretum in Flagstaff about her agave research. Her slides depicted people hiking out of the Grand Canyon with agave plants strapped to their backpacks, and research assistants teetering on 20-foot ladders capturing pollen and seed from the towering flower stalks. I was mesmerized. The agave plant has long since captured my imagination and that of many others. The stiff, succulent leaves spiral from the center of a rosette, fanning outward in perfect symmetry. The woody, burgundy-tinged spines arise from the leaf margins, and each leaf bears the imprint of the previous layer. These ghostly markings resemble the creases a sheet leaves on a lover's cheek the morning after a deep sleep. Agaves are monocarpic, meaning they only bloom once and then they die. Their common name, century plant, refers to the fact that it can take somewhere between ten and fifty years (okay, maybe a bit of exaggeration) for one to send up a towering, asparagus-like stalk that is heavy with nectar-laden flowers.

I corresponded with Wendy via email for at least two years before the opportunity surfaced to join her and a group of colleagues on a backpacking trip in the Grand Canyon. The quest was to locate a new population of the Grand Canyon's own century plant (*Agave phillipsiana*), rumored to be miles into the backcountry of Phantom Creek. This recently named species is what scientists call endemic, meaning it is unique to a narrow geographical region. In the case of *Agave phillipsiana* (named in honor of Arthur Phillips II, another avid Grand Canyon botanist), there are two known sites in the canyon where it has been found (Deer Creek and Clear Creek)[1], both in association with archeological sites. It has arching blue-green leaves that are more than a foot longer than the Utah or Kaibab agave, which also grow in the canyon. The towering flowering stalk produces hundreds of stout, cream-colored flowers that resemble lilies. The plants are usually found on terraces along permanent tributaries in association with pre-Columbian archeological sites.

When you hang around with botanists, you soon understand that many field trips have a pilgrimage quality to them, especially when you are looking for small things in a place as large as the Grand Canyon. The mission for this journey was especially sacred to Wendy. The fact that *Agave phillipsiana* more closely resembles Mexican agaves than

---

1. A new population was discovered in Shinumo Creek in the spring of 2013 by a river guide, Ariel Neill.

other agaves in Northern Arizona or the Colorado Plateau is of intense interest to her, and has been a major focus of her research for the past 20 years. This research provides evidence that *Agave phillipsiana* was a crop plant, introduced, farmed, and domesticated by pre-Columbian people. Evidence suggests the plant's closest relatives may reside in northern Mexico. Our Grand Canyon agave plant was probably acquired by the prehistoric inhabitants of the canyon from trade with Mexico, long before the existence of national borders or free trade agreements.

"Off we go like a herd of turtles," Wendy exclaims as we slowly make our way down the Bright Angel Trail. Spring is in full force with countless blooming wonders to behold. We stop every ten feet to admire a different flower, sometimes with a hand-lens and often times peeling back its petals to really get a good look. I wonder if we are going to get to Phantom Ranch before it gets dark. This cohort, comprised of both full-fledged and aspiring botanists, has been on many plant-driven adventures together from Grand Canyon to Mexico. Raul, originally from Veracruz, Mexico, curates the horticulture collection for the Desert Botanical Garden, which means he travels all over Arizona and Mexico in search of plants to grow. Daniela is the botanist for the Navajo Tribe, yet her attention to detail and strong accent reveal her German roots. Dawn, a woman with a big laugh and thick East Coast accent, is a recent retiree who helps Wendy and Raul in the herbarium and gardens at DBG. Amy is a desert aficionado and nurse with a plant problem, who speaks Latin as fluently as any professional botanist. I am the greenest of everyone in our group, and am grateful for the patience and generosity they demonstrate as I stumble over my Latin pronunciation.

What made a spiny agave plant such a valuable commodity item that an ancient inhabitant of a steep desert ditch would travel long distances to establish an agave farm? This question keeps me occupied as I negotiate the Redwall switchbacks with a heavy backpack. Agaves are unique plants in that they produce genetically similar clones, or pups, through underground stems or rhizomes. This characteristic makes the plants ripe for cultivation, as it keeps traits that were painstakingly selected by early farmers intact with each ensuing generation.

Early dwellers of Grand Canyon and other regions in the Southwest and Mexico utilized the plants for food, fiber, medicine, and beverages, both alcoholic and non-alcoholic. The long, broad, succulent leaves of *Agave phillipsiana* are easier to cut than the native agaves in the region, and its fibers may be more resistant to rot than those of other species found in the canyon. Agave species vary in taste, and the more savory varieties were an important trade item with other groups. Some were too bitter to eat, which necessitated long journeys to acquire a more favorable variety. *Agave phillipsiana* is one of the best-tasting agaves.

I try to imagine a plant being carried by someone to the Grand Canyon from Mexico a thousand years ago. What a splendid and heroic effort! Last summer on a road trip, I traded squash and apricot seeds with New Mexican farmers to augment my own garden in Flagstaff. While visiting from Vermont, my mother collected the graceful seed of needle-and-thread grass from the ponderosa forest for her backyard. Now we have gathered to traipse into the inner reaches of the canyon to find remnants of gardens from another human era. We may be a group of crazy plant nerds, but a journey for the sake of acquiring plants is nothing new.

The view of native inhabitants as either passive consumers or primitive resource extractors in an otherwise unblemished landscape is simple-minded. Human relationships with the plant world flourished long before the formal discipline of western science, as the existence of the Grand Canyon agave demonstrates. Why does such a botanical oddity capture the minds of scientists like Wendy? For botanists, plants can provide hints to the mysteries of human history, just as archeologists look for clues on petroglyphs carved into rocks. Our work is cut out for us; roughly three percent of New World human history is archived and recorded. The field of ethnobotany (the study of how indigenous and regional cultures utilize and perceive plants) is a relatively new discipline that incorporates a different cultural perspective and closer scrutiny of the landscape. The term "ethnobotany" dates back to 1852, but the history of this type of study of plants goes back to 500 BC.

Agave phillipsiana is only one of many types of rare plants. Wendy explains that each rare plant species tells its own story as to the elements which stand alone or in a mosaic to create a unique situation. She translates the theory into plain English: "Rare plants whisper to us:

Hey! Pay attention to me! I'm special for these reasons." Plants are usually rare because they are specialists, or because they are relicts from distant eras, and these factors, in combination with human pressures on their habitat, cause many to hover at the brink of extinction. The puzzle of rarity reminds botanists that no matter how hard we try to make categories for plant species, nature does not always fit neatly within our human-constructed definitions. Thankfully, plants continue to offer surprises that make us work harder to understand them. *Agave phillipsiana* is a unique type of endemic plant, in that its rare status is tied to its prehistoric human care and cultivation. In contrast to the situations in which many other rare plants find themselves, this agave's population could be threatened by *lack* of human contact or cultivation.

It is theorized that many of the agave species used for food and fiber have decreased in numbers after more than five centuries of cultivation by both Columbian and pre-Columbian peoples in the Southwest and Mexico. As cultivars and/or domesticates, they have diminished without care from humans. Within the Salt River Valley, where agaves are thought to have been cultivated, modern citrus, cotton, and alfalfa agriculture have further impacted agave populations. Wendy explains that as early as 1915 more than 250,000 acres of land in the Salt River Valley had been converted to agriculture, which was soon followed by sprawl. The Grand Canyon populations represent one of five known domesticated agaves north of Mexico today. Recently, Wendy and her comrades found other remnant populations of *Agave phillipsiana* on the west flanks of the Bradshaw Mountains along the Hassayampa River north of Phoenix, in the Verde Valley, and near Sedona, all of them probably cultivated by pre-Columbian peoples.

In our modern era of globalization and anonymous chain stores, there is something satisfying in seeking out the unique stories of rare plants, much like reveling in a tiny, old bookstore with out-of-print titles instead of clicking on your online Amazon cart. Searching for rare plants is like combing tag sales and antique shops for a particular type of limited-edition pottery. While you are on the hunt, you discover many other gems worthy of delight, like a sequined cashmere cardigan sweater from the 1940s or an old Schwinn one-speed bicycle. So it is with flowers—we are easily distracted by the trail of wonder.

Wendy is in her late fifties and emanates a rugged beauty much like the desert she loves. Her skin is brown and weathered, her graying blond hair bleached from the sun and tucked into a baseball hat that reads simply, *Grand Canyon*. Wendy is one of those people who glows with the inner satisfaction that she is living the life completely suited to her. She has energy reserves for the appreciation of plants and the Grand Canyon that I have not yet observed in another person. Even after dusk and a nine-mile hike to the bottom of the canyon, she still stops cold and groans a guttural appreciation, thankful for a blooming flower or a certain shadow of light on rock. Wendy is uncompromising in her belief that the most important element of being a scientist is to be observant and to listen to your gut feeling and let it guide your research. Chopping away at a blooming yucca stalk that she believes to be a hybrid, she says, "You don't want to only listen to the authorities" [referring to those in the field of botany who are increasingly relying on DNA to group and identify plants]. "Seeing plants in the field and collecting is critical to understanding a species or a group." As a woman, and an innovative botanist, this is the mantra that brings her back to the Grand Canyon trip after trip. Even after more than 50 years and five knee surgeries she returns, stronger and more determined each time.

Wendy chuckles at the irony of her own story: "I left my home in upstate New York to play college golf at Arizona State University. I found myself on manicured golf greens, gazing out at the harsh, yet strangely captivating Sonoran Desert." Intrigued by her surroundings, she gave up golf and took up biology, joining the lineage of desert rats in lifelong pursuit of rugged beauty. In all of her plant-driven travels, she has been drawn again and again to the Grand Canyon, where the isolation and diverse habitats provide a smorgasbord of botanical delights to feast upon. The canyon is a fascinating place to study plant diversity, as nearly half of the 4,000+ species that comprise Arizona's flora occur there, and new species of plants are welcomed into the arms of science continually. This distinctive landscape ranges in elevation from 1,200 feet at Lake Mead to over 8,000 feet on the Kaibab Plateau, creating countless microhabitats for plants to flourish. At the canyon, ecological influences from the Great Basin, Sonoran, and Mohave deserts converge. With plant life as your map, a hike from rim to river leads you on a path from Flagstaff to the Baja Peninsula in a mere nine miles.

After a night in the suburban-like accommodations of the campground at Phantom Ranch, I am eager to get away from flush toilets and crowds of other backpackers. We ascend quickly up the steep Banzai Route from Bright Angel Creek and pick our way through a clutter of immense sandstone blocks aptly named Piano Alley. Once on top, in Utah Flats, the reward for the scramble is the sweeping vista of red rock and clouds reflecting in water pockets. We meander north towards Cheops Pyramid, along an indistinct trail of cairns that crosses a narrow spine between two drainages. The landscape opens up to sprawling plains of blossoming pricklypear cactus (*Opuntia phaeacantha*) in a wide array of colors—coral red, fuchsia, salmon pink, translucent yellow. Negotiating the thin, prickly trail is like shuffling down the aisle of a packed airplane, but Wendy and Raul plop down in the midst of the spiny pads, smiling ear to ear. They are perplexed by the color variants the species exhibits and set out collecting samples they hope will help unravel the mystery.

Collecting has historically played an important role in the understanding of biological diversity. Since the days when the young biologist Alfred Wallace set out from his home in England to explore and collect in the Malay Archipelago, scientists have shed light on concepts of biological diversity and evolution through voucher specimens. In Grand Canyon botanical history, pioneering women and men helped create a great base of knowledge of the plant world by casting aside convention and venturing into the hard-to-reach places.

Elzada Clover and Lois Jotter were the second and third women to experience the Colorado River in 1938, and they completed the first botanical inventory of the river. I try to imagine the enormity of that experience for Elzada and Lois, 36 and 24 at the time. "Faculty Women to Face Danger on Stormy Colorado for Science" read the headlines from the campus newspaper, *The Michigan Daily*. Elzie, as she was known, was raised on a Nebraska farm. After the death of her mother, Elzie's father moved his farm to the Rio Grande Valley of Texas, where she discovered a passion for studying the cactus family. She received a Ph.D in Botany from the University of Michigan, where she later taught and was assistant curator of the botanical gardens. In the summer of 1937, she traveled west to the San Juan River to collect the desert plants she admired. At the Mexican Hat Lodge she encountered Norm Nevills, a local adventurer who aspired to run the Colorado River. Only a year later, the combination of Elzie's passion for plant exploration and Norm's desire to build boats and run rivers resulted in a historic plant-collecting expedition. We know less about Lois Jotter, a student of Dr. Clover's whom she recruited for the challenge. When people warned them of the danger, Elzie exclaimed, "Well, if we don't come back just toss a rose over into the canyon for us." On August 1, 1938, 42 days and 660 river-miles after they launched from Green River, Wyoming, the party emerged at what is now Hoover Dam, bearing with them many plant specimens, some of which were new to science, and plenty of stories of adventure.

Rose Collom was Grand Canyon's first paid botanist, hired by the Grand Canyon Natural History Association on a part-time basis from 1938 to 1953. A self-taught botanist, she learned the names of plants through books, and by corresponding with established botanists in the Southwest. A native of Georgia, she moved to Arizona with her husband, who was the assessor of the Silver Butte Mine in the Mazatzal Mountains for 42 years. Their humble house was six miles from the nearest neighbor and 90 miles from a railroad, but that did not seem to bother Rose, once a southern aristocrat. The flowers became her dear friends. In an interview published in the *Payson Roundup*, she expressed her deep connection to them:

> When one lives year after year apart from the world, miles from neighbors, towns, and railways, flowers become companions, and one not only enjoys them, but learns much from them. Our Arizona wild flowers are unique, beautiful and hardy, and courageous. They often grow, bloom and bear their fruit under most discouraging conditions. One watches for them and greets them as old and faithful friends, and surely from them one can derive strength and courage and faith.

Rose collected more than 750 specimens within Grand Canyon and Arizona, and several plants are named after her. She was the first botanist to collect *Agave phillipsiana* near Clear Creek in the Grand

Canyon, which she erroneously identified as *Agave deserti*. The fact that Rose walked these trails and collected this same species makes me feel connected to the stories of these early botanists; their curiosity and determination inspires us to keep assembling pieces to the puzzle.

Plant collecting is a brutal sport. Here in the depths of Phantom Canyon, a tributary of Bright Angel Creek, each new blooming plant that we encounter is plucked from its home in the earth and carefully pressed between layers of newspaper and cardboard. The spring breeze is crisp and a cerulean blue sky provides welcome sunshine. Yet my ears are ringing for the lives I am taking. I imagine the soundtrack of a high-pitched insect orchestra as the otherworldly screams of tortured plants. I adore and admire them as living things, and find it unsettling to think we will understand them better when they are two-dimensional. When the specimens are dried, keyed-out to the proper species, pressed, and glued onto acid-free paper, they will be archived in local herbaria as a record of our trip and a snapshot in time. I will learn their first and last names, their families; I'll revel in their flattened, dried beauty—colors more intense, the venation of leaves more pronounced, and the translucent petals resembling the delicate folds in an antique Victorian dress. Now, walking along the banks of Phantom Creek, I feel myself, a transplant from Vermont, becoming more rooted in this arid place that is not easy to live in. When I call out to a plant, it is as if I am greeting a neighbor met in passing. I am mindful of the niche it occupies in this narrow world and of the challenges it faces, as I discover my own.

We sleep next to the rushing creek and the next morning awake on polished Shinumo bedrock to sip coffee and gather ourselves for the day's work that lies ahead. A Utah agave with an arching 15-foot blooming stalk stands nearby, waking up to its own morning pollinator activity: dizzy with delight, huge black shiny carpenter bees hover around the yellow flowers. After a two-day approach, today is the day we look for *Agave phillipsiana*. We are all a bit giddy with excitement. We head up Phantom Creek, collecting many of the plants in our path. We arrive at the confluence where Haunted Canyon flows into Phantom Creek from the North Rim. This area is rife with diversity, due largely to the shelter of canyon walls and presence of year-round water. Working off of a description from Park Ranger Dean Reese, who first reported the sighting of "odd-looking agaves" in this location to Wendy, we split into different directions to comb the area. Within a matter of minutes, Wendy is calling out for us and gesturing wildly from a slope near an oak tree on the side of the creek. "They're here! Oh, my, look at them all!"

The plants are growing happily on the grassy slope, groupings of small families with mother plants and pups. They are robust and broad-leaved, each its own sculptural delight, with the grand towers of spent flowering stalks scattered among them. We all take turns counting them, reaching agreement at the number thirty. Wendy sets to work immediately to collect a herbarium specimen, cutting a few leaves at the base and making notes of all the other plant life associated with this site. None of the plants are flowering, as normally that happens in September. The larger rosettes are producing pups, and Wendy reluctantly digs up a small one. She carefully tapes together the burgundy spines that arise from the tip of each leaf, so as to prepare it for its journey out of the canyon in her backpack. This live plant will be cultivated at the Desert Botanical Garden so Wendy can study its phenology and other attributes. There, she can test the molecular structure in order to find more clues as to who its relatives may be. The site is mapped, and we fan out to look for the roasting pit we suspect is nearby. Within a few minutes someone notices a large depression littered with fire-cracked rock on the lower portion of the slope.[2] I am humbled to think of the rituals that must have been performed in this very place. As a passionate gardener, cook, and proponent of slow food, I deeply appreciate all the care that was taken to cultivate, propagate, harvest, and prepare this plant.

In her book *Food Plants of the Sonoran Desert*, Wendy researched and described the extensive preparation and effort involved in harvesting and preparing an agave plant for consumption. A tradition that continues in the region today with the Hualapai and Yavapai tribes, agave roasting is initiated with the harvest of whole plants as they begin to show signs of flowering, but generally before the stalk is evident. A pit up to three feet deep and twelve feet wide is excavated, which is

2. Archaeologist Helen Fairley reported that the roasting pits were Paiute. Subsequent surveys of the area revealed a granary further up Haunted Canyon and pre-Columbian rock terraces above the creek and a canal.

then lined with rocks. When the fire burns down, the hot stones are covered with green or wet vegetation. The agave heads are placed on top, covered with more vegetation (the Hualapai like to use barrel cactus pieces) and finally earth, and then cooked for two days. The most treasured part is the innermost non-fibrous core, which is tender and sweet, like an artichoke heart. The outer, fibrous sections are pounded out, sometimes coated in reserved juices, and dried, and can last a year as a dried fruit snack. Roasted agaves taste like a very sweet dried papaya or like molasses, which must have been a treasured treat for a prehistoric desert dweller.

That night we prepare dinners from an array of dehydrated backpacking foods in foil packages. I imagine what we might eat if we lacked these amenities. How many tiny orange wolfberry fruits would it take to satisfy our hunger after such a journey? In honor of our pilgrimage, I develop a watercolor game to test our botanical color associations. I spend a few moments mixing a potpourri of colors on the page, and we all huddle around my notebook discussing which plants are best associated with each paint hue. Flashes of recognition overcome us as we conjure the particular color of a fruit, leaf, or flower from each dab of paint. As the light fades away to evening, we celebrate the new *Agave phillipsiana* population by breaking out a flask of tequila. "Viva el Agave!" we shout as it is passed around. As the alcohol takes effect, we entertain ourselves with a game of limbo, grabbing a nearby dead Utah agave stalk, which works perfectly! We sing the Limbo Rock song "every limbo boy and girl all around the limbo world…," as individuals arch backwards to slide underneath the stalk, which lowers each round. Raul wins and later teaches us the national birthday song of Mexico, "Las Mananitas," which heralds the birthday person out of bed to greet the flowers blooming just for them. We stay up late amusing ourselves with "botany talk," i.e. why more people don't landscape with native plants, and what weeds (bad plants) we most despise.

Annie Dillard exclaimed from Tinker Creek, "I am not a scientist, I just explore the neighborhood!" There are many secrets the natural world can tell us, if we become observant and diligent, learning the names and personalities of the plants along our path. It is hard to believe that to really see the Grand Canyon requires a hand lens. Yet there are so many minute details in plants; to appreciate them, we must lean in close, observe carefully, and listen for the whisper. The discipline of botany requires the study of a visual world where a minute detail like the shape of a groove on a seed distinguishes one species from another. Plants are sentient, and are accurate indicators of the type and health of an ecosystem. Humans, birds, bats, lizards, insects, and mammals: we all depend on plants for our survival. I try to imagine being rooted in one place, not able to pick up and move with crummy weather, new annoying neighbors, or increased enemies. I might be overwhelmed with the little tricks I would develop to adapt better to my place in the world. But think of the patience it would require. "There are lots of things to see, unwrapped gifts and free surprises," Dillard wrote. "The world is fairly studded and strewn with pennies cast broadside from a generous hand."

I lie beneath the stars next to the rushing of Phantom Creek and welcome its steady clamor. This trip has been a semester's worth of botany in five days, and my head is throbbing from the exertion that my brain has weathered. I have committed to memory more than a few Latin names for plants, and these musical words are a new soundtrack I have on repeat. It is overwhelming to think of the endless ways we can know plants. As an aspiring botanist, I seek to know, name, collect and study them, and as a pilgrim I travel to these sacred places that harbor diversity as a kind of ritual. To know plants is to aspire to a different level of caring, patience, and optimism. The future of our wild landscapes as well as our backyards, neighborhoods, and urban watersheds rests in our willingness to be observant, passionate and courageous in what we do. When we take the time to look, we discover that the wild marvels of plants are everywhere, asking us to have enough faith to create beauty with only a seed.

A Redwall View
by
Eb Eberlein

I've been fascinated by the Redwall Limestone for some years now. This layer is possibly the most easily identifiable formation in the Grand Canyon and at the same time may hold the most secrets. Even its name is misleading; although its appearance is that of a massive red wall, the rock's true color is a light grey that can weather dark. Rain and snowmelt dissolve minerals from the Supai Layer above and deposit the resulting stain of red on the cliff. The natural grey can be seen on freshly exposed rock and in areas where the Supai has been long eroded away. The Redwall also holds the vast majority of Grand Canyon's caves. Many Redwall recesses are inaccessible to non-flying beasts, making them ideal nesting sites for birds. The California Condor seems to be fond of these aeries.

The rock forms one of the most formidable barriers to vertical travel in the Grand Canyon. Easily identified by even a tenderfoot visitor, the face of the limestone cliff is generally about 300 feet high with little in the way of features that would offer a route for even a bighorn sheep. Redwall Limestone generally weathers in a predictable manner. Faults create the breaks that allow for access through the wall. The exposed surface of the limestone becomes pitted due to exposure to the elements, creating sharp-edged ridges, points, and undulations, except in drainages where erosion polishes the rock to look like marble. A glancing contact with the limestone can be similar to rubbing a cheese grater against one's body. I knew this first-hand from an incident that had befallen me early in my canyon-hiking career. What I learned eventually is that this harsh and unyielding rock can also be a refuge.

Back in the late 1970s I had the good fortune to occasionally confer with Dr. Harvey Bouchart, the Obi Wan of the canyon, about inner canyon routes. His journals and maps continue to be among the most authoritative references. One of his principle occupations was identifying routes from the rim to the river. My friend George Lamont Mancuso and I explored many routes that we had learned about from Harvey. While George shared Harvey's interest in routes down through the gorge to the river, my interest was becoming more and more the Redwall Limestone. Routes through the Redwall help define many of Harvey's routes from rim to river.

In 1978, a couple of months after he had first encountered it, Harvey told me of a route which led out of upper Phantom Creek, through the Redwall, and up to the lower slopes of Shiva Temple. Harvey certainly would not have claimed its discovery, as he had a great respect for the native people who had been living in and exploring the canyon for centuries. This quickly became a favorite area for me, as it allowed me access to the Crystal Creek drainage without first driving to the North Rim. I was becoming more and more interested in the use of the top of the Redwall as a horizontal route for canyon travel. There is typically a convenient bench formed at the Supai Formation's contact with the Redwall. There are campsites on the flats of many points and, more importantly, water can be found in major plunge pools and small seeps in the drainages. I had found a calling, contouring the canyon on top of the Redwall.

I had a bad habit, which I have been unable to shake to this day: I did, and still do, a lot of solo hiking. While I have become more cautious, I was, at that time, honestly reckless. I did not even carry a first aid kit. My rationale was that there were two kinds of injuries I was likely to experience in the remote canyon: minor scratches and bruises which I could easily weather, or significant life-threatening injuries for which the signal mirror was the only cure. I advanced out of this naïve perspective while contouring the Redwall around Shiva Temple in 1979.

Shortly before this trip, I had picked up a small first aid kit at the thrift store in Flagstaff for fifty cents. I glanced inside and saw there was something in it, but made no effort to inventory or refurbish it. It went into my backpack, with the thought that my mother would approve of my growing maturity.

The plan for this trip was to get into Crystal Creek after circumnavigating Shiva Temple above the Redwall. I wanted to look at the route that Harvey had been unable to connect between Osiris Temple Saddle and the drainage below, as well as do continued exploration of the Dragon Arms. I had come up the easy way from Trinity Creek and the Isis-Shiva Saddle and was traversing clockwise around Shiva heading for Crystal Creek. It was autumn and water was to be found in the plunge pools. From my bivouac at Isis-Shiva Saddle, I had spent a full day reaching the southwest side of Shiva and found little to suggest that I would be connecting the route that Dr. Boucher had hoped might be possible. The next day I expected to easily finish the traverse and drop into Crystal Creek. There is a spot on the west side of Shiva where the Redwall bench is nearly nonexistent. Fairly easily identifiable on the topo map, I knew it would be the most challenging portion of the traverse. Sure enough, the Supai Formation disintegrates into a talus slope, quite steep and very loose, that feeds down into a chute, ending in a sheer drop. I surveyed the scene carefully before starting across as high as possible on the slope.

I've often said that all the rock in the canyon shares the goal of being washed in the river someday. About one quarter of the way across this exposed slope, I stepped onto a bathtub-sized slab that immediately began to slide. I jumped off, thinking only to let it go on its way. Unfortunately, the limestone face on my right had a sharp point that caught the bottom of my exposed forearm just below the elbow. A gash three inches long appeared that cleanly separated the skin to the muscle. I learned two things quickly: that limestone can be really sharp, and that when someone donates a first aid kit to the thrift store, there is not much of value remaining in it. The first aid item that is seldom used and exactly what I needed that day was about all that was left inside: butterfly closures. Upon reaching Shiva Saddle, I cut the trip short and turned toward home, and I still have that "Canyon Tattoo." I did rehab the first aid kit and have maintained a quality one ever since.

The abandon of my youth had given way to a more studied approach to canyon safety by the time I started my guide service, Sky Island Treks, in 1995.

It's not always hot down in the Grand Canyon. From October through April, temperatures can be anywhere from pleasant to chilly. That's why I generally advised potential clients for treks into the canyon to book dates after the equinox in September through early May.

In 2003 I had been operating Sky Island Treks as an overland guide service in Grand Canyon for seven years. Initially, our itineraries focused on the main trails, the Bright Angel and Kaibab Corridor, the Hermit, Grandview, Tanner, and North and South Bass. For our early clients, the Clear Creek Trail provided a higher level of challenge. In 2001 I created an assortment of extreme itineraries, trips that require a minimum of five days and involve primarily trail-less travel, hands-on segments, and occasional roping up.

With a limit of eleven people on Grand Canyon backcountry permits, we could reasonably have eight clients with three guides on these treks. In 2003 we booked a full trip for eight gents from back east in late October on an exemplary six-day route. We would cross Big Spring Canyon on the North Rim after heading south from Swamp Point Road and drop off Lancelot Point to the saddle of Elaine Castle. The next two days one drops into Modred Abyss and follows Shinumo Creek. Eventually you exit the canyon on the North Bass Trail.

In order to ensure that I would have a guide familiar with the route in case I was unable to be the lead, I booked a two-night permit in August and asked my right hand, Jeff Brucker, to scout it with me. As Jeff was not available, I asked a young man who had joined the outfit a year or so before to accompany me. Nick Bejarano is no stranger to the desert, having grown up in Globe, Arizona. Nick is an optimistic, cheerful, and ready-for-anything soul who jumped at the opportunity. On a hot August day we left the van and the comfortable temperatures of the North Rim and dropped off Lancelot Point. We made good time that day, covering the first two days of the October itinerary with ease, and stayed at the Elaine fork of the Modred arm that night. We took a bit of time to visit the spring a quarter-mile up the east arm the next morning. Water here rolls from a vertical crack near the base of the Redwall Limestone. The crack is wide enough and the flow sufficient that one could ride a kayak out from the cave. This is one of those hidden wonders that the folks in the air tours will never have a clue about.

On the second day, we were below the Redwall circumnavigating Holy Grail Temple on the Tonto Platform. There is a trace of the trail that William Bass had been improving east from Shinumo Amphitheater, and we were following it around Holy Grail to the west side, where there is a break in the Tapeats Sandstone which would allow us to get on the North Bass Trail at the famous narrows with the chock-stone wedged four stories up. The Kolb brothers' photo of this spot is one of their many iconic images. It was a bit past noon on that August day as we rounded the southernmost point of Holy Grail, and our feet were beginning to overheat. I carry a little Sherpa device which measures barometric pressure, altitude, wind speed, and, most importantly, temperature. At 11:30 it was reading 117 F. At that air temperature, the surface can be hotter than 140 degrees. The soles of your boots can get so hot that the bottoms of your feet get burned. We were becoming uncomfortable. No complaints came from Nick, but both of us realized the seriousness of the situation.

We got lucky. There on the Tonto Platform, south of Holy Grail Temple, sits a block of Redwall Limestone about the size of a large cathedral-ceiling living room. Blocks this big are rare. Contrary to first impressions, most erosion at the canyon is the steady mass wasting of small pieces. Major rockfalls are unusual events. This chunk had landed nearly intact. Luckily, it had a couple of good-sized cracks. Nick crawled into the crack on the north side, and I squeezed into one on the south side. Like lizards in the shade, at least 15 degrees cooler than standing in the sun, and certainly not in relaxing positions, we prepared to have our siesta.

Spending extended period with companions in tight places can test a friendship. On a climb of Argentina's Aconcagua in 2001, my partner Matt and I spent three days in a tent during a blizzard. Nearly continuous sixty mile-per-hour winds made this much like living inside a drum. With reading material and a backgammon board drawn on the sleeping mattress, we could entertain ourselves and found our friendship strengthened rather than frayed.

This was only one afternoon, a measly six or so hours spent in our prickly rock retreat. My major entertainment was a fence lizard that inhabited the rock. It too refused to go into the sun and scuttled through every once in a while. While numerous fossils, from trilobites and corals to fish, can be found in the Redwall, they are generally well spread out or concentrated in relatively small areas. Despite plenty of time for a close and careful inspection, I found none that day. I could see where slightly less resistant locations had been dissolved by rainwater. I made a careful inspection of the black stains, known as desert varnish, left by water that had run down surfaces. I gave excessive attention to small crystals imbedded in the matrix. I got bored.

Every twenty minutes or so I'd call out, "How you doing?"

Nick would reply with his typical, "Still here, Captain!"

"Be careful. There's some sharp points on this rock."

"I noticed."

There really wasn't a lot to say. Moving light and fast, we hadn't brought reading material, not that in our contorted state it would have been possible to focus on literature. They say time flies when you're having fun. Time crawled that day. Every movement invited an abrasion. But we had shade; hard shade, not the wispy soft shade of some scraggly little mesquite tree. And we had each other.

"How you doing?"

"Still here, Captain!"

"Dang it's warm."

"Warm over here too."

Why do we recall that day so fondly? It must say something about us both that it may have been one of the high points of our experiences as backcountry guides in the canyon. I don't recall if we shared the story with our clients two months later as we followed the same route in much more reasonable weather. But to this day I can picture that big old boulder, recall how we circled it and identified cracks that we could squeeze into, and envision the colors of the rock surface that were just inches from our faces. Thank you, Redwall Limestone.

Holy Water

by
John Yohe

Loose rock/stones on North Bass Trail, with soft dry dirt underneath, but not too steep. Down under the North Rim, away from the ponderosas, out in the hot Arizona sun, through thick manzanita, Gambel oak, scrub oak, locust (my old spiny enemy!) and the start of the pinyon/juniper tree mix, switch-backing into White Canyon proper, I stop and listen: Running water! A stream off to the left! I wasn't sure I'd be blessed at the beginning of the trip and so have loaded up with six quarts in my pack, enough to (maybe) get me through the first day and a half. Which it's about time to sample. And—that was quick—my first stupid mistake of the trip manifests: the four Arrowhead bottles of "spring water" I bought back in Kanab are not just spring water. No, I open one and it bubbles and fizzles out.

Aghast, I check the label. Oh. Oops. "Sparkling" spring water. I'm not a fan of tonic water unless it's in a gin and tonic, and I *could* still drink it but, well, here I am at *real* spring water right off the mountain. Meaning I'm dumping this sugary stuff right now. I know, I know, I hope Mother Earth forgives me. Who knows what kind of mutation I'm creating here, some two-headed lizard or something, which could be waiting for me five days from now when I come back. But I do it.

Hopefully this is my *only* big mistake. I usually have one every trip, but my consolation in this case is to sample the water of White Creek right now: Just scooping my hands into the water and raising it to my mouth. Cool, clean, deliciously pure. Or purely delicious. A wonderful treat after expecting basically arid desertness, and I'm tempted to lighten my load and just drink as I go, but who knows? Better to play things safe here in the Grand Canyon. I refill the bottles.

The trail parallels the creek down into the drainage bottom, shrubbery and small cottonwoods as well as a few brave ponderosas providing shade over boulders and rocks, and then climbs up onto red dirt PJ flats. And though some uphill is required to do this, walking on the trail is actually faster than jumping boulder to boulder. Weather today: mostly clear blue sky, with some high welcome Simpsons clouds. Birds: goldfinch, chickadees, and a big hawk circling above, not even flapping, just riding the hot air up and up. And flowers, still, at the end of May: reds, yellows, whites. Lunch break, check the map, and based on the fact that I am now at the Redwall descent (unmistakable because of the straight up and down red walls) I've only gone 3.5 miles! I re-check, using a big landmark, Emerald Point, up on the rim, directly across. Lining up the map, yes, I appear to be where I think I am. That can't be right. Hike all day, downhill, to only go 3.5 miles?? Time and Space seem to have no meaning down here. That means no Shinumo Creek tonight, which I'd thought a possibility, or maybe just a hope, because of its perennial water.

The Redwall, always the narrowest section of the side canyons. One misstep and I could go crashing down over the side! But, after some almosts, I'm down in the creek bed again, though water seems to have vanished, drizzled down underground. A few nice flat sandy open areas though, and HUGE red rock walls rising up, with a HUGE natural sandstone shell echoing even normal voice levels 200 yards away. A cathedral. In shade too—a relief from the hike over the hot flats, though still warm. Big contrast to last night up at Swamp Point where I froze my butt off!

Packless, I explore upstream, and find more blessed running water: just a trickle, but with some sandstone pools big enough to strip down and throw water on the ole corpse. Then kneeling, cupping and raising the hands. Feeling ghosts of others who have done the same here. Drinking water as a tradition. Drinking water as a spiritual experience. Quenched, at least temporarily, I sit in a last remaining sunny spot, naked, communing with dragonflies and butterflies, plus some fat black bumblebees.

Back in camp, feasting on Triscuit cracker-wafers, with Tillamook Monterey Jack cheese, working away at a huge chunk I've brought. Even cheese and crackers becomes a spiritual experience down here.

186

Backpacking as spiritual practice. And for dessert, Fig Newtons! I'm stuffed, though it's not really that much food. Weird how while backpacking I exert way more energy than at home, but eat less and feel better.

But the thirst. Drinking water all day and still this thirst. Gulping it down from my bottle. My urine was clear last time I checked, so not dehydrated yet. Out here even just lying on my sleeping bag is dehydrating. The air cooling some, but not too much. Sunlight reflecting on the clouds. A bumblebee buzzes by. Birds chirping, three different kinds at least. Crickets, spring peeper frogs, and . . . goats? No, frogs, bigger ones, farther upstream, echoing off the sandstone amphitheater. A frog chorus. Going to be a wonderful star night, if I can stay awake. And my friends the bats come out, flipping around. I doze off for a little bit but wake with darker sky and bright half-moon, cold, putting on my long underwear and zipping up my bag. Perfect—warm, but with cool night air on my face.

The next morning, after donning my pack, and in keeping with my tradition of thanking wonderful camp sites, I raise my hands to heart in prayer position, and bow deep at the waist, then turn and hike down between the narrow red walls. And I'd thought that there would be no more water until Shinumo Creek, but White Creek starts back up! Yes, with even a flat sandstone rock area and a dripping waterfall! Opportunities in life like this cannot be ignored—I must stop and stand under it! I de-pack and de-shirt, sticking my head into the drip. The water just slightly cool, not quite brisk. Goosebumply. A minor miracle. I raise my face, open my mouth, and gulp as much as I can.

This, alas, turns out to be the last of White Creek, as the path comes out of the Redwall narrows and onto the Tonto Platform. Flatter ground, following the now-dry creek bed. It's hot. And dry. Ugh. Cactus, mostly prickly-pear, some even blooming, but also hedgehog, spiny green penises. And another old enemy: catclaw! Arizona: where everything wants to bite, poke, or scratch you. But around lunchtime, another miracle: a small shady rock ledge. Thirty-degree difference in temperature under here! Feeling very lizard-like, I lunch and doze. Then more hot desert hiking, though soon heading downhill again, another steep descent, switchbacking over dark brown shale, and—finally!—a glimpse of Shinumo Creek! Glorious snaky shiny moving water in the desert. Coming down into the main campsite next to it, I drop my pack in the shade and get in on my hands and knees, like an animal, dunking my head and gulping cool clear water.

Plenty of time, the campsite still in full-on sun. Packless and light, I head upstream into the narrow side canyon on a small trail, wanting a nap more than anything, sun-groggy, but once I'm walking, curiosity takes over. The trail becomes more like a game trail, and actually ends after maybe a mile. A determined person could bushwhack farther, but this section of creek is deep enough to be considered a swim hole, so I'm determined to get naked and swim. In the desert, if there is a swim hole, one has a moral obligation. And lo, it is good. Refreshing and lovely, though once I find a nice rock ledge to sit on, keeping my feet in the water, my lower pale body in the sun, getting some air and sun on the man parts, I immediately start to doze, listening to water burble.

Back at camp, I set up near the creek, and dine on more cheese and crackers, dreaming of the decadence of river runners carrying coolers and coolers of iced foodstuffs, barbequing steaks and veggie burgers and drinking lots of cold beer. With plenty of sunlight still available, I'm tired, wanting to sleep really, but go down and do my best imitation of a crane, standing knee-high in the water and observing small fish jumping out, catching mosquito-looking bugs hovering over the water. One brave fish actually throwing itself onto a rock, trying to catch flies sipping at the stream edge. Plus, a stillwater pool of tadpoles, not moving much, just floating, maybe feeling the changes coming on, the appendages starting to grow. One big one hanging out at the edge, facing the dirt, as if hearing the call to crawl out of the slime. That's how I felt in high school.

Back in camp, air mercifully cooling down, sky deep blue, wispy pink cloud lines, then dark. Fat moon already glowing. Rapids both up and downstream. And here come the bats! I lie naked on my sleeping bag, watching planets and stars appear. Sky clear, no clouds. A light down-canyon breeze, warmer than the cool air settling in the creek bed. And more frogs! Another spring peeper choir to sing along with the crickets. What's missing is coyotes. Would be nice to hear them singing too. And wolves!

Morning sun almost over a nearby butte, which makes me think I must have slept a long time, but no, only six o'clock. Time flows differently here in the canyon. Sad to leave Shinumo Creek and its good water. Not sure if I'll be near it down at the Colorado or not. I can always filter river water, but I'd prefer this pure creek soma. Not quite goodbye, though. First, some creek crossings which, earlier in the year, with snowmelt off the North Rim, could even get sketchy-dangerous. Even now, a wrong step, a slippery slip, could put me face down with a heavy pack on, so I stay mindful.

And, even though I'm looking for it, I'm still surprised to come on Bass Camp, maybe because I was expecting some kind of structure, a shack or something. In fact, it's a cave-ish area under a big north-facing perpetually-shaded overhang. This Bass guy was one of the big (white) explorers back in the day, owned a ranch over on the South Rim, and had guests and customers over to this side, for hunting, and maybe just as the first tourists. This "camp" still includes a collection of old tools—an axe head, three different pick heads, a stove, some pry bars, plus a bunch of glass fragments from really old bottles, all laid out on some benches. The hard thing to believe, although the guidebooks say so, is that Bass had an orchard here, with apple, peach, and fig trees, whereas all that's here now is some mesquite and catclaw, on sand. Can peach trees grow in hot desert sand? But how amazing would it be to sink my teeth into a nice juicy peach right now?

This is the last place to fill up my bottle and dunk my head before the push for the Colorado. And the sun is a hot bastard. I dunk my t-shirt and floppy hat in the water, as well as my head, for some evaporation action as I continue on the trail, which soon splits: The path-most-traveled heading up and over a pass to, supposedly, sandy beaches. I'm sorely tempted to just stay on the path-less-traveled following the Shinumo, but I've heard rumors of women in bikinis on those beaches. That is, the possibility was mentioned, and it has become a Great Promise. Maybe I'll even encounter one of those all-women groups. Good odds! Surely one would want to rebel against all that women's empowerment energy and invite a scruffy backpacker dude into her tent. And anyways, why couldn't that be empowering?

But first, up 700 feet—a good dry run for the hike out, and yeah, it's hot, and yeah, it's uphill, but in fact after a half hour, lo! Thar be the mighty Colorado down below! A shiny, wide, deep green strip curling through red-brown and black rock, two sets of mild rapids visible, and glimpses of white sandy beaches (so it's true!), with a flotilla of rafts even gathering above the top rapids! I descend, switchbacking through shale, watching them take the whitewater one by one. Lordy, that looks so much more fun than hiking in the desert with forty pounds on my back right now.

At the bottom, another fork: One way going down to the main bigger beach right below, where the rafters usually camp, but there's another smaller beach just below the top rapids, and I love the idea of a beach of one's own, though that lowers the chances of being invited for dinner and beers by bikinied vixens. Sigh. I hike the extra mile upstream and find a little trail that weaves down onto a beach, with bonus little shady cliff overhangs. I drop pack and shed clothes asap, heading to my baptism. By the way, that sand is blazing hot! No stopping now, though! I get on a rock bluff, the water clear and deep below, and dive.

Holymotherofgod it's COLD! My appendages, all five of them, throbbing. But I swim! Not too far out: the strong fast current a wee bit scary. Would be really cool (and dangerous) to go all the way to the other shore, but that's just not possible here. These little beach areas are hemmed in by tall rock ledges, especially on the south side.

I reach the shore and pull myself out of the depths, out of the water, and rise, naked, reborn. This is it, the holy land. Cliff walls and mountains rising up all around. The wide green Colorado, rapids and clear sky. The enormity of this Canyon, and this River that carved it, and the Time it took. Hallelujah!

Thus Spake Zarathustra
by
Mark Jenkins

"The big day," John said.

"Yup," I replied, rubbing my eyes.

It was three in the morning. We were standing on the South Rim of the Grand Canyon aiming the beams of our headlamps down the South Kaibab Trail—a mule-stomped trough of glistening ice running between snowbanks. The trailhead sign read:

ICY TRAIL: CRAMPONS RECOMMENDED.

In the previous few days, with spring a week away, the South Rim had received a half-foot of snow; over on the North Rim, a foot had fallen. Crampons would have just slowed us down. We had light metal instep cleats strapped to our hiking boots, and trekking poles.

The trail descended into blackness. We looked out across the vast reservoir of cold night air toward the distant North Rim, distinguishable only as a horizontal line above which the stars were scattered. We searched the inky chasm for Zoroaster Temple, the formation we'd come to climb.

"Can you make it out?" I asked.

"Nope," said John.

Zoroaster Temple is a Grand Canyon landmark, an immense mountain rising inside the colossal rift. It's shaped like a pyramid and topped with a 700-foot, custard-colored sandstone tower that was first climbed by Dave Ganci and Rick Tidrick in 1958; before that, very little technical rock climbing had been attempted in the Grand Canyon. After a pilgrimage to Yosemite had expanded the pair's conception of what was possible on big rock, Ganci and Tidrick, both in their early twenties, traded their clothesline for a nylon rope, and loaded their packs with World War II army angles and giant pitons forged by a Scottsdale blacksmith. Their epic ascent took seven days.

Geographically part of the North Rim, Zoroaster is more easily accessed from the South Rim. Although there are only six pitches of technical climbing, a round-trip climb of Zoroaster requires almost 30 miles of hiking and over 17,000 vertical feet of elevation gain and loss—more than the trip up the south face of Everest and back from Camp II.

Just to reach the base of Zoroaster's final tower, Ganci and Tidrick had had to scout out the tricky passageways up through the shelflike layers of shale, sandstone, and limestone. Once the route had been reconnoitered, subsequent ascents cut the rim-to-rim time in half. It's still considered by some the grand prize of climbing in the Grand Canyon. According to John Annerino's 1996 guidebook *Adventuring in Arizona*, 7,123-foot Zoroaster is "a remote, backcountry peak that requires at least three days."

We were going to attempt it in one.

There was half a moon, but its silver light was less useful than we had expected. Our headlamps illuminated the trail itself and nothing more, as if we were tromping down a mine shaft. On one side there were boulders; on the other, a black abyss. We didn't talk. We hiked, single file, John in front.

Right here, before we go any further, I must say that you don't march off on a mad caper with just anyone. Not if you want to succeed, or sometimes simply come home. It has to be someone whose bravery outstrips his banter. Someone whose strength and stamina are indubitable. Someone who has gotten himself into a hundred fixes and each time figured a way out. My 45-year-old partner, John Harlin—writer, editor, extreme skier, mountaineer, and all-around miscreant—is such a fellow. We had climbed on other continents together and knew each other well. More salient, we were matched in skill, temperament, and speed.

A two-man team leaves little room for error. On the other hand, if you're a seasoned pair, there's no weak link. Add another person—or, God forbid, a few—and fast, clean, continuous movement becomes impossible. Somebody always has to stop to take a leak, tie a shoe, tighten a buckle—minor delays that burn precious moonlight. If you're in sync, two is the perfect-size team.

Before John and I walked into the Grand Canyon, we spent three days climbing in the Arizona desert together, working out the kinks, getting dialed. The night we dropped off the rim we felt ready. The temperature was 25 degrees, perfect for hiking. We sank into the cold, dark air as if it were a liquid. The season and the time of day were part of the plan.

In the desert, the two things most likely to kill you are heat and dehydration. Hiking at night, especially in March, neutralizes both factors. You don't overheat, so you don't get overly thirsty. Why do so few people hike at night? Perhaps it's a reluctance rooted deep in our psyches, a genetically imprinted trait that can be traced back for millennia to a time when humans were predators by day but prey at night. Today the saber-toothed tiger is gone, replaced by its shrunken descendant the mountain lion, which is generally not up for taking on full-grown humans.

Nevertheless, "people have strange phobias about darkness," says Ken Walters, who teaches outdoor skills for the South Rim-based Grand Canyon Field Institute. "I tell them it's just deep shade. Hiking in the desert, you're always looking for shade—trying to get some chunk of rock between you and the sun. When you hike at night, you're putting a very big chunk of rock, the Earth, between you and the sun. It's always a huge breakthrough when people stop being hung up on daylight."

Thus our dark descent along the South Kaibab Trail. After we dropped 500 feet, the ice turned to mud and we removed our cleats. It was our only stop. Like two stones pushed off the rim, John and I rolled down to the river without effort. We crossed the suspension bridge over the quiet Colorado at 5:30 AM and followed the smell of bacon up to the Phantom Ranch mess hall. It was packed with people, light and noise streaming through the windows. We didn't go in. We stripped off our gaiters, changed socks, ate a bagel, checked the map, and chugged some Gatorade. As we were refilling our bottles from an outdoor faucet, two cowboys stepped from the lodge into the darkness, their coffee cups steaming.

"What're you boys up to?" one of them asked.

"Hikin'," John replied.

They sat down on some rocks and looked up through the trees at the dwindling stars. Likely as not they'd been awake as long as we had.

Three hours earlier, driving past the trailhead on the rim, we'd met a cowboy already loading his pack animals. We'd asked him if there was any place to park where we wouldn't get a ticket. "Don't s'pose there is," he said. After a long silence, he told us, "You boys look all right to me. Guess you could park up there beside my cabin."

Now these two cowboys watched us reload our packs and asked just enough questions to figure out what we were really up to.

"Sounds like some kinda endurance thang," one of them remarked, tossing the coffee grounds from his cup.

"We'll see," John replied.

"I, myself," the cowboy said slowly, "ain't into self-abuse. But good luck to you anyhow."

We tipped our baseball caps and galloped away.

A quarter-mile past Phantom Ranch we doglegged onto the Clear Creek Trail and began zigzagging up the north wall of the canyon. Light was pouring from the sky, washing out the night. The shapely buttes, scalloped slopes, and crenelated shelf lines of the South Rim glowed red as a Mexican dancer's dress.

We arrived at Sumner Wash around 7:30 and stopped beside a tinaja, an ephemeral rainwater pool, to fill up our as-yet-unused two-quart water bags. We'd been forewarned to carry enough water for the entire climb from Phantom Ranch. But given the recent snow, we gambled on finding water in Sumner Wash, and did.

Lack of water is a hazard in the Grand Canyon.

"We do over 400 rescues a year," Ken Phillips, search-and-rescue coordinator for Grand Canyon National Park, told me by phone. "Most occur in June, July, and August." Around 12 people die every year in the park. "Half of these are preventable—people who die of dehydration, hyponatremia [critical loss of sodium], heat exhaustion, physical exhaustion, or some combination of the above."

Ganci and Tidrick nearly learned a fatal lesson themselves when they summited Zoroaster back in late September of 1958.

"It was the first and only time I've ever experienced absolute thirst," Tidrick, now 63, told me when I called him at his home in Colorado. "We had hundred-degree temperatures. I lost 15 pounds in six days."

"Rain was predicted," Ganci, 64, said on the phone from Prescott, Arizona. "So we carried this five-gallon metal jerry jeep can and a tarp for collecting the rainwater. We had 65-pound packs and looked like a couple of Sherpas."

But the rain came four days late, after they had completed the climb and were on their way down.

"We were in the red zone, advanced stages of dehydration, tunnel vision, and euphoria, stumbling, floating along," Ganci recalled.

Impressed by their suffering, I'd started my own specialized training program: I quit drinking water. I'd go ice climbing or backcountry skiing for the whole day, without water. To compensate for the missing weight, I'd load my pack with useless climbing gear. Back at the house after a long, demolishingly parched day, I'd attempt to accurately mimic one of the mental side effects of dehydration (i.e. euphoria) by drinking only beer—a clinically tested diuretic. I found it to be one of the most enjoyable training programs I've ever attempted.

John and I filled our two-quart bags with green, insect-rich water and tossed in a few capfuls of iodine solution (later we would dump in a package of sweet-tasting electrolyte powder). We dried our socks in the sun, ate another bagel, and surveyed the landscape. We were surrounded on three sides by a 500-foot limestone band of cliffs called the Redwall.

"Looks like there's only one way through it," said John.

He pointed to a dark slot halfway between the broad back of Sumner Butte and the squat, white steeple of Zoroaster. Our photocopy of the route description warned, "The climbing here is Class 4. Use a rope if you feel at all insecure with a heavy pack."

A heavy pack. Make that the third thing that'll kill you in the desert, or anywhere else. If there's one good reason why doing something in one big day rather than in several small ones makes sense, it's to avoid the utter misery of humping a heavy pack.

For some masochistic reason, John had been impressed by the huge loads that Ganci and Tidrick had carried, and his own training regimen reflected this. He lives on a farm in Oregon and is currently building a fireplace from river rocks. The river is 200 feet below and a half-mile away from his house. John took to loading a backpack with 120 pounds of rocks and hauling them up to his house. Your average washing machine weighs about 120 pounds. He'd make several trips.

For this climb, however, our packs were well under 20 pounds. We'd taken the lightest iteration of each piece of gear. Twin, 145-foot ultrathin climbing ropes, featherweight wire-gate carabiners, Spectra slings, a frighteningly small rack of protection. We had no camping or bivouac gear whatsoever. Bring it and you'll use it—if only because the extra weight will slow you down so much that you'll be forced to stop. The self-evident secret of going fast is to go light. To carry just enough. Too much and you fail, too little and you fail. Besides climbing gear, we brought insulated coats, fleece hats and mittens, sardines, bagels, M&Ms, water, ibuprofen, and a pocketknife for compound fractures or field appendectomies.

Knowing how much to bring comes from knowing yourself. How far above your protection you can climb before you freak. How cold you tend to get. How much food and water you need to keep going. The answers are individual and only acquired through experience.

We dodged our way through agave and cacti, climbed the chimney sans ropes, and began moving up a ridge of sandstone shelves. Unlike Ganci and Tidrick, all we had to do was follow the route description and stride along in the sunshine with one eye out for the next cairn. At 10:30 AM we contoured around to the shadowed north face of Zoroaster Temple.

"Back into winter," I whined.

"Ya sissy!" bellowed John.

There was a foot of snow on the north side of the tower, and the cairns were buried. We picked our way along, clambering up breaches in the bands of ice-cloaked sandstone, until we could post-hole diagonally to the base of the northeast arête. It was below freezing. We pulled on caps and gloves, burrowed into our coats, and studied the route.

"Looks like some of the cracks have ice in 'em," exclaimed John, obviously thrilled.

We weren't sure of the route. A slab of rock had fallen out and changed the start. No matter. At noon sharp, John stripped off his gloves and coat and attacked the first frigid pitch. He climbed up to an overhanging 5.8-ish finger crack; clawed out the ice and snow, breaking off chunks of rotten rock; pulled over; scampered to a tree; and belayed me up. Then I led a wide, generously verglassed 5.7 crack.

John got off-route during the next pitch and we ended up pumping through a drippy, peeling-off-in-our-hands 5.9 overhang and hauling into a two-foot snowdrift on top. The next two pitches were 5.8 stemmy chimney/hand cracks which could have been beautiful desert climbing had there not been ice or snow every place you needed to put your hands and feet.

Pitch five was supposed to be an airy 30-foot traverse protected by two bolts. John got out his monocular and searched the wall.

"Damn. Where are they?"

On any climb worth a story, it is axiomatic that there will come a point when the protagonists are confronted with something they really don't want to do. This, of course, is God giving you a chance to back off. You will lose face, but you'll save your ass. Wounded pride or peril, your choice. The mythic dilemma.

Infelicitously, it was my lead. I admit my pride is more sensitive than my flesh. I plugged in a little piece of dubious protection and moved out on a band of blank rock above the snow. The sandstone was wet, but the knobs were solid. I skittered sideways like a crab, only to discover that the last five feet of the traverse, invisible from the belay, were glazed with ice.

It was the predictable point of no return, the place where the fear of going backward outweighs the fear of going forward. A few easy moves (hindsight bravado) and I was through.

The final pitch was described as a "strenuous off-width, 5.9R." ("R" stands for runout, which means you can take a long fall if you slip.) It was John's lead. Even half-filled with snow it turned out to be not strenuous, not off-width, not 5.9, and thankfully not a runout.

Above the crack we plunged through two feet of snow, cut over to the summit block, scrambled up a chimney, and popped out into the sun atop Zoroaster.

"Four o'clock," said John, checking his watch, "Not bad."

We shook hands like men are supposed to do on summits, snapped photos, sat down, and ate the last of our bagels and sardines while soaking up the sun and the phantasmagorical view of the Grand Canyon.

"You know who Zoroaster was?" I asked John.

"Zorro's father?" John quipped.

Like Brahma, Buddha, and other divinely christened formations within the canyon, Zoroaster was named after a sacred figure, in this case the Persian prophet who lived in the sixth century B.C.

"Otherwise known as Zarathustra," I added. "Remember your Nietzsche? The Übermensch?"

"I remember Zorro the Gay Blade," wisecracked John.

"'Man is a rope, tied between beast and overman—a rope over an abyss.' Thus Spake Zarathustra."

Much is made of summiting, but the fact is you're only halfway home. We started rappelling at 4:30 PM, reached the base of the Temple at 5:30, hustled back across the snowy north face, trotted along the descending ridge to the Redwall gully, and were off the final raps by nightfall.

Hiking steadily, dreaming of cheeseburgers, we were back at Phantom Ranch by 8:30. The kitchen was already closed. As a consolation prize, the cashier offered us free Oreos and hot chocolate.

We recrossed the suspension bridge at 9:30 and methodically ground out the 5,000-foot ascent, reaching our car on the South Rim at one in the morning, 22 hours after we'd left it. We weren't sore, blistered, or exhausted, merely bushed. There had been no real drama. Drama happens when things go wrong. Drama happens when people make mistakes, when reach exceeds grasp. Ours was an epic non-epic.

On the way out, near the top, we noticed a large trail sign we had somehow cruised right by on our way down:

WARNING: DANGER! DO NOT ATTEMPT TO HIKE FROM THE CANYON RIM TO THE RIVER AND BACK IN ONE DAY. EACH YEAR HIKERS SUFFER SERIOUS ILLNESS OR DEATH FROM EXHAUSTION.

V

Encounters

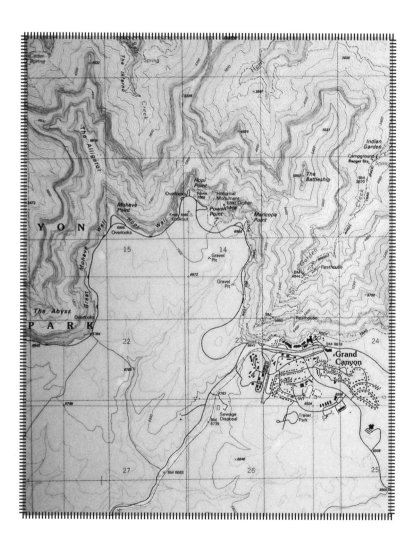

On Being a Trail Guide in Grand Canyon
by
Wayne Ranney

I have the best job in the whole wide world. That's not my appraisal of its many and varied privileges: it's simply what I'm told all the time from the people who listen to what I do for a living. Think about it: my boss is many miles away every single day that I show up for work, and he has absolutely no possible way to give orders to me—no phone, no fax, not even e-mail can reach me when I'm hard at work. In most respects, I don't even consider that I have a boss since *I'm the one* who ultimately decides exactly how my workday evolves and the pace that suits me.

Those who are around me hang on every word I say and consider me to be a knowledgeable authority who is also caring, comforting, and intimately invested in promoting their own success (my job runs smoother when they perform their best). The walls of my "office" are painted in the brightest, most interesting colors, and the ceiling is the widest dome of blue sky you've ever seen. These walls hardly ever feel confining, but in those rare, sought-after instances when they are, it's a good thing! I often shake my head in disbelief that I have the good fortune of being a trail guide deep within the Grand Canyon.

My journey into this unique "job" began with one simple creed: "Do what you love and the money will follow." Not a lot of money mind you; nobody gets rich in a material sense being a trail guide. But the intangible rewards—heaps of fresh air, significant exercise, healthful sunshine, beauty beyond description, and a satisfying intellectual freedom while working on the job—may be the perfect antidote to the many detractions found in an increasingly unrewarding work environment. I wouldn't trade my job for all the money of a lawyer, a politician, or a weapons manufacturer.

How did I get here? In a sentence, I just followed my heart. In high school and even college, I never enrolled in courses with the primary interest of defining a career path. I remember feeling incredibly lost as friends around me identified their life choices at the young age of 18 or 19. Heck, I didn't even know what the options were at that age. So I just took classes in the things I was interested in and worked at jobs that were satisfying and not just a paycheck. I did what pleased me and identified the things that I definitely *could not do*. (Subjects whose textbooks had no pictures were definitely out.) This had the unintended but fortunate effect of leaving me dozens of choices for the things that I *could do*. And in those wilder and freer times of the early 1970s, I discovered and wandered into the Grand Canyon.

Instead of a career path, I got a footpath. Who would have thought that a rather spontaneous four-day hike that I undertook as a 21-year old kid would turn into a career? I sure didn't, but because I was able to let my young life "flow" wherever it wanted to go, I found satisfaction far beyond a fat bank account, a fancy car, or a fabulous house. No. If a person wants to live an extraordinary life they should make extraordinary choices, rooted in the heart and without regard to status, wealth, or fame. That's what I did, and that's why I became a Grand Canyon trail guide.

So what's it like working in paradise? Many times each year I drive up to the canyon from my home in Flagstaff and enter an orientation room with nine or ten strange faces staring back at me. They have that look of intensity, wondering what the hell they've just signed up for. Some of them are there because they've backpacked the Appalachian Trail and want to try their luck out west. Others are unwilling spouses, sisters, or dads who've signed on reluctantly at the urging of their relative. And occasionally, a few of them are in denial about their advancing age and figure that if they can drop one vertical mile in just seven miles of trail, then maybe they still "have it." You see all types of people who come to a Grand Canyon trail hike, and if I've had one unexpected and pleasant surprise in this line of work, it's that I couldn't have known that I'd be so damn interested in working with and learning about people. This job definitely brings out the best in people, along with a few of their quirks and limitations.

The first day of a typical trek to the bottom of the Grand Canyon is devoted to getting to know one another in a classroom setting. I look at their gear and make sure they do not bring too much stuff.

(Stuff is heavy, and the lighter you go down, the happier you are). It's a great exercise to pare down your needs to a bare minimum, but at the same time it's a fine line between sneaking through the canyon with that hardcover edition of "War and Peace" (camp reading) and leaving behind your boots (it happened once to someone who didn't realize it until they arrived at the North Rim with their boots back at the South Rim).

In the course of looking at all that trail mix and underwear, I slowly get a picture of who my trail companions will be. Sometimes it makes you worry when you realize that the last time this person was on a trail was when the Boy Scouts still thought hatchets were a good thing to bring along for cutting down trees to make firewood. Most of the time, it gets you really excited to know that you're about to take people on the trip of a lifetime, one that they will accomplish on their own two feet. I love it.

After a day in class, it's time to head down the trail. Invariably, someone is late to meet at the appointed time, and more often than not it's a married couple with one of them moving a whole lot slower than the other. Or, if there was anyone you might have had some concerns about the day before, they're late too. I've noticed that folks who fail to show up on time for this little deadline are also the ones who were likely conflicted in deciding whether to attempt the trip or not. No matter, that's a concern to deal with later on down the trail. It's time to start the fun!

At the trailhead, people are keen to take a picture of themselves and the group while they're still clean (and the cleanest they'll ever be until the trip is over). I usually do the honors, but oftentimes there are rim-bound individuals nearby who are recruited for the job. This is a great opportunity for me to have a little fun with everyone. If the chubby visitor who soon has nine cameras dangling down from his wrist doesn't ask, I always throw out a baited comment like, "We're going down for four days!" This usually yields the intended result: "Four days? And you have everything you'll need in those packs?"

I don't have to say another word because by now the group is really pumped up about camping under the stars, seeing Bright Angel Creek, and enjoying a cold beer at the bottom of the Grand Canyon. Suddenly the person who volunteered to take our picture is getting an earful about our itinerary. It has the intended effect of crystallizing in the participants' minds just how unusual this venture is going to be and how lucky they are to experience it. (In fact, less than one percent of the people who visit the Grand Canyon actually sleep on the ground inside of it).

Thoroughly imbued with confidence, we begin our descent. The South Kaibab Trail was constructed in the 1920s in response to an über-capitalist who insisted that he owned the rights to the Bright Angel Trail and collected one dollar from anyone taking a mule on it. So the National Park Service built a trail of their own that, unlike most other canyon trails, does not follow a fault and thus was constructed on a protruding ridge of rock. The effect is that it is one of the steepest, most straightforward descents found in all of Grand Canyon.

The trail starts out steep and never lets up. And occasionally, I'll look up after descending through The Chimney and see that someone is already inordinately behind. Oh-oh, what could that be about? (All sections of the Kaibab and Bright Angel trails have colorful names for reference, and The Chimney is the very first portion of the South Kaibab Trail that leads to Phantom Ranch).

So I stop at Oh-Ah Point and wait. I show the others what's visible from here besides all of creation. We look east towards the Desert View Watchtower and in those 25 miles of unfathomable space numerous side canyons slash their way down to the Colorado River in deep but regular intervals. Between each of these drainages, jagged rows of rock project up from the recesses, with their familiar lineup of weird-looking but spectacular buttes, spires, mesas, knobs, and temples. Yes, even temples. Zoroaster. Vishnu. Brahma. Deva. Isis. Shiva. The list goes on.

Many times in these instances, I wish I weren't a guide. I wish I could be out here on my own, with my own schedule and not constantly having to tell people to tie their laces or keep drinking water. I wish I could just stop here at Oh-Ah Point with my hands crossed and look in perfect reverence at a landscape that I have become intimate with through almost four decades of hiking in it. In this imaginary solo journey, I am a prayerful and silent worshiper paying homage to bare naked rock—the most essential of all earthly gifts, providing soil for our crops, foundations for our homes, and, once upon a time, silt for our rivers.

Nowhere else is rock exposed in such a grand and sublime fashion as here in the Grand Canyon. But then I come to my senses and realize that were I not a guide, I most likely would not be privileged to know the canyon as deeply as I do. It's a small price to pay to experience this joyful intimacy in a great rock cathedral. I bring others into the temple, and while they experience its magnificent beauty and many charms, I become intimate with it in the process. It is a circular perfection that never seems to lose its charm or meaning to me.

Wait a minute—what about "Susie"? I forgot all about her way back up on the trail. She's missed out on all of these subtle musings as she fussed with her hiking poles or emptied the red dirt out of her boots. I'm beginning to worry, with the slow pace we've started with, whether we'll make it to the cantina at Phantom Ranch before it closes at four o'clock. Wanting to speed things up, I ask her, "Hey Susie. How's it going?" She looks at the group and wonders if maybe she should apologize for holding us up. "Come on over here Susie and check out this view," one of her companions exhorts her. Sure enough, Susie is impressed with the view. But I'm far more impressed at the lessons my group repeatedly teach me on each and every trip: camaraderie on the trail is more important than speed, and togetherness is better than aloneness. I smile. It's going to be a good trip.

After a pee stop at the Cedar Ridge toilet, we descend through the Supai Group of rock layers. My ticket into this breathtaking world of sculpted rock was that I became fascinated with earth history while working as a backcountry ranger for the National Park Service. There were many things of interest to me in those early days of my career, but I always gravitated more towards the geologic stories that I heard from those who lived here. I always paid a little more attention to them and just had a knack for easily remembering the rock names and the ancient stories they whispered to me as I walked the trails. *Shinumo. Tapeats. Muav. Hakatai. Coconino.* These words may sound foreign to visitors, but to those deeply connected with the Grand Canyon they are cherished sounds. The rock layers are like old friends you can count on every trip down. Even in side canyons that I've never visited, I know with geologic certainty what colors there will be around the corner and what textures the rock walls will contain. Such is the magic of being in love with stratified terrain.

One of these layers, the Redwall Limestone, stands as a great barrier to foot travel in the Grand Canyon. The ravens, of course, don't even notice the Redwall as they dive-bomb into the canyon at 60 mph with their black wings swept back and sharp beaks pointed downwards with poise and confidence—those cheaters! But to mere mortals, the Redwall is over 500 feet thick, composed of pure limestone and durable chert that rises up like a skyscraper into the dry desert air. In a more humid climate, this cliff face would be chemically decayed into a gently sloped ruin, but here on the Colorado Plateau you can barely break it with a large rock hammer.

Thus, the legendary Red and Whites, switchbacks of dynamited torture almost a mile in length that twist and turn through the sun-drenched Redwall cliff. Invariably, someone will get a blister here and we'll need to stop and tend to it. But inside my head I'm always trying to get the group to go just a little bit farther down the trail. I'm way too invested in a strategy of delayed gratification. I think to myself, *Slow down. Slow down.*

This time it's Mike. He's the one who came to the trip reluctantly with his wife, losing out to her desire to go with a group and a guide. I can hear the words in his mind now: *Only sissies need a guide. We just wasted $600 bucks each going down with this group of Girl Scouts.* Beating back my inner feelings of glee that the blister belongs to him, I point out an arch in the rocks high above the trail. "I actually walked up there once," I tell the group, and they and I stare in disbelief at my own exuberant youthfulness back then.

They can't even imagine such a side trek, since, by now, the question of "How much farther?" easily spills from the recesses of their minds to the forefront of their lips. I look down to the trail below us and point out the toilet at the Tip Off. "Let's all rendezvous down there," I say. "Once we get there it's only about two miles to Phantom Ranch." I'm always framing our endeavors in the most positive light, lifting their spirits with every opportunity they give me.

Although it might seem logical to eat lunch at the Tip Off (I mean really, it's a toilet in the heart of the Grand Canyon!), I have a special place just 200 meters farther on that I'd like to take them to. It has a view of the Colorado River, but more than that, I know of a little geologic secret I want to share with them. For sure, 99.9% of all the people who walk by there will miss this little gem entirely, and I don't want my group to be part of that crowd. So, if we are lucky enough and strong enough to have lunch this far down the trail (5.5 miles), it's where I like to stop.

The view is fantastic, and we can now pick out our campground in the trees below us next to the creek. After everyone finishes their sandwich, I draw their attention to a small cliff of purple quartzite that has provided us with some welcome shade. I show them where pieces of this dense, purple rock had fallen from an ancient cliff a very long time ago. The fallen boulders then became engulfed in a swash of brown sand that was being deposited along the shoreline of an ancient beach. Like the chocolate chips found in cookie dough, there are dozens of purple quartzite boulders that stick up in relief here from within the brown sandstone.

And I tell them that on a single day, 525 million years ago, storm waves lashed this same cliff face and battered it, causing the purple boulders to become dislodged and fall into the soft sand below. After burial, the brown sand became lithified (turned to stone), and the entire event was preserved for 524.9 million years or so, only to become re-exposed by the relatively recent incision of the Colorado River. Some of them will understand this story, some of them won't. Their feet are talking to them, and it's probably time to move on.

The day before, I told the group that the hike down would be the hardest of the whole trip. They weren't expecting to hear that and probably wondered if I was telling the truth. But I assured them that the relentless drop for seven miles took its toll, and that if they were to get a blister, or a sprained ankle, or a bum knee, it would be on the way down into the canyon and not the way out. At Panorama Point I remind them of this, and they now get it. Down is hard—at least as hard as up. They're already learning about life down here, and they've only just arrived.

I've always liked that about the Grand Canyon. It chews you up and spits you out, scrapes your skin, and gives only a rocky place to lay your bed. It's steep, it's rocky, it's hot, and most of the plants have spines that never seem to need water. But by doing this, the canyon teaches you what it is like to be a very small being in a very large place. I suppose that if everyone could come down here, most of them wouldn't like it. Yet of all the people who do, just about every one of them can't wait to come back. How can a place be so cruel and so welcoming at the same time? I wonder.

Finally. The bridge. The Colorado River has taken six million years to carve its path through the rocks we just walked down in six hours. We are a fast species, I remind my tired hikers. They laugh at me again as we walk across the bridge, entering another world of babbling streams and cold beer. First we visit our campsite and set up the tents. I only bring one if it's going to rain, and it hardly ever does. In over 30 years, I've been caught without shelter only a couple of times, and at four pounds per hike, I figure that I've saved well over a ton of weight by not carrying one.

One of the times that I should have brought a tent was with a girlfriend who left me afterwards—the most expensive four pounds I ever left behind. (I'll bet she still brags about it though . . . Nah).

After the boots come off, I encourage everyone to go down to the creek and place their tired, sweaty "dogs" in the cool spring water. It has the magical effect of washing away a lot of the pain inflicted by the trail. A breeze rattles the leaves in the cottonwood trees overhead, and I have to remind myself that I'm at work. This is work!

Wandering up to the cantina at Phantom Ranch is like going back in time to when small human villages were set discreetly upon the much larger landscape (and you actually had to look hard for them from the heights). Some people bristle at the notion of a commercial "lemonade stand" in the bottom of the Grand Canyon, but I never harbored such feelings. It seems the place was home to me before I even arrived. When I worked here in the 1970s, I was a very young soul, and the character of my life had not yet formed. This place in a sense created and shaped me as a person, and for that, Phantom will never be just a lemonade stand to me.

Now comes the fun part. We'll be inside the Grand Canyon without having our packs or boots on for almost 48 hours. There's so much to do! We can explore other nearby trails (unbelievably, many of these are somewhat flat), visit a secret waterfall, rest by Bright Angel Creek or the banks of the mighty Colorado River, discover 900-year-old Indian ruins, write postcards, enjoy a glass of wine or beer, or just do _nothing_. How long has it been since any of us just did nothing?

In this modern world, we move too fast, and of all the things that I could possibly teach those on this trip, it would be this: life is fast, slow down. I have just four days to be with them, and I would hate to see them spend all of their time down here in a hurry, which is how most of them live at home. So I lay out all of the possibilities, and within minutes we're headed up to the cantina for postcards and beer.

We'll eventually get around to the trails, the ruins, and the Colorado River, but there is never enough time. This place has everything I need— blue sky, salubrious air, a running stream, lots of happy folks stumbling around drunk on blissfulness. Every time I come down here I say to myself that I will return to volunteer at the Ranch, living day to day as a compassionate sage offering encouragement to weary hikers, while I pull weeds along the side of the path leading to the cantina. When it's time to pack up and go, I always vow to return, and so far that's held true. In fact, there will only be one time in my life that this won't happen.

No matter how much I tell the group that the hike out will be much easier than they think, they never believe me, and they fret when they see that one-mile vertical wall looming ahead. The easiest way to get people out of the Grand Canyon is to break the nine-and-a-half-mile hike into little parts, and the Bright Angel Trail lends itself well to this kind of beneficial division. In slow, deliberate words, I tell them: one and half miles along the River Trail (easy, scenic); one and half miles along gurgling Pipe Creek (easy again); one mile up the Devil's Corkscrew (nine brutal switchbacks but over in only 30 to 40 minutes); and another easy mile along Garden Creek (waterfalls, ruins, chirping birds!). Which brings us to Indian Garden, more than halfway to the top. Five miles completed, and most of them did it in just two hours. When I tell them that they are more than halfway out at this point, they actually start believing that they're going to make it. Smiles all around.

Until Mike reminds us all that even though we've accomplished more than half the distance, we still have three quarters of the climb to go. Upon hearing this, Susie slumps back against her pack and just glares at the last four-and-a-half miles and the 3,000 vertical feet. Thanks, Mike.

"Ah yes," I remind them. "Mike is right. But we'll break this part up into three bite-size pieces as well." Which has the effect of making the hike out pure joy if you let it feel that way. Okay, I exaggerate. But they *will* feel joy when they actually do "top out." I remind them, "Remember to always look down at what you've done already, rather than up towards what you still have to do." It's a tried-and-true trick of the trail, and has a magical way of making the ominous walls gradually recede into the postcard view of the canyon that we all grew up with. "I've never had to leave anyone down here before," I say, "and I don't think any of you will be the first. You're doing too good." Mike frowns, but everyone else is smiling again.

Of course, as the guide I have to stay with the slowest hikers, so I'm only too happy to tell Mike, "Go on ahead and lead the way for us." He's happy to oblige, although I notice just a bit of apprehension when he realizes he has to walk alone with only his own wits now. The rest of us (including his wife) are happy to let him go and have a moment when he can stretch it out and just be alone with the canyon. Throughout the trip I have encouraged everyone to have some "alone time" in the canyon—just them and their thoughts and the big beautiful gorge. These moments are when they too begin their own intimate relationship with the Grand Canyon.

And when we finally do reach the top, there are hugs all around from everyone, even Mike. We assemble near the flagstone sign at the Bright Angel trailhead, and this time I do not need to do the asking—they all run right up to the nearest over-perfumed visitor and ask her to take their picture with their knotty hair and scraped knees. Everyone's laughing and feels good about the experience. I point out to them a couple of non-guided inexperienced hikers who invariably walked in "too fast" at the start of their day, necessitating a hike "too slow" to end it. They look haggard from the experience, nothing at all like the festive group we've become.

True, not everyone needs a guide to complete this trip successfully, but having one can create a much different experience that cannot be easily duplicated without one. Pacing is important in the Grand Canyon, and the proper tempo is only learned from repeated experiences and an intimate knowledge of the trail.

Invariably, it is the "Susies" of the group who end up being the most touched by the whole journey, and they don't even try to fight back the tears. The "Mikes" of the trip usually do come around to being great trail companions, only too happy to help those with less experience. Walking back to the classroom, I see a raven fly towards the lip of the canyon, ready for another dive. I take one last look as we retreat back from the edge. And the thought enters my mind that I do have the best job in the world.

Going Rim to Rim, Barefoot
by
Thea Gavin

Obsessions. My latest one was ridiculous, which would have made it awkward to talk about around the copy machine at work.

So I didn't.

Instead, I logged a bunch of miles on local trails, overdid it, felt a stress fracture coming on, tried to keep the miles going anyway (just at a slower pace), and then showed up at the North Rim one 38-degrees-and-cloudy October morning, ready to obsess my way across the Grand Canyon.

Barefoot.

That this might be slightly unusual/dangerous/stupid was borne out by the questions and comments of other dedicated rim-to-rimmers I met along the way:

"Where's your shoes?"

"How do you do that barefoot?"

"Can I get your picture, sweetheart? I won't get your face, just your feet." (This one weirded me out a bit.)

"You're brave." (Perhaps a code word for "stupid"?)

And my favorite, stated without sarcasm and not a shred of self-awareness: "Barefoot, huh?"

When I was a kid and got an idea fixed in my head, I'd bike to the library and check out my limit of books on the subject du jour (usually horse-related). How cool that online research came along so I could become an arm-chair expert on . . . running injuries. Barefoot running. Crossing the Grand Canyon. Alzheimer's disease—how to deal with parents who suffer from it, and how to keep from getting it myself. Exercise helps? I can do that.

Stuffed with knowledge, I had Kaibab Plateau-high hopes of running at least part of the way. And I did, at least until the notorious switchbacks that plunge through the red dust below Supai Tunnel. I appreciated the warmer temps (in the 50s now), the result of dropping 1,500 feet in elevation, but my left knee started twinging with a sharp pain behind the kneecap that came and went with increasing frequency and ferocity as the downhill miles snaked on.

My hiking poles, which I had thrown in the car at the last minute (who needs hiking poles if they're running?) were suddenly essential, repurposed as crutches. I began to worry about the ugly underbelly of what I had learned in my internet education: Grand Canyon rangers are not pleased with idiots who get themselves stuck in the canyon and need rescuing. And those idiots must, literally, pay for their mistakes and pick up the rescue tab. Helicopter and all.

Then there was the skin toughness issue. During my training hikes I had wondered if the soles of my feet could take so many miles of trail without wearing clean off. Here my research had been encouraging; I discovered a handful of crazies who ran or hiked prodigious distances shoelessly, and whose skin stayed on. Not as encouraging: my longest training hike had been only 18 miles, with sandals required halfway as the sharp-rocked trail baked in the July sun.

The North Kaibab in October was anything but hot, however, and my mostly trail-tough tootsies were thrilled by the damp grit and fun puddles, the result of intermittent showers almost the whole 14 miles down—which was fine as long as the chilly wind didn't gust too hard. Usually it didn't. But I was never sure if the weather was about to turn from playful pitter-pats to canyon-carving deluge, so I tried to keep my pace purposeful, scarfing dried fruit and nut mix on the move, as I had read about and practiced all summer.

Dang. There I was in the midst of all that stratified, stark, eroded beauty and there was no time for poignant pauses to savor the damp-rock-scented canyon air, or to ponder which cliff crevice was acting as an amplifier for the haunting canyon wren music; my soles felt studly, but my knee might be a ticking time bomb, and my long history of left patella pain was not going to re-write itself just because I had a crazy dream to trot 24 shoeless miles through the grand location of my *Brighty*-fueled childhood dreams. (Thanks, Marguerite Henry. I blame your book for sparking this Grand Canyon fixation early on.)

So I wasn't all that surprised when my knee went south on the switchbacks only two miles into the trek. Depressed, yes. Surprised, no.

In fact, the whole barefoot running thing had been inspired by the spiraling desperation I felt in regards to my chronically painful knee. I'd read about, and tried, a wallet-load of non-surgical remedies: traditional physical therapy, acupuncture, rooster comb injections, non-traditional physical therapy (ART, Rolfing). Barefoot running would save me. I wanted to believe it.

My knee remained a skeptic.

It was right: patella salvation would not be accomplished by the mere removal of shoes. The 5,800-foot elevation loss between the North Rim and Phantom Ranch helped me realize that.

What I tried to tell myself, though, was that this was OK. So what if legions of loping folks in short shorts passed me all day? They could follow their own obsession and rush rim-to-rim—or rim-to-rim-to-rim, 40+ miles—getting their endorphin freak on, while I sauntered (or limped, depending on the steepness factor) along, splashing in the puddles, marveling how the rocks always allowed for a smooth place for my feet to fall. Only the infamous Box held a section where the trail surface was nothing but chunky scree.

It's a mystery of barefooting that I don't quite understand, but thoroughly enjoy: my toes somehow find little landing platforms, whether on rocks or between them, without my having to consciously place them. What everyday miracles our brains and bodies are capable of, and we don't notice! But hiking alone for miles and hours, I had plenty of time to think about what a gift it was to even be able to walk, especially as I recalled my father's former good health and the recent deterioration of his brain and body. When I needed to chase away crazy ideas of my left kneecap exploding, leaving me begging for a helicopter ride out, I focused on appreciating my slow but steady downhill progress, each footfall a blessing of sensation. I'd tripped and ripped off the ends of assorted toes more times than I could count, on trails far rockier than the North Kaibab, so I knew that all it took was one second of wool-gathering for the trail to rise and bite my unprotected toes.

Besides the immediate logistics of where to step, any rim-to-rim adventure at Grand Canyon requires delicious hours of planning. First priority: strategize an escape from work that allows not only trail time, but the 9+ hour drive to and from Southern California. Decide how you want to spend the night before the hike—camping, cabin-ing, car-slumming. Think about obtaining back-country permits or Phantom Ranch lodging to break up the inner canyon journey. Finally, figure out how to either a) hitchhike or shuttle bus back to the rim where you left your car or b) convince some kind soul to drive 200+ miles around to pick you up on the other side.

Back when I must have been on some kind of runner's high from a mid-summer barefoot gallop, I thought I would be making a one-day outing of it. On the actual drive, heading north under threatening clouds on Interstate 15 through Las Vegas, it began to seem that an overnight break would be prudent. Of course that meant I would have to throw more dollars at this divertissement: besides gasoline and night-before reservations at the North Rim Lodge, I now had to make a moderately desperate phone call to claim a last-minute bunkbed and hot meal at Phantom Ranch. Done.

My chauffeur went along with all this nonsense: he cheerfully slept with me at the Lodge and delivered me to the North Kaibab trailhead at first light. Little did either of us know how he would shiver through the coming snowstorm as he hung out at the Lodge all day, and then attempt to keep warm that night in our station wagon before making the early morning 4.5-hour drive to pick me up over yonder on the South Rim . . . and then motor us 500 more miles back to Southern California. After almost 40 years of marriage, it's little gestures like this that make me OK with not getting flowers on Valentine's Day.

My first photo—a grinning self-portrait as I crouch by the North Kaibab trailhead sign—is time-stamped 6:39 AM; a hundred or so pictures later, I have a shot of the humble outbuildings of Phantom Ranch, taken at 2:10 PM. Almost eight hours to make 14 miles. That's not going to set any speed records, but I like to believe it is the FKT (fastest known time) in the category of barefoot 53-year-old grandmas.

But was I barefoot the whole way? The Phantom Ranch Cantina has a sign out in front with some nonsense about shoes being required to enter this most holy place . . . so I guess it was a good thing I'd lashed a pair of sandals to my day-pack. My feet immediately started sweating, though, as soon as I situated my lonely self at the long "family style" dining table. Before I said a prayer of thanks and pitched into my vegetarian chili, I had to slide out of my sandals and let my toes go free again.

My lucky toes! They had just experienced 14 miles of rock-rainbow intimacy, caresses from boulders to pebbles in a kaleidoscope of shades: rust, cream, pink, black, ochre . . . all weathering down to sand, which is the Grand Canyon on the move toward the sea. This disturbed my sleep a little (or maybe it was the snoring from some of the other tired ladies in the bunkhouse): I'd heard of the un-fun, deep sand-trap that was the Bright Angel Trail along the Colorado River. But the morning after rain, untainted by hoof print or footprint, it proved to be an ecstasy of smooth-packed delight. The only thing that made this section difficult was trying to see through some pesky tears of gratitude: I'd just spent the night at the legendary Phantom Ranch where Brighty the donkey used to frolic; I was more than half-way across the canyon; all the downhill-induced knee agony surely must be over.

Before I hit the sand, the thinnest of crescent moons had greeted me as I minced over the Colorado River on the silver suspension bridge. Its span of almost 500 feet provided the harshest sensory challenge of the whole journey: highly engineered metal grid-work. The deep-lugged Vibram crowd who were waiting their turn to mount the silver beast seemed too dismayed by my lack of shoe-sense to even say "good morning." Either that, or they were awestruck. Sure, that was it.

The discomfort ("pain" is not allowed to enter the lexicon when I am extolling the virtues of barefooting) of the bridge was immediately forgotten as I embarked on the glorious lower Bright Angel Trail. Downriver, a few cliffs caught the sun's early rays and double-glowed, courtesy of the reflective green river. More hikers, probably full of a good Phantom Ranch breakfast, passed me as I set up my camera to take some self-portraits with all that dawn beauty in the background.

How could I ever capture it? What a wonder-filled contrast—ancient rock and us young humans. (Canyon geology always makes this grandma feel brand new on the scene.) Come on, little camera—help me take away images of both people and bedrock illuminated in the splendid clarity that only comes after a storm; help me record an answer to Gerard Manly Hopkins: "What is all this juice and all this joy?"

So much morning-light jubilation left no room for a pain that over the years has seemed downright vindictive in its capricious appearance during moments of trail bliss. Even my non-canyon life's background haze of worry about declining, demented parents dissipated in the river shine.

Up until an hour previous, I had not decided whether to ascend via the South Kaibab or Bright Angel trails. Early rising bunk mates convinced me that although Bright Angel was two miles longer, its accessibility to water made it the better choice.

While I'm sure they were referring to the piped-in drinking water at several rest stops along the trail, I was pleased to discover there was also water *to be crossed*. One of the utmost delights of wandering barefoot on trails is soothing my soles in streams of cool water . . . it makes me want to accost every foot-coffined hiker and stiffly shod runner: "Lose your shoes! Find your feet! Get wet, for goodness sake!"

But that would be rude, and below the rim at Grand Canyon is no place for rudeness (well, except for the occasional flagrant flouting of uphill/downhill trail etiquette as to who yields to whom, but that seemed more ignorance than maliciousness on the part of those clueless amblers).

So I stood and soaked awhile in each blessed rivulet, trying not to give off gloating vibes as the shod masses passed me by, stepping gingerly from rock to rock, sometimes pausing to discuss my (lack of) footwear.

Stream crossings, photo ops, trail chats, intermittent stabbing knee pain on those darned rock step-ups . . . in four hours I had sashayed a whopping four miles, almost to Indian Garden. Which left almost five miles to go—with a knee that seemed jealous of all the attention the canyon views were receiving; now it wanted me to only focus on its dark dazzles of hurt.

To distract myself, I tried to imagine how my husband was doing; was he cruising past the Vermillion Cliffs right now, admiring them as we had done together just a year before on a drive from North to South Rim? Who would make it first to our rendezvous at the Bright Angel Lodge fireplace at noon? Noon?! That would be . . . two hours from now?

Yikes. I needed to quit shooting the breeze. Although some of my fellow hikers had fairly inane throw-away comments, others had good honest questions, including the always-perplexing, "Why?"

As I am still trying to work this out for myself, I have long and short versions of my answer; these versions also have sub-categories of explicitness. I try to use my teacherly instinct—when the other person's eye contact diminishes (especially if they're headed in the opposite direction), I try to wind up my explanation within the hour.

So. It was 10 AM and I had five miles left. Scientifically speaking, my knee felt like Bugs Bunny had hired little winged guys with pitchforks to flutter around and randomly stab at it. When they did, I just leaned a bit more on my crutches. I mean, hiking poles. The elevation increase—Indian Garden is at almost 4,000 feet; the South Rim is 6,800 feet—was starting to affect my breathing, but there was this big guy in a ranger shirt (and heavy-duty hiking boots) a few switchbacks ahead of me, and I made it my new life's goal to try to catch him and introduce him to a shoeless hiking paradigm.

Rock ledge. Step up. Stab. Both the bad knee AND good knee buckled. Only my death grip on the hiking poles kept me from hitting the ground. How was I going to make it to the top, much less shift people's paradigms, with this kind of patella shenanigans going on?

I'd already resigned myself to not running rim to rim. Now I had to lower my expectations again. Forget about showing off what an awesome barefoot hiker I was; I just needed to find some way to less painfully drag that left foot up and over the (many) human-engineered ledges on this last section of trail. The solution came after a bit of clumsy experimentation: angle my left foot out about 30 degrees. And, of course, keep placing one foot in front of the other—above all else, this remains a key to life and hiking. My almost-ninety-year-old parents have been doing this their whole life; their steps are much slower now, and throw rugs can really mess up this philosophy, but I appreciate their example of unglamorous, faithful endurance. Maybe, somehow, I could inspire others as well: shoes or no shoes, we need to keep heading toward our goal, and either we'll get there or have to be evacuated by helicopter . . .wait, that's not how it's supposed to end.

Did I mention that it was getting colder and colder? The low October sun angle meant shade the rest of the way, but I didn't want to stop and pull my long underwear back on. (Yes, I had been quite the fashion icon in the rain yesterday: black running shorts over gray woollies, along with an electric blue rain jacket draped hunchback-style over my small day-pack.)

The ground was now cold enough to start to numb my weary feet—and I hate that feeling almost as much as I hate my left knee twinges—but finally, after 23 miles of hiking solo, my pace matched up with someone for the last mile: John, a teacher from Chicago. Now I could chat *and* walk. We discussed students these days, and his trek to Indian Garden just now, and whether he should attempt to hike all the way to the river tomorrow. He had planned this trip to the Grand Canyon for a long time—the canyon does that to you: grabs your attention at whatever flatland desk you work at and gives you something to dream about—and he wanted to get the most out of it.

So it snuck up on me, the Bright Angel trailhead, my Grand Canyon goal. John and I wished each other well. I picked my smiling husband out of the crowd—such a horde of rim-only tourists with clean shoes. (How did he know to meet me there? Which trail I would pick? After all these years of marriage, are our brains melding?)

Thus ended my rim-to-rim obsession.

Having completed this iconic pilgrimage—R2R, something I'd read about for years—I regretted that my knee let me down, that it took me two days of painful plodding to find my way across.

But even those fifteen hours now seem as brief as the rainfall I'd witnessed at the bottom of the canyon, when I sat on the beach by Phantom Ranch with my feet feeling the pull of the Colorado River, when I watched raindrops evaporate before they could become part of the current. How they caught the light, if only for a few seconds; how they made a high sparkle against the dark eroding shoulders of the old cliffs. Here's a new obsession: to remember how the damp trail meandered all those miles, how the green river was alive with swirls and swells, how my bare toes felt it all.

Uphill Battle
by
Matt Berman

In the winter and spring of 2009, I worked at Grand Canyon National Park, building and maintaining hiking trails out of a backcountry post called Indian Garden, which is about half way between the rim and the river. That May, as daily temperatures soared well above one hundred degrees, I started to feel like the canyon was something like a trap. We were working just one mile uptrail from the Colorado River, on a steep and winding section of Bright Angel Trail chiseled into the side of a pink and red and white cliff of decomposing granite called the Devil's Corkscrew.

Every day I prayed I could make it back from our worksite to our trail crew bunkhouse at Indian Garden that overlooked a sea of red rock buttes and purple prickly pear cactus. It was an uphill hike in the heat of the day, beginning in the afternoon, when I was already tired from a day's work. Each day I returned to that oasis and saw that trickling creek and those stout cottonwood trees, which seemed as completely out of place in the desert as I was, I felt grateful to have survived.

As the heat intensified, I began to obsess about moving north again. By the end of the month I planned to be back in Grand Teton National Park in Wyoming to begin my summer job, in a latitude I felt more comfortable in. But for now I was toiling in the canyon for nine days at a time, installing juniper log stairs into the ancient trail, part of a crew of five. We were helping to check the erosion caused by the same factors—wind and water—that had combined to carve out the canyon over the last five million years, with a little help from the impact of mules' hooves and hikers' feet.

As the weeks brought us all closer to summer in the desert, I began to appreciate those who attempted that hike, facing so many obstacles on their way from the canyon rim down to the Colorado River and back again—heat, sun, exposure, elevation, a heart-thumping cardio-workout. The Grand Canyon can seem like a disturbing chasm in the earth, but surprisingly, it's irresistibly attractive to enter; hikers, experienced or otherwise, practically have no choice but to amble on down the path. The magical environment is too inviting, the morning sun reflecting the color of Mars too intriguing. Once on the edge, it's easy to be called into the wild.

Dropping away from the rim feels great on the mind and the body, especially in the early morning. The steps down come easily along the Bright Angel Trail, as it faces north most of the way and therefore the shade covers it for a good portion of the morning. Leave the rim early enough, and it's possible to get halfway down before seeing the first beams of desert light hit the ground. The air is cool and full of high-altitude gusts at that time of day, being that the rim is close to seven thousand feet above sea level and the river is more than four thousand feet below us. We aren't sweating yet, and so we don't drink enough water.

It's after a few hours of hiking, when we begin to climb back out of the immense natural amphitheater, that all of nature's forces align against us. This is when we begin to struggle. We are tested against ourselves and against the earth. Most of the time in our modern society, we easily coexist within our environment. We don't directly look death in the face very often. But that is not the case as we hike back toward the rim, on an eight-mile climb from the river. It's afternoon, and the Arizona sun has burned any remnant of shade away. All those downhill steps become uphill battles, each one seemingly taller than the last.

One afternoon, we were working about a mile up-trail from the river, along that first major slog through the lowest stretch of the Bright Angel, using mules to haul the gravel we were shoveling in behind our newly-constructed juniper steps, when a heavy-set hiker in his early twenties walked into our worksite. He wanted to know if he could ride out of the canyon on one of Eric's mules. Eric was surly in general, like most horse packers, but friendly enough to that struggling hiker, even though he had to tell him, "Can't. I don't even have another saddle." Each of the mules carried a bag on both sides of their round bellies. They looked passively toward the troubled hiker. "These guys are just rigged up to carry dirt."

Damon was my crew boss. He'd been working on trail crews for ten years, a few more than me, though we were both thirty years old. He had the straight black hair of a Hopi, the descendants of the ancient Anasazi who lived in the canyon for hundreds of years, in immaculately-constructed dwellings. He told the hiker, "There's no way you're getting out of here on a mule—we just can't. But keep hiking," he said, "and, if you feel really bad, come on back and we can try to help you out, somehow." Damon was well-versed in the art of Search and Rescue.

That hiker had barely disappeared out of sight around the first bend in the canyon before he returned to our worksite to repeat Damon's words back to him: "I feel really bad." He told us his chest was hurting and his right arm felt tingly.

As Damon ran down to the bottom of the Grand Canyon, looking for a place to call a dispatch operator to request a helicopter, and as he searched for a good place for that helicopter to land, I thought of how he was not the first person to run through the canyon searching for help. On average, almost one person is rescued from the maw of the Grand Canyon each day. In the summer, multiple people may be saved in one day. My guess is the Anasazi wouldn't have dared to carry so much on their back through the heat of the day, and they probably wouldn't have walked from the rim to the river and back again in one day, either. To survive in such a hostile place they had to have been infinitely more adapted to their environment than we could ever hope to be.

Damon quickly found both his radio communication point and his helicopter landing zone, and that hiker was whisked to the rim and on to the hospital within the hour, a much better option than bouncing three hours up that winding trail on the back of a mule, or the option of dying, trapped at the bottom of the Grand Canyon.

For the rest of my time at the Grand Canyon, I thought about that hiker, and I thought about my friend and co-worker Jake Quilter, whose heart had given out farther south, in Saguaro National Park outside of Tucson, as he hiked an equally challenging desert trail. Jake had also worked on Damon's crew at the canyon. The day he died, he was on his way to start a week-long backcountry tour like the ones Damon and I still worked, four years after. Damon showed me some of Jake's work—a rock wall holding in the trail and a covered bench the crew named Jake's Shade. That desert pushed hikers up to and beyond their limits; over the years, no doubt, Jake's Shade gave just enough relief from the sun to save at least one hiker.

The day I thought about my survival the most, and about Jake and the heart-attack-kid, was when Della, a park ranger, called us from Phantom Ranch to say that one of the canyon's largest cottonwood trees just up from the river had crashed to the ground in the night, blocking the hiking trail. I carried a chainsaw from our worksite down to the bottom of the canyon to cut the tree out of the way.

A line of hikers waited. They watched as my saw screamed through that old, dying tree, sending a stream of woodchips through the air. When the first cut-rounds of tree dropped to the ground with a thud, my audience—anxious to get going because the cool morning air was already rising, replaced by rushing, toaster-oven air—applauded. I let that first wave through, then continued cutting. I could hear my heart beating away as I baked in the sun. An hour later, I sat with Della under another still-standing cottonwood tree, a sister of the fallen giant, to eat lunch. For the moment, I was in the shade. That's something that never lasts long in the Grand Canyon.

On the hike back up from that assignment, I counted my blessings for conquering each step. As I moved through the heat waves, carrying my backpack and a chainsaw, I lived and breathed my mortality. Thankfully, my pack was empty; I'd eaten my lunch and drunk most of my water. By the time I rejoined my crew, they looked dusty and tired, having dug in a few more juniper steps. They asked me if I'd saved the day. "Saved it," I told them, raising an eyebrow and smiling slightly, conserving my energy for the rest of the hike.

I didn't hesitate longer than to put down that chainsaw before I continued on to the bunkhouse in Indian Gardens, an hour's hike away and up a thousand feet. Tired as I was, I noticed how the western redbud had already dropped its signature magenta flowers and begun growing clover-shaped leaves to catch the summer sun. At the junction, I decided to hike the Old Bright Angel Trail, breaking away from the new trail just below a section of Tapeats Sandstone called the Narrows. I walked past several seldom-visited Anasazi granaries, some of the small rooms still in perfect shape, their square doorways midnight black against the face of the orange cliffside.

We were living in the Grand Canyon, like the ancients, although in 2010 we were cheating, sleeping at night in a bunkhouse with electricity and running water. Instead of farming corn and hunting small game, we had a helicopter bring us nine days' of food at a time, straight from the grocery store. Unlike the ancients, we now have the ability to save a man from nature's wrath. The trail crew, beyond surviving, only hoped any structure we built would last as long as those ruins.

The Grand Canyon can nurture life just as well as she can take it away. I thought more about life and death there than in anyplace else I'd ever been. Life sometimes came through just as powerfully. Near our worksite my friend and I discovered an incredible oasis bursting through the barren desert, when we squeezed through a crack in the boulders toward the sound of trickling water. Yellow columbines and magenta monkey flowers grew there in thick carpets, their broad, green leaves locking moisture into the air of that dark desert cave, making it humid, dank, and drastically cooler than it was outside in the sun.

We found that oasis the same week that three young kids on a field trip from Phoenix were swept away by the Colorado River when they tried to swim across, instead of hiking the suspension bridge like everyone else. We ran from our worksite a mile down to the river and searched the surface of the water for them for hours, but, sadly, they'd disappeared in an instant, and there was nothing anyone could do to change it.

All around us was the story of life enduring through desolation, swift death, and drought: the spines of the cactus, the retreating of the ancient ones, the look on the faces of the struggling hikers, the lost kids from Phoenix. But life persisted. The heart attack-kid survived. And those clusters of colorful wildflowers drank forever from their secret cracks in the rock.

Canyon Karma
by
Marjorie "Slim" Woodruff

Some people don't even notice.

The little things. A water bottle lid. A cigarette butt. The tear-top of a goo packet. Little things that lay on the trail, unnoticed and unseen. Except I see them. The animals see them, and they eat them, too. Some of our condors have been taken in to rehab with a crop full of "micro trash." Our deer have been shot. Our bighorns have been euthanized, their stomachs full of micro trash.

Runners and racers are the worst. On every rim-to-rim hike I pick up countless empty water bottles and goo packets. Some are hidden, but most are abandoned in the middle of the trail by some who can't spare a few seconds to stop and put their trash in the pack. Assuming they are carrying a pack. There is no place to put trash in those skimpy little running shorts.

One of the Search and Rescue rangers put it best: "The runners prance along throwing little pieces of crap over their shoulder." Don't bother writing me letters: prove me wrong by picking up after yourself and your friends.

Big things, too. The unopened MREs left by the trail. The full or almost full bottles of stove fuel. "Someone else can use this," they tell themselves, and abandon it. Except if they don't want to carry it out, chances are no one else does.

So I do. Grumbling and griping, muttering ancient curses under my breath, and sometimes above it, I carry it out. The leftover food, the water bottles, the Kleenex and the cigarette butts (the latter treated as toxic waste, which they are, with plastic gloves and ziplocks). Old socks and underwear (and what is the story behind that?).

I also try to educate. To the charming small child carving her name into a rock: "The canyon belongs to everyone: it's not fair for one person to write her name on the rock." To the pimply adolescent scratching four-letter words onto the Coconino: "Have you ever tried to walk out of the Grand Canyon with a broken leg?" To the smoker who drops a butt: "You probably don't realize that condors feed those to their chicks." To the speed demons cutting switchbacks: "That causes dangerous rock slides, and people have died on this trail." (Not from slides, but they don't have to know that.)

Perhaps my favorite intervention is the Stealth Squirrel Chase. I carry a little squirt bottle in a waist holster, presumably to cool others and myself on the trail with a refreshing mist. It is also useful for erasing graffiti and discouraging overly friendly squirrels.

Of course, the last time I was at Mile-and-a-Half Resthouse, I spent most of my rest break gaily squirting squirrels up and down the path in a vain attempt to break them of their habit of demanding food from unwary hikers. My spies informed me later that after I left, a gentleman began feeding peanut-butter crackers to every animal in sight. His rationale: "They couldn't get a thing to eat with that crazy woman chasing them."

Sometimes it doesn't seem worth it. Every rim-to-rim I still get a full bag of water bottles and energy bar wrappers. Every time I come out the Bright Angel (by far the most-used and therefore most-abused trail) I pick up the butts and the bottles and the underwear. Not the same underwear, but still . . .

But the canyon knows. The canyon punishes and the canyon metes reward. It is called Canyon Karma. Treat the canyon right, and the canyon will do right by you.

I always have beautiful weather. I usually get my favorite campsite. I find fossils no one else knows about, and I see flowers and animals that other people miss. Coincidence? Experience? Or Canyon Karma? You decide. You, of course, carry out all your own trash, because you are a righteous, worthy person. Try carrying out other trash that you see, and you'll find out. Canyon Karma—it's for real.

Bright Angel and the Heat Spirit
by
Seth Muller

I wake at Indian Garden during a March group backpack trip. The early sky holds thick and gray clouds. A fine mist of rain falls. The weather does not matter. The hike up and out from Indian Garden to the South Rim marks our last of five days in the canyon, the trip a Hermit-Tonto-Bright Angel loop.

I walk out of the campground to a place where I can see the El Tovar Hotel lights, the ones that shine on the American flag. I look for the places where the Bright Angel Trail clings to the outcropping of land along the cliff face. I squint. In the dull light, it does not appear.

The storm gathers around the edges of the canyon. Although morning, the sky darkens instead of lightens in the passing minutes. I return to camp and boil water with the last of my camp stove fuel. I empty two bags of oatmeal into the hot water. I add some trail mix and dried mango. I eat my last Clif bar. The only food I have left for the hike out is a bag with a few handfuls of cashews.

"Think it's snowing up there?" I ask Wayne Ranney, who leads the trip as the expert geologist.

He cranes his neck to look up at the rim. "If it's not, it will be."

I nod. I want snow. I want to walk into a land transformed, to step into the quiet beauty of it.

Two days before, I sat at a beach near Colorado River's Granite Rapid. I wore sandals and shorts. The temperature neared 70.

I clean out my cook pot and finish packing my gear. I wear only pants and a thin Capeliene top layer over a T-shirt. The cool and damp air gives me a chill. But, in minutes, I will accelerate my blood flow. I will be hiking uphill with thirty pounds on my back—normally more except the food is gone and I will hike with only the water I need to get out.

One person in our crew of five wakes early and leaves before the rest of us. Wayne stays with a woman on our trip named Marcy, who plans to take it slow. This leaves Nick and me to stick together for companionship as we hike out.

The trek from Indian Garden to the South Rim begins easily. The trail crosses a wash and moves along the slopes below the looming cliffs. The elevation gain is steady, and soon, looking back, the trees of Indian Garden lower and the views stretch beyond Indian Garden, out to the edge of the Tonto Platform.

As we walk, the rain finds steady rhythm. I make high steps over the water bars in the trail. They prevent erosion. In the big ascent up the Bright Angel, I think of the footprints that marked the trail before me. The millions of hiking boots, the endless progression of mule hooves. But the Grand Canyon fights to claim the path. Floods devour sections and require rebuilding. Rock falls will take out layer after layer of switchback. In a few lifetimes of ignoring and neglecting a trail, it could grow broken and impassable. Not buried by the loam and plants of a lush climate, but battered away by stone, sudden water, and gravity.

The sky lightens with the expanding day, but still appears like slate. I narrow my eyes and look at the tops of the highest cliffs for signs of snow. I see nothing, save for the isolated patches from the previous week's storm.

The Grand Canyon takes on a different kind of foreboding under a stormy sky. The colors of its rocks are muted. The canyon appears draconian, mystic. Most visitors see it with cloudless conditions, when the canyon has a different kind of perilous feel. A sense that hiking it could bake a person alive under the relentless sun. A sense that a body could turn from flesh to blanched bones in weeks.

I follow Nick up the trail in the first serious climb. It picked up the nickname "Jacob's Ladder," after the ladder to heaven in the Book of Genesis. Every few hundred feet, we make a hairpin turn to the right or the left. We do this over and over, a dozen times, until we reach Three-Mile Rest House. I stop, remove my pack, and eat cashews.

I look up for the top of the cliffs, for the end of the trip. I take time to wipe off the rain from my glasses with my shirt. I rub my hands and feel the five days' growth of beard. It reminds me of the shave and hot shower that waits for me at home.

I glance to the rim one last time before shouldering my pack. After five days, the pack becomes a comfort, a reassuring weight. I clip the waist belt and the load balances between my hips and shoulders. I stare at the view into the canyon and the places directly below us. Indian Garden becomes a cluster of trees in a valley among cliffs. When I trace the scene up to the cliffs, I notice gray specters drifting down from the clouds.

Snow.

I follow Nick for the next leg of the hike. I revel in it. With each step away from Three-Mile Rest House, I move closer to the halfway point between Indian Garden and the South Rim.

We step into the rusted-red realm of the Supai Group. It is the rock saturated with iron, like blood, turned red from the oxygen in the water and air. I daydream of iron as a connecting mineral. It is in the earth and it is in our blood.

The ascent becomes more gradual. Here, the switchbacks are longer. We make the steady climb toward the Mile-and-a-Half Rest House. The drizzle turns intermittent. We pass our first wave of day hikers and Phantom Ranch guests on their way down. Part of me wishes I could turn and follow them, forever looping through the Grand Canyon's interior, never surfacing at the rim. But the rest of my life waits outside of it.

At the second rest house, I drop my pack. My stomach roils and gurgles, from too much water or too many cashews. I use the bathroom. The water spigot is shut off because of the cold temperatures and possible freezing pipes, and I am nearly out of water.

My legs and back ache and my stomach hurts, but my thoughts remain buoyed. My hike of thirty miles winnows down to less than two. Foot traffic from the rim coming down increases. We hear the first clops and calls of a mule train descending. We will finish our hike in a little more than an hour.

Nick and I re-shoulder our packs and travel with a steady creak and a rhythm. A short elevation gain from the rest house, we cross the rain-snow line.

The drizzle picks up an icy mix. After a few more switchbacks, small flakes spiral from the sky. They hit the ground and melt on the wet earth.

We walk to a tighter set of turns, where we make a left or right every hundred feet. The coiling of the trail leads up to the first of two tunnels blasted out of the rock, where the trail moves out of the Coconino Sandstone layer and into the Toroweap Sandstone.

As I follow Nick, I notice it. A magic moment to observe. Every day in the Grand Canyon has one, or many. Each time Nick turns to the next level of trail, I see the outline of his body where the snow melts in the air. His body heat lingers where he has passed. It warms up the space that partial degree to change the snow to rain. With each switchback he turns, I see this outline.

It appears like an inverted ghost.

By the time we reach the tunnel, the heat spirit is gone. I say nothing to Nick. I want it to be more than a quirky phenomenon, more than a "hey, neat" moment. I want to think of it as meaning something, to think of that part of ourselves that floats off into the canyon. I want it to be a reminder that our place in the canyon is temporary—or that miracles are always lingering.

Patina

by

Sara Whitestone

I look down from the South Rim of the Grand Canyon feeling completely displaced. I am with a group of students from my college who are taking a weeklong field course. The professors include two geologists, two biologists, and one astrophysicist. All of the students are science majors—biology, geology, geophysics—except me; I am studying to be an elementary school teacher. What am I doing here?

Even though I'm not a scientist, I can't pass up the opportunity to hike to the bottom of the canyon and learn what I can along the way. The others in the group treat me as an equal, and soon I am throwing out names like Supai and Vishnu Schist as casually as the rest of them.

I spend a lot of time with David, an unconventional geology professor. Before the trip, he sent out a list of items everyone should pack. Just for fun, he included a crow bar on the list, and one poor student thought it was required. David had to apologetically encourage him to leave it behind at the top. I had worked hard to gather together what I considered to be sensible gear, knowing that thirty-five pounds will feel much heavier later on.

The April air is cool at the rim. We hike down the Bright Angel Trail leisurely, stopping often to hear the observations of the professors. Several of the layers, like the Kaibab Limestone and the Hermit Shale, enclose fossils of all kinds—reptiles, plants, amphibians, and marine animals—each layer recording history. We discuss the idea that an ocean was once here. When we reach the Redwall Limestone, which is known for its rusty color, we learn that the real ruddiness comes from the strata above, where iron oxide leaches out, staining the limestone below.

Just before dark we set up camp on the canyon floor and then eat dinner by lantern light. Gary, a professor of biology, feels strongly about protecting me and the only other young woman on the trip, so he chaperones us in his tent. A strong wind rises, and every time I wake up, I see Gary struggling to hold on to the center pole so that the tent won't fly away.

The next day is not leisurely. Even in April the canyon floor is hot, and we have to trek the nine miles up to the rim by nightfall. When I summit a mountain, I know that the hardest part is over, and I can let myself relax both physically and mentally on the way back down. But this morning, when I look up at the steep canyon walls, I am unprepared psychologically for mountain climbing backwards.

Steve is the head geologist and leader of the team. He hikes quickly, lets us pantingly catch up, delivers several scientific annotations, and then takes off again. I find discouragement in switchbacks. At one point I count over thirty. After that I decide to focus on the beauty of the multicolored strata—the butter yellow of the Coconino Sandstone and the way that the Redwall turns to orange fire in the sun. Some layers are not as thick as others, and some rough-hewn walls give way to smooth. But each tier, with its own unique color and texture, adds to the next—layer upon layer—all building into the grandeur of the canyon as a whole.

I picture my own life in layers—the hard foundation of the formative years, the fragile sandstone of adolescence, and the metamorphic rock shaped by the pressures of adulthood. Memories, like thousands of fossils, are preserved within. I have experienced enough now to have gained perspective. I see that the bottom levels support who I have grown to be, while the upper tiers patina what is below, using wisdom to soften the look of the past. As I begin to climb again, I envision, through faith, the solid, colorful layers of my life to come.

On our hike we meet many park rangers who patrol the canyon at all hours. My group notes with a mixture of admiration and envy that they trek up and down the trail without even breathing heavily. Their jobs are twofold: to guard the canyon from human damage and to aid hikers in need.

At a rest break, Professor David takes out a little bottle and asks those closest to him to see what happens when he pours acid on a rock. A ranger suddenly appears (where did he come from?) and tells David in stern terms that he is close to being permanently expelled from the canyon. The other professors are grim, and from then on David quietly concentrates on the ascent.

Several times each summer rangers must rescue exuberant hikers who have overestimated their abilities. I worry that Ken, the other biology professor, will become one of them. He is in his late fifties and has suffered a previous heart attack. Some of the students divvy up his gear, and I end up strapping on his large foam pad. Even though it is lightweight, it acts like a sail on the mast of my pack. As I top one ridge, the wind hits the mattress, lifts me off my feet, and then pins me to the ground. In that moment I sympathize with every capsized turtle I have ever seen. I simply cannot get up under my own volition. I can't even turn sideways. All I can do is wiggle my limbs in the air.

Another sturdier student takes me by the arms, pulls me to my feet, and generously stows the mattress with his own equipment. We begin to get to know one another as we walk along the trail. He is a graduate geology student, and his enthusiasm for the canyon is infectious. Our pleasant conversation eases the difficulty of the upward climb.

It's ironic that just when I'm congratulating myself for helping someone else, I find that I am the one in need of rescue. I dislike the feeling of indebtedness and work toward being as independent as possible. But it's when I admit my limitations and, with vulnerability, open myself to the service of others, that I find not only the aid I seek, but friendship as well—and more memories to imbed in the strata of my life.

In the cold evening air I take my last step out of the canyon and back onto the rim, thinking about layers, each building onto the next and adding to the grandeur of the whole.

About the Authors

Since 2001, **Matt Berman** has moved every spring and every fall, living seasonally in national parks across the American West, from the Grand Canyon to the Grand Tetons, building and maintaining hiking trails. He aims to bring the world of working seasonally amongst nature's finest cathedrals and the feeling of perpetual motion to the page. In 2013, Matt earned an MFA in Writing Creative Nonfiction at Spalding University in Louisville, Kentucky.

Bob Bordasch grew up in California, where he began backpacking at age thirteen, hiking extensively in the Sespe Wilderness and the Sierra. He moved to Boulder, Colorado in 1978, where he worked as an engineer. He soon discovered southern Utah and Grand Canyon. He has since made over 40 week-long excursions into Grand Canyon, accumulating over 300 hiking days below the rim. He moved from Boulder to New Mexico in 2013.

Nathaniel Brodie worked on the Grand Canyon National Park Service Trail Crew for seven years. He received his MFA in Nonfiction Creative Writing from the University of Arizona, where he served as a Beverly Rodgers Fellow and an 1885 Graduate Fellow in the Arts and Humanities.

A native Midwesterner, **Rick Dean** came west to continue an education and stayed for the landscape. He holds a Master's of Science from the University of Missouri and a Ph.D. in Philosophy of Religion from Claremont Graduate University. Currently living in Southern California with his family, where he manages a nature center, he retreats to the Colorado Plateau to hike and explore its slot canyons.

"Compulsive trekker" **Mark Robert "Eb" Eberlein** has been a teacher, wilderness guide, wild-land firefighter, and taxi driver as well as enjoying numerous other short term occupations which account for his scattered resume. From his first glimpse of Grand Canyon in 1971, he has been smitten with "canyon fever," resulting in an estimated 2,000 nights spent below the rim. He was owner-operator of Sky Island Treks, a guide service for overland trekking in Grand Canyon from 1995-2005.

Thea Gavin is a native of Orange, CA; the nearby foothills of the Santa Ana Mountains are her barefoot hiking and running playground—and inspiration to write. In June of 2011 she was privileged to spend three weeks as Artist-in-Residence at Grand Canyon's North Rim, and since then she has returned as often as possible to wander and write.

Margaret (Molly) Hollenbach is a freelance writer from the West Coast United States. A nomadic soul, she has loved every place she lived. Her love affair with the Grand Canyon began with a month-long stay at the North Rim as a Volunteer-in-Park in 1988. She has a PhD in cultural anthropology from the University of Washington and an MFA in writing from Pacific University in Forest Grove, Oregon.

Mark Jenkins is a field staff writer for National Geographic Magazine and Writer-in-Residence at the University of Wyoming. A critically acclaimed author and internationally recognized journalist, Jenkins covers geopolitics and adventure. His four books are *A Man's Life* (Modern Times, 2007), *The Hard Way* (Simon and Schuster, 2002), *To Timbuktu* (William Morrow 1997) and *Off The Map* (William Morrow, 1992).

Rick Jurgen, a past teacher of Biology and Marine Biology, now spends part of the year living and working on the coast of Maine, where he produces and sells seashells and other marine products. The remainder of his year is spent seeking beauty below the rim of Grand Canyon.

Editor **Rick Kempa** has been hiking in and writing about the Grand Canyon since 1974. With Peter Anderson, he is co-editor of the anthology *Poetry of the Grand Canyon* (Lithic Press, 2015). A poet and essayist, he has also published two books of poems, *Keeping the Quiet* and *Ten Thousand Voices*. He is accessible at www.RickKempa.com.

Clint King was born in Indianapolis, Indiana. He studied History/Political Science and American Literature at Miami University in Oxford, Ohio. Among countless adventures, he's worked as a waiter in Glacier National Park, Montana, coached basketball in Indiana, and sold advertising in San Francisco. Clint is a writer and currently lives in Los Angeles.

Nic Korte is a groundwater geochemist with more than ten years of experience as a private consultant following 20-plus years of groundwater research, principally with Oak Ridge National Laboratory. He has hiked and backpacked in much of the Western United States, including nearly 150 nights in the Grand Canyon. Other hobbies include birdwatching/nature study, gardening, and reading. He and his wife reside in Grand Junction, Colorado. His nature blog, "Birds and More," can be found at http://www.gjsentinel.com/blogs/

D.J. Lee is professor of literature and creative writing at Washington State University. She is author of numerous articles and three books on the literature and history of the 19th century. She also writes creative nonfiction about her experiences in the wildernesses of the American West. She has hiked several of the wilderness trails in the Grand Canyon with her father, and they have more planned for the future.

Writer and photographer **Laurie McClellan** lives in Arlington, Virginia. An avid hiker, she writes most often about travel, nature, and science. One of her first adventures in the outdoors was a trip to the Grand Canyon in 1991, which set her on the path of exploring the wilderness. Laurie's articles and essays have appeared in numerous literary journals including *The South Dakota Review* and *Front Range Review*.

Molly McCormick grew up in Kansas and received a degree in Southwest Studies from the Colorado College. Following a need for adventure and education, she landed at Grand Canyon in 1999. Molly has been a biologist, backpacking guide, Phantom Rancher, and volunteer at the Park. She currently practices restoration across the state of Arizona, and occasionally writes articles for newspapers and magazines about her adventures, and the goings-on in the world of ecological restoration.

Dillon Metcalfe is an all-around adventure specialist with a passion for the Colorado Plateau. He has been climbing, scrambling, boating, rappelling, cycling, running, leaping, and slithering for all of his adult life—and exploring off-trail since he could walk. He has worked as an environmental educator for the National Park Service at Grand Canyon, and also as a professional backpacking guide there. He lives in Flagstaff, Arizona with his wife Anya.

Journalist and author **Seth Muller** moved from the East Coast to northern Arizona in 2001 for a new life of exploring Grand Canyon and the Colorado Plateau. His love for the open country has blended with his passion for storytelling. He has written *Canyon Crossing: Stories about Grand Canyon from Rim to Rim* and a children's book series, *Keepers of the Windclaw Chronicles*, set on the Navajo Reservation. He lives with his family in Flagstaff.

Chris Propst is an English professor, currently climbing the trail at Western Wyoming Community College. A fiction writer and sometimes performance poet, he has had work published in *Owen Wister Review*, *Flint Hills Review*, wyohistory.org and elsewhere. He grew up in Alaska, but has since turned towards the clean sand and warmer temperatures of the desert Southwest.

Wayne Ranney is a geologist, river guide, and trail guide based in Flagstaff. He became interested in geology while working as a backcountry ranger at Grand Canyon National Park and later received his Bachelor's and Master's degrees from Northern Arizona University. He has led thousands of people down the trails and river in Grand Canyon and is the author of eight books, including *Carving Grand Canyon*, *Ancient Landscapes of the Colorado Plateau*, and *Sedona Through Time*.

Arnie Richards made his first backpack trip into the Grand Canyon in 1967 at the age of 18. Since then, he has hiked the canyon more than forty times, mostly off-trail, and primarily in the western part of the park between Deer Creek and Tuckup Canyon, in addition to studying and exploring the various routes from the Shivwits Plateau into Separation Canyon.

Kristi Rugg is a lifelong learner, photographer, wilderness first responder, author, adventure seeker, NPS park ranger, and baritone ukulele player. Her greatest aspiration is to explore continents capturing her experiences through lens and pen. When not elbows-deep in technology, Kristi bakes ridiculous quantities of pie, doodles, jams, and has a rugged good time. Kristi connects with nature and people, and whenever possible, finds herself adventuring into the great unknown.

Scott Thybony has traveled throughout North America writing award-winning articles for major magazines. His book for the National Geographic Society on the canyon country sold hundreds of thousands of copies. As a river guide he won the coveted Colorado River JerryRigging Award for fixing a broken motor mount with beer cans and driftwood. His commentaries are heard regularly on Arizona Public Radio.

Kate Watters is a botanist, restoration practitioner, backcountry cook, community organizer, artist, and musician. She spent ten years living and working in the Grand Canyon, building trail and leading plant research and restoration projects for the Park Service. She is the co-author of *River and Desert Plants of the Grand Canyon*.

Sara Whitestone is a writer, photographer, and teacher. In exchange for instruction in English, her international students introduce her to the mysteries of the world. Whether she is in a desert in Saudi Arabia or a castle in Italy, Whitestone discovers writing through travel. Each time she visits Grand Canyon, with its strata so magnificently laid, she hopes the small layers of her life have taken on a little more of the canyon's ancient patina.

Marjorie "Slim" Woodruff was born in Arizona, where she became comfortable with things that crawl, sting, bite, and gnaw. This served her well when she started working with adolescents. She has been hiking in the Grand Canyon for forty-five years, and works as an instructor for the Grand Canyon Field Institute, where she teaches about geology, history, natural history, Mary Colter, and of course, Canyon Karma.

Born in Puerto Rico, **John Yohe** grew up in Michigan and currently lives in Portland, Oregon. He has worked as a wildland firefighter, deckhand/oiler, runner/busboy, bike messenger, wilderness ranger, and as a teacher of writing. After many years of fighting fires on the North and South Rims, he finally made it down inside the Grand Canyon in 2013. A complete list of his published writing, with samples, can be found at his website: www.johnyohe.com.

Dave Zucconi hiked the Grand Canyon for the first time in 1959. What he calls the canyon's "bigness" made a lasting impression on him, and he's averaged one hike a year since then. Although each trip is a long drive from his home in Tulsa, he says it's worth it, as he looks forward to the next fifty or so canyon hikes.

Acknowledgments

Nathaniel Brodie's "Sparks," first appeared in *Creative Nonfiction*, Issue #44, Spring 2012.

Mark Jenkin's "Thus Spake Zarathustra" first appeared in *Outside Magazine* in June 2001, and later was included in *A Man's Life: Dispatches from Dangerous Places* (Modern Times, 2007).

Rick Kempa's "Claim Your Due: A Backpacker's View of River Runners" first appeared in *Camas*, the literary journal of the Environmental Studies Program at the University of Montana, in Fall 2010.

Debbie Lee's "The Edge is What We Have" first appeared in *Tinge Magazine*, December 2012.

Laurie McClellan's "Time's Factory" first appeared in *The Christian Science Monitor* (June 3, 2010).

Seth Muller's "Bright Angel and the Heat Spirit" is excerpted from *Canyon Crossing: Experiencing Grand Canyon Rim to Rim* (Grand Canyon Association, 2011).

Wayne Ranney's "On Being a Trail Guide in the Grand Canyon" was published in slightly different form, as "The Best Job in the World," in *Outdoors in the Southwest: An Adventure Anthology* (University of Oklahoma, 2014).

The search for fossil trackways in Grand Canyon that inspired Scott Thybony's essay was supported by an exploration grant from the National Geographic Expeditions Council.

Kate Watter's "In Pursuit of Plants" was originally published in 2004 in *Grand Canyon: The Art of Living in Place*, a collection of essays for her Master's thesis at Northern Arizona University.